WHAT ABOUT DIVORCE ?

San Jose Bible College
Memorial Library

Clayton Walters

Presented by

M/M Harry Sanders

WHAT ABOUT DIVORCE ?

BY
SPIROS ZODHIATES, TH.,D.

An exegetical exposition of Old and New Testament pertinent passages. The Greek text of Matthew 5:27-32; 19:2-12; Mark 10:2-12; Luke 16:18; Romans 7:1-3 and other scriptures.

This is Volume I on the subject of marriage, divorce and remarriage.

Volume II, entitled "May I Divorce and Remarry?" is a companion book on I Corinthians 7 from the Greek text.

AMG PUBLISHERS
CHATTANOOGA, TN 37422, U.S.A.

First Printing 1984

COPYRIGHT 1984 by SPIROS ZODHIATES
PRINTED IN THE UNITED STATES OF AMERICA

ISBN-0-89957-574-9

AMG Publishers, Chattanooga, TN 37422, U.S.A.

Canadian orders
Purpose Products
81 Temperence
Aurora, Ont. L46 2R1

Dedicated to Murray C. and Dorothy Fletcher as a token of deep appreciation for their unselfish service to AMG International; Murray having served on its Board of Directors for almost a quarter of a century.

PREFACE

God hates divorce! There is no doubt about it. Have you ever read Malachi 2:14 to 16? ". . . The Lord hath been witness between thee and the wife of thy youth, against whom thou hast dealt treacherously: yet is she thy companion, and the wife of thy covenant. And did not he make one? Yet had he the residue of the spirit. And wherefore one? That he might seek a godly seed. Therefore take heed to your spirit, and let none deal treacherously against the wife of his youth. For the Lord, the God of Israel, saith that he hateth putting away: for one covereth violence with his garment, saith the Lord of hosts: therefore take heed to your spirit, that ye deal not teacherously." Surely this leaves no doubt as to God's attitude regarding adultery and divorce. And is there anyone else who doesn't hate it?

The young man and woman who fall in love with each other are deadly serious about it when they decide to get married, but all too often their idyllic dreams are shattered.

What actually constitutes marriage? Is it a man-made institution that either husband or wife can break at will?

No, marriage is instituted by God. He only can be the cohesive power binding a man and a woman into one flesh and unity of life. Follow the instructions of the Manufacturer who designed marriage and there is nothing to fear.

Disregard the Designer's instructions, and the plane called marriage which soared aloft so beautifully will crash. And when it is destroyed because one of the two chooses to pull apart, what can the other person do?

God grieves over sin too. He detests crime. But if someone should attack me and I become the victim of that crime, would His justice then punish both the criminal and me, the victim of the crime?

Above everything, God is a just God. Deuteronomy 32:4 says: "He is the Rock, his work is perfect; for all his ways are judgment: a God of truth and without iniquity, just and right is he."

When Jesus Christ came to earth for the purpose of reconciling man to God, God's justice had to be satisfied. Man had to be punished for his sin. God could not accept defiled mankind into His spotless family without someone bearing the punishment to atone for man's cleansing. And that was the role undertaken by Jesus Christ. Now, whoever accepts by faith the payment made for man's sin by the Lord Jesus Christ satisfies God and is extended His forgiveness.

In the matter of divorce, a crime is committed often involving a guilty party and an innocent party. It is possible, of course, that both parties may be guilty, in which case both need to repent and start their lives over.

But what happens when marriage is broken by the sin of one of the two members without any guilt on the part of the other? Is the innocent one to suffer because of the sin of his former marital partner?

The words spoken by Christ on this subject are among the most misunderstood of His teachings. The translators, for the most part, have so mistranslated Christ's words originally recorded in Greek that they have presented Him as adding salt to the wound of a marital partner who has been deserted for no justifiable reason. The amazing thing is that Christ is thus presented as bringing upon both divorce parties, guilty and innocent alike, the same punishment. Such is not the case. He fully agreed with the precepts taught in the Old Testament.

We have fully examined every word of the pertinent texts from the Greek New Testament to find out what Jesus really said. Sometimes it becomes rather technical as it examines grammar and syntax. Truth requires careful and faithful grammatical and lexical analysis, however. This is what you have in this book. Study it carefully from beginning to end without critical, preconceived ideas.

There is hardly an issue in our day as devastating and perplexing to the non-Christian and Christian as that of divorce and possible remarriage.

The views are varied, and in preparing this book, I put aside all prevailing views and practices in an endeavor to find out exactly what the Word of God said.

What one's cultural and religious setting permits or does not permit is not of primary importance. It is what God says in His Word. Many people have based their opinions on a casual reading of one or the other versions of the New Testament. As a Greek who has studied his Greek New Testament for 46 years, I felt I owed a debt, under God, to the world to examine the Greek text and delve into these turbulent waters. I have been as diligent and honest as I possibly could.

You will find in this book a word-for-word examination of the New Testament Scriptures in addition to Old Testament passages. The following New Testament texts are examined in detail: Matthew 5:27-32; 19:3-12, Mark 10:2-12, Luke 16:18, and Romans 7:1-3. Of course, many other relevant Scriptures are also examined.

This volume, however, does not deal with that very difficult but pertinent discussion of the Apostle Paul on marriage, divorce, and remarriage in I Corinthians 7. I have separated my study of that chapter into a separate volume which completes this one. The title given to that study is, *May I Divorce and Remarry?*

It would have been awkward every time reference is made to a man putting away his wife to also say that the same applies to a woman putting away her husband, or in other cases to refer to both the man and woman. Probably in those days more men were putting away their wives rather than the reverse since women in Old Testament times were "disposable chattels," and thus the Scriptures refer primarily to the man.

Christ corrects such a despicable view of women. He elevates a woman to equality with man as far as behavior toward Him is concerned. He spells out the special behavior of a husband toward the wife and vice versa. He never places a woman so low that she is to be kicked about by her husband, but places her only under him, close to his heart so that she can be loved and simultaneously experience his protective umbrella of strength since he has been divinely endowed with superior physical strength by nature of his God-given constitution.

As far as the laws regulating divorce are concerned, the same ones apply for women as for men as is definitely affirmed by Mark 10:12 speaking of a woman dismissing her husband

and marrying another.

Please, therefore, understand that the terms, man or woman, and the respective personal or relative pronouns, he, she, him or her, used in their generic sense, refer to either man or woman.

I praise God for His grace in giving me a wonderfully happy marriage. As I release this two-volume study, my one-and-only beloved wife and I have celebrated 36 years of marriage. Therefore, what I have written does not have as its motive the justification of a position which I desire to defend in my own life.

I want to express my sincerest thanks to my dear wife, Joan, who has labored many long months in editing this material. As a result, we have grown to love each other more in greater mutual esteem in the Lord whom we both love dearly and endeavor to serve faithfully.

Our prayer is that you, too, will have a greater appreciation of God's wonderful gift of marriage.

If an unhappy marriage or divorce has been your unfortunate experience, remember that our God can rebuild a life by remolding the clay, as long as you allow Him to shape you according to His image and not insist upon your own wishes. Human failure provides God with divine opportunities.

What He can do with a life totally controlled by Him may amaze you. I am reminded here of a story I read many years ago. A well-known artist visiting a family with a small child brought a handkerchief to the little girl as a gift. Accidently, she spilled a bit of ink on her new handkerchief. Tears welled up in her eyes as she saw her brand new gift already destroyed. Gently the famous artist took the damaged handkerchief into his skilled hands and began to work with it as the child quietly and patiently waited. In a few moments, he had changed the ungainly spot into a beautiful flower.

If you have experienced the devastation of an unhappy marriage or divorce, remember, God can still make your life a thing of beauty for His glory and honor.

My prayer is that such would be the result of a careful perusal of this study as it is committed to the glory of God.

Spiros Zodhiates

Chattanooga, TN, U.S.A.

X

CONTENTS

INDICIES

1

BETROTHAL AND MARRIAGE IN THE OLD AND NEW TESTAMENTS

The first stage called the betrothal in the formation of a marriage union had a prominent position among the Jews as among other peoples at the same stage of social development.

Three Hebrew words translated as "betrothed" in the Authorized Version are correctly rendered by the following expressions: "and so gain the right of possession" (Deut. 20:7; Hos. 2:19, 20); "designate" (Ex. 21:8, 9); and "acquire" (Lev. 19:20). In II Samuel 3:14 it is translated as "espoused." The betrothal was also designated by one Greek verb *mneesteuein* translated "espoused" (Matt. 1:18; Luke 1:27; 2:5). In the Revised Version "betroth" is exclusively used where the reference is to the initial stage (II Sam. 3:14; Matt. 1:18, etc.), while "espouse" is restricted to the passages which imply completed marriage (Ex. 21:8, 9). The ceremony of betrothal has no name in the Old Testament. The Talmudists refer to it under the names of "consecration or betrothal," and "compact or conditions."

No restrictions on the age of marriage are given in the Old Testament, though early marriage is sometimes spoken of with approval (Prov. 5:18; Isa. 62:5).

The custom of allowing the individuals concerned to arrange a marriage according to inclination is a late and exceptional concession. In societies in which the family organization is strong and stable, the betrothal is treated as a concern of the family group or the tribe.

The powers are vested in the head of the tribe, or they may devolve upon particular members of a family group—under the patriarchal system upon the father or nearest paternal relative; under the matriarchal upon the maternal uncle or the eldest uterine brother. The betrothal is viewed from this standpoint in the Old Testament. In the exercise of his patriarchal function, Abraham through a servant negotiates with Bethuel for the hand of Rebekah, and Laban as her brother is taken into counsel (Gen. 24); Hamor endeavors in treaty with Jacob and his sons to arrange a marriage on behalf of his son Shechem (Gen. 34:6ff); even the lawless Samson requests his father to procure for him to wife a woman in Timnath (Judges 14:2). The advances, furthermore, were made by the house of the bridegroom except in cases where the superior rank of the bride's family justified them in taking the first step (Ex. 2:21; Josh. 15:17; I Sam. 18:27).

Resentment was expressed when a man repudiated the rights of the natural guardians and took the matter into his own hands (Gen. 26:34, 35). The protests were not unreasonable in view of the interest of the family in the alliance that might be formed and of the interest of the women in the bride with whom, in a patriarchal society, they were to be so closely associated (Gen. 27:46). In reality, society in those days was similar to the city-states of Europe in past days, and inter-marriage between families or tribes bore strong political influences or alliances.

Yet, while the system required that the machinery of the family should be employed, it might easily happen, as the cases of Shechem and Samson show, that it might be set in motion by a lover. This was the more so in that in ancient Israel the association of the sexes was comparatively unrestrained, which naturally led to personal attachments which sought satisfaction in marriage (Gen. 24:15; 29:10, 11; II Sam. 13). Among the Hebrews, in any case, the tyranny of family rule does not appear to have dispensed with the consent of the parties (Gen. 24:8), which under this regime is often treated as a matter of indifference, at least as far as the bride is concerned.

Mixed Marriages

The Israelites in the Old Testament had frequently been urged not to intermarry with heathen nations, especially with the Canaanites (Num. 25:6ff; Deut. 7:3). Mixed marriages were one of the great troubles of Ezra and Nehemiah after captive Isreal was restored (Ezra 9:1ff; Neh. 13:23ff). The strict Jew would, like Peter, think it unlawful "to join himself or come unto

20

one of another nation" (Acts 10:28).

Yet there were, both in the Old and New Testament times, many cases of mixed marriages. The marriage of Timothy's Greek father and Jewish mother is a later example (Acts 16:1). There seems to be a reference to it in Galatians 2:3 where Paul says that Titus, being a Greek, was not compelled to be circumcised. He was doubtless thinking of Timothy's circumcision (Acts 16:3).

For Old Testament mixed marriages in practice, see Ruth 1:4; I Kings 7:14; II Chronicles 24:26, besides the alliances of the kings.

Marriage between a believer and an unbeliever is forbidden: "Be not unequally yoked with unbelievers" (II Cor. 6:14, an admonition which has a wider application than marriage.)

In dealing with Christian marriage, Paul tolerates the union of Christians with heathen only when it has been entered into before conversion.

In such a case, the parties should continue to live together if the unbelieving partner is willing (I Cor. 7:12–16). The reason given is not only the well-being of the non-Christian spouse, but also that of the children (v. 14). "Now are they holy" are words which may refer to the probability that the children will be brought up in the faith by the believing parent, whereas separation may mean that they will be brought up by the non-Christian parent.

If a widow remarries, it must be "in the Lord," i.e., the second husband must be a Christian (I Cor. 7:39).

Peter refers to mixed marriages (I Peter 3:1), a passage which is parallel with I Corinthians 7:12ff. He probably is dealing here with a marriage before conversion.

Monogamy and Polygamy and Bigamy

The New Testament supports monogamous marriage. It does not refer to polygamy and bigamy directly, but by virtue of its support of monogamy declares itself against both polygamy and bigamy.

Among the Jews polygamy had greatly decreased since the time of the patriarchs, and at the commencement of the Christian era was little practiced.

Polygamy among Jews in the second century A.D. is,

21

however, mentioned by Justin Martyr (Dial. 134). For Christians it was inconsistent with Jesus' elevated teaching about marriage which assumes monogamy. In the Old Testament itself, the polygamy of the patriarchs is spoken about apologetically. Noah was monogamous (Gen. 7:7). Monogamy was held to be symbolical of God's union with Israel (Hosea 2:19ff), while polygamy was symbolical of idolatry.

2

PROHIBITED MARRIAGES

The New Testament is silent in as far as the provisions of the Old Testament in regard to certain marriages.

A Son and a Mother or Stepmother

However, in I Corinthians 5:1–5 and 13 Paul deals with the case of a Corinthian who temporarily took as a sexual partner his father's wife, either his stepmother or perhaps even his own mother. It is not quite clear if the father was alive. If II Corinthians 7:12 refers to the same incident, as it appears to, he was alive. However, it is not clear whether the father had divorced his wife and the son had married her or if they simply cohabited. In any case, the inference is that even if it were a case of marriage between a son and his stepmother, it would be repugnant to the Apostle as it would be even to the better heathen. The marriage or adultery of persons so closely related by affinity had shocked both Christians and heathen alike.

Marrying a Sister-in-Law

Another case is that of Herod Antipas and Herodias, his brother Philip's wife (Mark 6:17ff). Here again it is immaterial whether Philip was still alive or dead, or whether Herodias had been divorced; the connection would be prohibited in any event (Lev. 18:16): "It is not lawful for thee to have thy brother's wife." (She was also niece of both of her husbands.)

In the Old Testament there is what is known as the levirate marriage (from the Latin *levir*, "brother-in-law"). It refers to the marriage of a man with his deceased brother's widow in the event of his dying childless. The widow was not to remarry outside the family, and the unmarried brother was to perform the duties of a husband to her to raise up children to the deceased in order to perpetuate his name in Israel. If the man refused, the woman was entitled to subject him to public disgrace before the elders (Deut. 25:5–10).

The Old Testament contains two instances of the practice. In the patriarchal period, Onan deliberately spilled his semen on the ground lest the offspring should be counted as his brother's. His own subsequent death was pronounced a divine judgment on him (Gen. 38:8ff). The book of Ruth tells the story of Ruth offering herself to Boaz, believing him to be the nearest kinsman to her deceased husband. However, Boaz at first declined on the grounds that there was a nearer kinsman. Only when the latter refused did Boaz take Ruth to wife (Ruth 4:1–13).

The practice of the levirate marriage was perhaps still practiced in New Testament times. It was presupposed in the query of the Sadducees concerning the marital status in the resurrection of a woman who had married seven brothers, each dying childless (Matt. 22:23–33; Mark 12:18–27; Luke 20:27–38). Jesus' reply rebuked the Sadducees for not knowing the Scriptures or the power of God, for in the resurrection the present marital relationships with their physical ties are transcended and the resurrected dead are like the angels (Matt. 22:30; Mark 12:25; Luke 20:36). Nevertheless, they live because God is God of the living (Matt. 22:32; Mark 12:27; Luke 20:38).

3

A SECOND MARRIAGE

The remarriage of widows and widowers stands on an entirely different basis from polygamy, and though it was disliked by many Christians in the early ages of the church, it was regarded by all, or almost all, as permissible. Paul allows it to widows (Rom. 7:2ff; I Cor. 7:39). No reproach was attached to the widows who did remarry, although the Apostle thinks that widowhood will give greater happiness than remarriage (I Cor. 7:40).

If, however, we take the term *neooteras,* the "younger women" in I Timothy 5:14 to refer to "younger widows," Paul encourages or even commands a second marriage in some cases. "I desire that they marry, bear children, rule the household." But apparently Paul, according to I Timothy 5:9 and 16, did not approve of a second marriage for his local church officials or the widows who were on the church payroll. These widows must be over threescore years old, "having been the wife of one man." It excludes bigamy, digamy, and marriage after divorce alike.

What does Paul mean in I Timothy 3:2 and Titus 1:6 when he says that the bishop or elder must be the husband of one wife? This qualification is repeated in the case of deacons in I Timothy 3:12.

In these pastoral epistles Paul recommends marriage for the local clergy. He also advises it for young women (I Tim. 5:14), or as we have seen, for young widows.

From the whole context of these pastoral epistles, it appears that the term "husband of one wife" presents Paul as desiring his local church officials, the elders (bishops) and deacons, to be, at least as a rule, married men.

This phrase can hardly be taken to refer to polygamy although the Jews sometimes practiced it in the apostolic period. It is also probable that some Christians followed their example. But there is no evidence of Christian polygamy found in the New Testament. The very fact that the apostles did not find it necessary to forbid it explicitly prevents us from thinking that Paul merely means that a bishop or elder or deacon must not be a polygamist. If this were the meaning, the prohibition of polygamy to the church officials would imply that it was not uncommon among the laity and, in fact, even permissible. We may therefore safely dismiss this view. No Christian, church official or not, was allowed to be a polygamist.

In the apostolic age there was considerable prejudice against a second marriage. This is seen by what Paul says about widows in I Timothy 5:9 and 16 that if they remarried they would not need to be helped by the local church. This would not be considered as an ironclad rule, but as a local regulation. In the case of the second marriage of church officials, it was likewise. Paul did not want to give unnecessary offense to public opinion.

The prejudice against a second marriage may be seen in Josephus (Ant. XVII, XIII. 4) where Glaphyra is reprimanded in a vision by her first husband for remarriage. This was also a case of forbidden degrees, for her first and third husbands were brothers. Perseverance in widowhood was commended not only in the New Testament (Luke 2:37; I Cor. 7:40), but by the heathen Romans (Josephus, Ant. XVIII, vi. 6: Antonia, widow of Drusus).

In the second century A.D. Hermas says (Mand iv. 4) that digamy, or a second marriage, is not a sin, but that a widow or widower who remains single is commended. So Clement of Alexandria (Strom iii. 12), commenting on Paul, says that one who remarries does not sin but on the other hand, does not follow the most perfect course.

Digamy, or a second marriage, in a man was much less disliked than in a woman.[1]

[1]See *Dictionary of the Apostolic Church,* James Hastings, Vol. II, "Marriage".

4

THE DOWRY

The first important stage in the betrothal procedure was the settlement of the amount of the so-called dowry, and the payment or part payment of the same.

The dowry of the Old Testament (Gen. 34:12; Ex. 22:16, 17; I Sam. 18:25) was not a portion brought by the bride into the husband's family, but a price or ransom paid to the father or brothers of the bride. In primitive conditions, it was naturally claimed as compensation for the loss to a family of a valuable member.

An Arab father regards his daughters much as he would his sheep or cattle, selling them for a greater or lesser price according to his rank and fortune and their beauty (*Eastern Customs* by Tristram, p. 92).

In the Old Testament, Hamor offers to pay for Dinah, "never so much dowry" (Gen. 34:12); in Exodus 22:17 it is referred to as a settled custom. Deuteronomy 22:29 assesses the damages for seduction which are payable to the father, and thus fixes the amount. For the common people, the sum to be paid was doubtless settled by custom, while in the case of important alliances it was a matter of negotiation (Gen. 34:11, 12).

The dowry was not necessarily paid in money or kind, but might take the form of service, as in the case of Jacob (Gen. 29) and David (I Sam. 17:25).

As time passed on, the dowry, if not in its entirety, at least in portion, was appropriated to insure the comfort and security of the bride. It was conserved as capital and in the event of the death of the husband or an arbitrary divorce, it furnished a useful provision for the wife.

While the settlement and payment, in whole or in part, of the dowry was the decisive act in the betrothal, there was probably also an additional ceremony of a more or less formal kind. Of the procedure, various elements appear to be preserved in the narrative of Rebekah's betrothal (Gen. 24). The terms in which she is asked and gives her consent, in all likelihood preserve an ancient and familiar formula—"Wilt thou go with this man?" "I will go" (verse 58). The same applies to the blessing which is pronounced upon her when she is handed over or "sent away" (verse 60). The conjecture that a ring was given to the bride finds no obvious support in the Scriptures, yet the use of the ring, which plays an important part in the Talmudic formalities, may well have been of considerable antiquity (Gen. 24).

In the procedure sanctioned by the Talmudic authorities, the bridegroom handed to the bride an article of value, such as a ring or a written document, adding: "By this ring, etc., may she be consecrated (or betrothed) to me." The presence of two male witnesses was required so that the appropriate benedictions might be pronounced on the union.

According to the Mishna, there were three modes of betrothal—by the payment of money, by the conveyance of a contract, and by coition; but the third was prohibited by later Rabbis under penalties.

If betrothal or the promise to marry someone involved immediate sexual privileges, then there would be ground in believing that Jesus was the son of Joseph. The Scriptures, however, state beyond a shadow of a doubt that Jesus Christ was conceived of the Holy Ghost. Joseph wanted to put Mary away privily because he knew that he had had no relations with her.

After the betrothal, the bride was under the same restrictions as a wife. If unfaithful, she ranked and was punished as an adulteress (Deut. 22:23, 24); and on the other hand, the bridegroom, if he wished to break the contract, had the same privileges and had also to observe the same formalities as in the case of divorce. The situation is illustrated in the history of Joseph and Mary who were betrothed (Matt. 1:19).

d the festivities of the event. In the case of the
is possible that the expense of the festivity was
utions by the guests themselves, which was
e gifts that we give at weddings today.

seven days following the wedding, the young
ated by the villagers as king and queen. The
r, probably because it was a large, flat area
ted, where they are married is their court, and the
dge is their throne. March was the favorite month.
as then set up whose business was to ascertain that
had been consummated (Deut. 22:13–21).[2]

geneetai, third person singular, second aorist
e of ginomai, "to become". This in the Revised
translated to be "joined to a man;" gamizomai or
nai, to be "given in marriage" (Mark 12:25); and
"to give in marriage" (I Cor. 7:38).

Dictionary of the Bible by James Hastings.

NUPTIAL RIGHTS
AND CUSTOMS

Upon the betrothal followed, after a longer or shorter period, the marriage proper or wedding, the customs of which we may gather partly from incidental allusions in Scripture and partly from survivals of ancient customs in Talmudic literature and in the Middle East.

The Hebrews used various terms to indicate the term that we call today and commonly translate "to marry." The Hebrew words were: "to take" (Gen. 19:14, II Chron. 13:21); "I became to a man" or "am married" (Hos. 3:3; Num. 36:3, 6, 11); "to become master of," expressive of the husband's authority (Deut. 22:22, etc.); and in later literature "make to dwell, give a dwelling to" (Psa. 113:9; Ezra 10:2, 10, 14, 17, 18; Neh. 13:23, 27); "to form marriage alliance with" (Gen. 34:9); and "given to marriage," the Authorized Version of Psalm 78:63.

The New Testament Word for "Marry"

In the New Testament, gameoo is used of either sex (Matt. 5:32; 19:9, 10, etc.). Also, in Romans 7:3 where it says: "So then if, while her husband liveth, she be married to another man . . ." That expression "she be married to another man" in Greek is "if she becomes to another man."[1]

Isaac and Rebekah

In the case of Isaac and Rebekah the formalities were over with the betrothal, and on the bride's arrival at her new home she was simply conducted to her tent (Gen. 24:63–67).

David and Michal

Similarly, as soon as David had fulfilled the conditions

imposed by Saul, he received Michal to wife (I Sam. 18:27). That this was, however, not universal practice appears from Genesis 29:27. The later practice was to draw a clear distinction between betrothal and marriage (Deut. 20:7; 28:30), to magnify the final function and invest it increasingly with publicity and pomp.

The Wedding Procession and Feast

In the Biblical references to the marriage celebrations, two functions stand out prominently—the wedding procession and the wedding feast or marriage supper. As to the nature and place of the ceremony by which the woman was transferred to the husband (the counterpart of our marriage service), the biblical references leave us uninformed.

The wedding procession naturally fell into two parts. First, the bridegroom and his friends may be supposed to have marched to the house of the bride; then in a return procession the festal company, reinforced by the bride's friends, conducted the pair to their future home. We catch a glimpse of the garlanded bridegroom in his splendid attire (Isa. 61:10), and of his veiled bride surrounded by the friends of her youth (Psa. 45:14 and 15); the attendant throng gives vent to its jubilant feelings in dancing and shouting, and songs are struck up (some perhaps preserved in the "Song of Solomon") which sound the praise of wedded love and the newly wedded pair.

The relation of the wedding procession to the situation presupposed in the Parable of the Ten Virgins requires illucidation. More rarely a procession conducted the bride to meet the bridegroom as he approached with his friends (I Maccabees 9:37ff). In the evening such a procession sometimes took place by lamp and torchlight. The explanation here suggested is that the marriage took place late at night and that the bride's company was preparing to go out to meet the bridegroom on his first appearance.

The marriage supper which took place in the house of the husband was a great social event in the life of a family and, where the standing and means allowed it, might have been planned on the most lavish scale. In the Parable of the Marriage of the King's Son we have an example of boundless hospitality, and also an indication of the resentment felt when the invitation

was slighted (
gives us a glimp
in humbler hom

The Ancient Mar
the Modern Marri

The marriage cer
to be summarily impo
doubtless nearer the n
being in early times the
peoples the public meal
it was quite in harmony w
feast of which bridegroom
their friends as the right by
conjugal footing. The view is
period the feast was still tre
proceedings that *gamos,* the
marriage, stands equally for the
22:4). In the course of time, inev
instituted. The most natural occas
at which the bridegroom came to ta
But evidence goes to show that the
so long as her parents, who accompa
her side. The act upon which attentio
the decisive and uniting act was the le
"chamber," which in the old period wa
for the wedded pair. This is why sor
described as "the tenting." Out of th
naturally develop to form a ritual. From a
supposed that the pair entered into a solem
also probable that the good wishes of the co
crystallized into definite benedictions invoki
posterity. After the exile of the Jewish people
was embodied in a written contract (Tobit 7:1
Septuagint as *suggraphee,* "a document put to

The Wedding Festivities

The wedding festivities which followed were long
out. The usual period for the rejoicing was a week.
music, and dancing, such as celebrated the return of th

son, characterize
poorer people, i
met by contrib
equivalent to t
During the
couple are tr
threshing flo
centrally loca
threshing sle
A tribunal w
the marriag

¹*Ean,* "if,
subjunctiv
Version is
gamisko
gamizoo

²Source

6

THE DUTIES OF THE HUSBAND AND WIFE IN THE OLD TESTAMENT

The duties of the husband in the Old Testament were generally recognized to include all that is involved in the support of the home. Exodus 21:10 enumerates as the minimum obligation the provision of food, raiment and cohabitation.

In regard to sexual morality, the Old Testament theory as well as frequent practice fell far short of the standard of equality of treatment. The chastity of the wife was jealously guarded by the heaviest penalties, but custom and law recognized no parallel obligation of conjugal fidelity as resting on the husband—provided he always respected the rights of other men. At the same time, conjugal fidelity was naturally involved in the loving relations of the husband toward his wife, depicted in more than one touching instance (II Sam. 3:14ff).

However, the prophetic conscience was possessed by a deep sense of the abomination of whoredom; and finally a principle which claimed absolute marital fidelity was laid down by Malachi when he taught that neglect and inconstancy have God for their witness and avenger (Mal. 2:14, 15).

The duties of the wife were not so specifically stated. The fundamental ones were chastity and submission (Gen. 3:16), with devotion to the husband's family and interests. And by general consent, the standard maintained by Hebrew wives was high.

7

MARRIAGE IN CHRISTIANITY

Christianity began a new epoch in the history of marriage. The changes which it introduced were due partly to the express enactment by Christ and His apostles and partly to the obvious implications of fundamental Christian principles.

The Christian system involved the adoption of monogamy and the prohibition of polygamy and bigamy (Matt. 19:4, 5). Duties of the married state were also revised in the spirit of Christianity.

Under Christianity, the husband is instructed to love his wife as himself. Paul says in Ephesians 5:28, "So ought men to love their wives as their own bodies. He that loveth his wife loveth himself." The husband's love for his wife is further likened to the love of Christ for His Church (Eph. 5:25). In Colossians 3:19 Paul admonishes: "Husbands, love your wives, and be not bitter against them." In all these Scriptures, the Greek word for love is *agapaoo*, a love which meets the needs of a wife as he who is her provider recognizes it.

In I Corinthians 7:3–5 Paul asserts the law of conjugal rights. "Let the husband render unto the wife due benevolence: and likewise also the wife unto the husband. The wife hath not power of her own body, but the husband: and likewise also the husband hath not power of his own body, but the wife. Defraud ye not one the other except it be with consent for a time, that ye may give yourselves to fasting and prayer; and come together again, that Satan tempt you not for your incontinency."

In I Timothy 5:8, Paul prescribes that it is the husband's duty to provide for his own family. "But if any provide not for his own, and especially for those of his own house, he hath denied the faith, and is worse than an infidel."

The difficult question concerns the privilege of the spouse in dissolving the marriage in case the partner does not fulfill all or some of the fundamental duties in marriage. This we shall examine later as we study the pronouncements of the Lord Jesus and the Apostles.

Faithfulness in Marriage Obligatory in Christianity

In the New Testament, faithfulness of the marriage partners is obligatory. It seems that such faithfulness was not taken seriously at first, at least not among the Gentile Christians. It therefore became necessary for the Council of Jerusalem to educate the conscience of these new Christians by making it clear that fornication did indeed belong to the class of things to which they should pay strict attention. "That ye abstain . . . from fornication: from which if ye keep yourselves, ye shall do well" (Acts 15:29).

Paul threatens with excommunication those who conduct themselves immorally. He writes in I Corinthians 5:9–13: "Not to keep company . . . altogether with fornicators of this world . . . if any man that is called a brother be a fornicator . . . put away from among yourselves that wicked person." Of course, Paul here was not speaking of a spouse putting away her partner, but of excommunicating a fornicator from a local church assembly.

In I Thessalonians 4:3 Paul says, "For this is the will of God, even your sanctification, that ye should abstain from fornication." In Galatians 5:19–21 he tells us that they who engage in "adultery, fornication, uncleanness, lasciviousness . . . shall not inherit the kingdom of God." "Marriage is honourable in all, and the bed is undefiled: but whoremongers and adulterers God will judge" (Heb. 13:4).

Anyone reading Paul's Corinthian Epistles could easily conclude that the loose morals prevailing in that cosmopolitan city had affected the Church and the believers. This is why Paul, as an apostle, extends the detailed teaching on marriage and divorce beyond the limits with which the Lord Jesus dealt with them. Paul develops the doctrine of the human body as an integral and abiding element of personality. It is incompatible, he claims, to be a follower of Christ and simultaneously to engage in sexual license. He says in I Corinthians 6:13: "Now the body is not for fornication, but for the Lord; and the Lord for the body."

Paul repeatedly urges constancy of conjugal love as the practical expression in the recognition of the perpetuity of the marriage bond.

What Is to Be the Status of the Woman?

The duties of the wife, in spite of the improvement of the status of woman which Christianity brought about, continued to be developed from the presupposition of her subordination and were summed up, not in love, but in obedience. But this obedience is in response to the husband's love. Her subordination is not in blind submission but in recognition that she is physically the weaker vessel who finds protection and fulfillment under the care of the stronger spouse, her husband.

Thus, we read in Ephesians 5:22: "Wives, submit yourselves unto your own husbands, as unto the Lord." The Greek verb for "submit yourselves" is *hupotassesthe*, which really means "find your proper category under." But is this under a husband's tyranny or loving protection? There is no doubt Paul means the latter since in verse 25 he says, "Husbands, love your wives, even as Christ also loved the church, and gave himself for it." The husband must not take advantage of the wife's physically weaker position but be willing to give himself in protecting her. And in Colossians 3:18 the same Greek word is used: "Wives, submit yourselves unto your own husbands, as is fit in the Lord." Again, the same word is used in I Peter 3:1: "Likewise, ye wives, be in subjection to your own husbands; that, if any obey not the word, they also may, without the word, be won by the conversation of the wives."

Christianity included various elements which tended to elevate and indeed revolutionize the woman's position in contrast to the attitude of previous ages—especially the fact that in the spiritual sphere she was on the same platform as the man, being redeemed by the same Saviour, saved by the same faith, and destined to the same everlasting inheritance. Peter in his first epistle, 3:7, admonishes: "Likewise, ye husbands, dwell with them according to knowledge giving honour unto the wife, as unto the weaker vessel, and as being heirs together of the grace of life; that your prayers be not hindered." In view of this stupendous fact which Paul refers to in Galatians 3:28, the wife could no longer be treated as an acquired piece of property, but was in herself a loved and redeemed child of God. "There is neither Jew nor Greek, there is neither bond nor free, there is neither male nor female: for ye are all one in Christ Jesus."

Paul, however, does not imply that a man and a woman were created equal or are to be treated equally as far as their bodies and their physical endurance are concerned. God made them different, each fitting a special category of role in life and work. Even in the marriage union they are not to be regarded as co-equal partners. The one complements the other simply because they are unequal. God made all things and people different. I Corinthians 4:7 asserts this beyond the shadow of a doubt: "For who maketh thee to differ from another? And what hast thou that thou didst not receive? Now if thou didst receive it, why dost thou glory, as if thou hadst not received it?"

The subjection of the wife to the husband, according to the Apostle Paul, was founded upon the original purpose and decree of God in creation, which could not be annulled. He says in I Corinthians 11:9, "Neither was the man created for the woman; but the woman for the man." Woman's constitution was modeled upon that of the man. It was not like his. It was created to complement his which was an immediate reproduction of the image of God.

That man and woman are created to fully complement each other is made clear in I Corinthians 11:11 "Nevertheless neither is the man without the woman, neither the woman without the man, in the Lord." This means that in the Lord a man needs a woman just as much as a woman needs a man. This, however, does not annul the fact that they are different. Because they are they can complement each other.

8

A WOMAN AS A WIFE
IN THE OLD TESTAMENT

In the culture of the Old Testament man took the woman of his liking or his parents' choice to become his wife. He was master in his relationship with women, and various circumstances tended to depress the status of the wife. One reason for this was the logic of the patriarchal system. Another was the custom of the dowry.

Another circumstance that tended to depress the status of a wife was the institution of polygamy which divided her legitimate influence among several claimants. In theory, she was the owned one while the husband was the owner. In the Decalogue she is numbered with his possessions (Ex. 20:17). In certain strata of the population, the wife was little more than chattel.

But among the wealthier classes, the wife had no small liberty of action (I Sam. 25:18; II Kings 4:22). And where a woman possessed exceptional capacity or knew how to increase her husband's affection, she asserted her title to a very different status. The wives of the patriarchs are not only consulted in matters of importance, but often impress us as accomplishing their purpose by their superior force of character (Gen. 21:10; 27:13, 46). In the period of the judges, the interest centers more than once in a strong woman (Judges 4:4, 17).

The Man Had the Right to Divorce

As the Jewish law gave the husband the traditional prerogative to choose or accept a woman as a wife, so also it gave him the right to dismiss her from being his wife. In reaction to the irresponsible exercise of this right, we see, in the Old Testament, prophetic protest and legislative enactment, ending with the effective protection of the wife's position.

The custom of polygamy (one man having many wives) made its appearance as a result of the fall (Gen. 4:23) in the lawless line of the descendants of Cain.

It is, however, not without significance that Noah, the second father of the human race, represents monogamy (Gen. 7:7).

That the power of divorce should have been regarded in ancient times as a traditional right of the husband was in harmony with the general ideas and practices of the time in regard to woman's status. She was regarded as property, and as the husband could get rid of other property, he could dispense with his wife also.

The father of the Jewish nation, Abraham, summarily dismisses Hagar. We read in Genesis 21:14: "Abraham rose up early in the morning, and took bread, and a bottle of water, and gave it unto Hagar, putting it on her shoulder, and the child, and sent her away: and she departed, and wandered in the wilderness of Beersheba." Abraham's bigamy is explained by Sarah's desire for children (Gen. 16:2) as an apologetic. So also is Jacob's bigamy by the deceit of Laban (Gen. 29:23).

Saul took away his daughter Michal from David her husband and gave her to Phalti, the son of Laish (I Sam. 25:44). Here the father took the liberty to dissolve his daughter's marriage.

The Practice of Divorce Did Not Bear God's Approval

In spite of the fact that this was the way women were treated in their role as wives, it did not mean that the treatment and practice necessarily bore God's approval. What God permits, including polygamy and reckless dismissal of a wife, does not necessarily mean He condones. He allowed man to fall by giving him the gift of free choice. Obedience would not be a virtue if there were no possibility of disobedience.

Monogamous marriage, nevertheless, was extensively used in the prophetic teaching as the symbol of the union of God with Israel (Hosea 2; Isa. 50:1), while polygamy had its counterpart in idolatry. The imagery shows that monogamous marriage was felt to be the highest form, and on the other hand, the detestation of idolatry naturally strenghtened the dislike of the form of marriage by which it was so eloquently typified.

The religious code in Deuteronomy 24 thus acknowledged a husband's right to divorce. That did not necessarily mean that it was God's original purpose for the state of matrimony to be dissolved by any cause other than the death of the one party. God's original purpose and intent are clearly stated in Genesis 1:27: "So God created man in his own image, in the image of God created he him; male and female created he them." Also, in Genesis 2:18 and 24 we read: "And the Lord God said, It is not good that the man should be alone; I will make him an helpmeet for him . . . Therefore, shall a man leave his father and his mother, and shall cleave unto his wife: and they shall be one flesh."

These verses describe the state of mankind and the estate of marriage prior to man's fall as a result of his disobedience. It is because of man's fall that the estate of marriage deteriorated and continues to deteriorate. It will continue to do so as the prophetic Scriptures foretell, even as all evil will become worse and worse until the Lord puts an end to this world as we know it.

God did not immediately destroy man because of his sin. He was, by virtue of the fall, separated from God's presence. Man's spirit became divorced from God's spirit in his spiritual death.

Laws Are Necessitated by the Presence of Sin

Because of man's alienation from God, his conduct had to be regulated by law. Had man not sinned, he would have never needed the Ten Commandments or any rules and regulations. He would have always done that which is perfect in God's sight and all his actions would have been beneficial to his fellow humans and never harmful.

Divorce and the dissolution of marriage by any human cause are the direct result of man's fall. Consequently, God had to make regulatory laws as in many other aspects of man's behavior.

The only perfect matching of two individuals was the union of the first pair, Adam and Eve. There has never been another. That's why God's Word contains a great deal of counsel concerning marriage. Christ can, however, restore us to that first estate of marital happiness by reverting us to the divinely instituted original union. He is the only One who restores man to what He originally meant him to be, and the more a husband and wife seek to be what God originally intended them to be, the happier their marriage will be. The limitation, however, is our

41

continuing human nature, fallen but redeemed. Our redemption is only partial since we still have the ability to fall short of God's goal for us. And we do fall short because of the yet unaccomplished redemption of our bodies and the environment in which we as humans live.

Therefore, our imperfect union in marriage needed God's regulation. In our next chapter we shall see how God regulated it.

9

THE DETERIORATION OF
THE ORIGINAL MARRIAGE

God ordained marriage. He made woman to complement man—one man to one woman and one woman to one man.

Genesis 2:24 is absolutely clear: "Therefore shall a man leave his father and his mother, and shall cleave unto his wife: and they shall be one flesh."

The Lord Jesus confirmed this Old Testament verse and stated it to be His concept of marriage. In Matthew 19:5 we read: "And (Jesus) said, For this cause shall a man leave father and mother, and shall cleave to his wife: and they twain (the two of them) shall be one flesh." That is marriage as God originally instituted it and as Christ affirmed it.

In the Old Testament we read that many kings took to themselves many wives, but this was not with the consent of God, but in spite of His prohibition. "Neither shall he (the king) multiply wives to himself, that his heart turn not away" (Deut. 17:17a).

Why Did God Institute Marriage?

First, it was His means for the propagation of the race. We read in Genesis 1:27b–28a: "Male and female created he them. And God blessed them, and God said unto them, Be fruitful, and multiply, and replenish the earth . . . ."

This relationship together between husband and wife is the only way God intended children to be born into the world. Not one man with any woman or women, but one man with one woman. Sexual union alone does not constitute marriage, but the union of a male and female with the blessing of God is the only divinely approved context of the exercise of sex.

The second function of marriage as instituted by God is to help each other. This is indicated in Genesis 2:18: "And the Lord God said, It is not good that the man should be alone; I will make him an help meet for him." God put a man and a woman together to provide each other with a unique companionship. This companionship is for life, while the companionship of a child-parent relationship is temporary (Gen. 2:24).

Any sexual relationship outside of marriage is sin. Paul says in I Corinthians 7:2, "To avoid fornication, let every man have his own wife, and let every woman have her own husband."

Marriage is valid for all people. The Apostle says in Hebrews 13:4: "Marriage is honourable in all, and the bed undefiled: but whoremongers and adulterers God will judge."

Paul in writing to Timothy tells him that in the latter times there will be an attempt made "forbidding to marry" (I Tim. 4:1–3). Why marry since two can have sex and live together in companionship and avoid the trouble and trauma of divorce if it doesn't work out according to their plans? That is a prophecy of not only the deterioration of the bond of marriage, but of the abolition of it.

An original duty is bound upon believers to marry only in the Lord. Paul in speaking about the duty of a widowed, believing woman says: "She is at liberty to be married to whom she will; only in the Lord" (I Cor. 7:39b). And in II Corinthians 6:14, Paul says: "Be ye not unequally yoked together with unbelievers: for what fellowship hath righteousness with unrighteousness? and what communion hath light with darkness?"

10

DIVORCE IN THE OLD AND NEW TESTAMENT TIMES AND TODAY

A basic reason for the current misunderstanding of the Biblical teaching of divorce is due to the change of the terminology used.

The word "divorce" as we use it today did not exist in olden times.

Today by divorce we mean the official declaration by a judge that a marriage performed either by a practitioner of religion or an empowered authority of the government has become legally dissolved. When that divorce is granted by a judge, there may be total freedom one from the other, or the judge may impose certain conditions. He may adjure that properties commonly held be divided according to a certain percentage. He may demand that alimony be paid by the husband to the wife and for the support of children if they should exist.

With the heathen, divorce was the easiest possible thing; it was open to a husband or to a wife to terminate the marriage at will. And things were not much better with the Jews, although there was a difference of opinion among the Rabbis. Some held that a man could "put away his wife for every cause," interpreting the "unseemly thing" of Deuteronomy 24:1 as anything for which a husband may dislike his wife. Others held that the husband could give his wife a bill of divorcement only if she were guilty of adultery, interpreting "the unseemly thing" in this stricter sense (Edersheim ii. 332ff). Jewish law absolutely forbade the marriage of the adulterer with the adulteress (Edersheim ii. 335).

In a modern divorce, it is the judge who decides the case as a result of the matter being brought before him by either spouse or by both of them.

However, that was not the procedure in Biblical times. The

45

dismissing was usually done by the husband. It was a matter between the two marital spouses, and most often, an arbitrary action by the husband not subject to the wife's consent. (See Gen. 21:14ff.) It was not a matter to be adjured by a judge of the state. The reason for this was that marriage as such was not a matter of civil authorization, but a recognition of the families or tribes or the society concerned as we have seen in our historical study of marriage.

When a husband in particular wanted to dismiss his wife for any reason, no one could hinder him from doing it. He simply sent her away. This sending away in the New Testament is expressed by two different words: "put away," *aphieemi;* "to cause to stand away from him" and "to dismiss;" *apoluoo,* "to send away from him." In the case of the wife or the dismissed partner leaving, it is the verb "to separate oneself" (*choorizomai*) that is used. It then refers rather to the one who wants to dissolve the marriage as just leaving the marital partner. All three words, when applied to marriage, signify its dissolution.

According to our understanding of the Old Testament, if the husband dismissed his wife for fornication or marital infidelity, he did not have to give her a bill of divorcement because such a certificate would actually declare an adulterous wife innocent and would give her permission to remarry without incurring any guilt upon herself.

If the wife was dismissed for reason of fornication or infidelity on her part, then the prescribed punishment was death by stoning. A man also who committed fornication or adultery was to be stoned. This was decreed in the law of God through Moses, but because of man's rebellion was not practiced.

At no time in either the Old or the New Testament do we find the case of the separation of the marital partners referred to civil authorities as is done today. No judge pronounced the separation valid as is the current practice. Judges sometimes, as we see in this study, examined the nature of the case in order to find out the validity of the guilt with a view of determining who should be declared innocent and who guilty. Always, utmost care was to be exercised in attributing guilt to the right person. God demands punishment only of the guilty party and the declaration of the freedom of the innocent party. Christ in the New Testament, which is the fulfillment of the Old Testament, cannot reverse the character of the God of the Old Testament.

46

The God of the New Testament is the God of justice of the Old Testament. However, in the New Testament we have the exception that Christ gave Himself to pay for the penalty of the sinner who, on the acceptance of Christ's grace, is justified before God and becomes just in that he is miraculously changed into a new creature. The God of the New Testament continues to be a God of justice, but because of the redemptive work of Christ, also becomes a forgiving and regenerating God. For, as the Word of God tells us, all have sinned, all need to repent.

But in the case of marriage where two individuals are concerned in their one-to-one relationship, when they separate, that separation may be due to the guilt of both.

As we read Numbers 5 and Deuteronomy 22, we see how meticulously God provided for finding who the guilty party was in the case of marital jealousy. If the husband suspected that his wife was unfaithful to him, there was a definite procedure whereby the truth could be found as to whether it was a matter of jealousy on the part of the husband or real guilt on the part of the woman. If the woman was not guilty she was free of the marital relationship whether so pronounced by her husband or not. God never punishes the innocent party in the conjugal relationship. In the case of guilt on the part of one spouse, the innocent would be declared free by the examiners and the guilty punished. The dismissal with trumped-up charges was forbidden by the guilty party without giving the innocent spouse a bill of divorcement (Deut. 24:1).

This was not something that a judge did as is the case today, but the dismissing, guilty spouse put away his innocent wife. To put away or dismiss, therefore, was an action taken by the guilty partner. The giving of the divorce document enabled the innocent party to remarry without any stigma of guilt. "Then let him write her a bill of divorcement, and give it in her hand, and send her out of his house. And when she is departed out of his house, she may go and be another man's wife" (Deut. 24:1b, 2).

We see, therefore, that to divorce one's marriage partner was not equivalent to today's divorce. Today in some countries a divorce does not spell out who is guilty and who is innocent of the two partners. The judge does not consider this essential to find out and make public. He simply dissolves the marriage legally. Such a thing does not exist in the Bible.

Biblical teaching distinguishes between the guilty and the

innocent party. The guilty party was known to God and sooner or later would bear the consequence of his or her guilt. And the guilt was that much greater if, by not granting the certificate of divorce, the dismissing partner refused to clear his or her spouse from the supposed guilt of marital separation.

Since the only legitimate cause of separation in the New Testament was and is fornication, or sexual infidelity, the mere dismissal of a marital partner automatically bears upon it the guilt of adultery. This is why any woman, according to Christ's words in Matthew 5:32, who is dismissed and is married by another causes that new husband to assume her presumed guilt. If she, however, is not merely dismissed, but dismissed with a certificate of divorcement in her hand by her husband, then she would really be divorced officially as we understand it today. That divorce would bear on it the stamp of innocence as far as she was concerned.

Thus in Biblical times, if a person was said to be divorced or had a bill of divorcement in her hands, that meant she was innocent and free to remarry. If she was merely dismissed without a certificate of divorce, then she could belong to one of two categories. First, she would be guilty because she was unfaithful to her husband in which case her husband did not have to give her divorce papers, or she was innocent but because her husband did not give her divorce papers, she was considered guilty.

The only thing that such an innocent wife could do in the latter case was to exercise the freedom to remarry denied to her by her guilty and unscrupulous husband, but inherently provided to her by a just God.

In Leviticus 20 and 21 there are all kinds of sexual sins delineated and prohibited. Guilt brings its prescribed punishment.

When it comes to the priests and their marriages, we read in Leviticus 21:7: "They shall not take a wife that is a whore, or profane; neither shall they take a woman put away from her husband: for he is holy unto his God."

Observe that there is a distinction made between a "whore," which means a proven sinner who wallows and finds pleasure in the sins of the flesh. But it also says that priests should not take "a woman put away from her husband." There must be a difference between the two. The second one is not a guilty one,

48

but one who bears upon her the appearance of evil, most probably being the unjustifiably dismissed one of Matthew 5:32b.

If one remembers Paul's admonition in I Thessalonians 5:22, "Abstain from all appearance of evil," one would better understand his admonition about the marriage status of a bishop (I Tim. 3:2) and an elder (Titus 1:6) to be one woman's husband. This basically means to be currently married to one woman, to be monogamous and not married to more than one woman.

But it is not inconceivable that Paul had in mind the Old Testament regulation that the priests should not even marry a woman who was put away by her husband, one who was innocent and yet bore the possible appearance of guilt because she was put away without a bill of divorcement. These two verses, in our opinion, cannot lead to any strict regulation of prohibiting those bishops or elders who are married to an innocent, dismissed woman, from the service of the Lord.

This matter becomes discretionary rather than mandatory, especially as one remembers that the bishops or elders of the New Testament are not the successors or exact equivalent of the priests of the Old Testament.

When God in the Old Testament uses the term "divorce" in His relationship to His people Israel, we must remember that in a figurative sense the word has a fundamentally different meaning than the literal use pertaining to the conjugal relationship between two human beings. In this latter relationship, the guilt may be on both parties or on only one. The innocent party is always exonerated by God and is set free, whereas the guilty has punishment proscribed.

In the simile of God being married to Israel or Christ to His Church, when the relationship goes sour, it is never God's or Christ's fault, but Israel's or the Church's. Therefore God entreats His people to come back to Him from whoredom to Himself.

In Jeremiah 3:6 we read: ". . . Hast thou seen that which backsliding Israel hath done? She is gone up upon every high mountain and under every green tree, and there hath played the harlot." And then in verse 8 we read, "And I saw, when for all the causes whereby backsliding Israel committed adultery I had put her away, and given her a bill of divorce; yet her treacherous

49

sister Judah feared not, but went and played the harlot also."

The giving of a divorce in this symbolic use of spiritual harlotry has the meaning exactly opposite to the meaning when a guilty husband faces an innocent wife whom he dismisses.

God is not a guilty spouse. He is holy and the reason He puts away His people to whom He is married is always due to their guilt and backsliding. The certificate of divorce given by God to His people is rather a confirmation of the guilt of His people.

But when a guilty marital partner puts away his or her spouse for a reason other than fornication, the required bill of divorcement is to demonstrate publicly that he or she is innocent and is free to remarry.

When God chose Israel and the Jews for His wife as Hosea the prophet describes, it was not because the Jews were so upright and holy. They did not deserve it any more than any other people, but God had joined them to Himself under an unconditional covenant in Abraham. Thus we find God married to a defiled people. "Go, take unto thee a wife of whoredoms and children of whoredoms: for the land hath committed great whoredom, departing from the Lord" (Hosea 1:2). Then God gave His people the conditional Sinaitic covenant. His blessings under that depended on the condition of the fulfillment of the prescribed laws.

Let us therefore not in any way confuse the meaning of God's attitude toward a disobedient people (whom He loves and pleads for their return in spite of the spiritual divorce that exists between them) and the relationship between a husband and wife in which case either the husband or wife may prove to be the guilty party in the relationsip. And in any human marriage, while a partner may be innocent of sexual sins, in no way could that one be totally free of all sin and so the analogy breaks down.

In all that we say about a husband putting away his wife unjustifiably or justifiably, it must be understood that the treatment and justice of God is equal no matter who is the guilty or the innocent party, the man or the woman. God is not a respecter of persons. He does not have one standard of justice for men and another for women. The sin of fornication or adultery is no less serious because it is perpetrated by a man and more serious when perpetrated by a woman. We have spoken about a guilty husband and a non-guilty wife because it is more frequently present in this manner in the Scriptures. It may be the husband is less faithful than the wife in the marital relationship because he is less likely to be discovered and bear openly and for a lifetime the consequence of his sin.

11

GOD PROTECTS THE INNOCENT PARTY

What the Old Testament records, as the Lord Jesus later affirmed, is that divorce was practiced then even as it is practiced today. So was polygamy, but it did not bear upon it God's sanction and approval. What God was and is concerned about is that justice, as much as possible, be rendered to the victim of divorce by the perpetrator and initiator of it.

God prescribes what man must do in order to mitigate the evil consequences of his sinful choice, and that is to protect the innocent party who suffers because of his action. Thus He maintains His justice since man has chosen a life of sinfulness.

In Leviticus 21:7 we read: "They (the priests) shall not take a wife that is a whore, or profane; neither shall they take a woman put away from her husband: for he is holy unto his God." No doubt the woman put away from her husband was an innocent party put away without being given a bill of divorcement.

And in verse 14, continuing to speak of the priest, it says, "A widow, or a divorced woman, or profane, or an harlot, these shall he not take; but he shall take a virgin of his own people to wife." It is evident that God's choice for a priest was nothing less than a virgin since even a widow was excluded.

Of course, this has limited application to a priest of that time and is not in any way binding in the New Testament dispensation where we are given further apostolic enlightenment as to elders and deacons. (See I Tim. 3:2 and Titus 1:6.) These are not to be equated with the priests of the Levitical order.

Further instructions concerning the priests and their families are found in Leviticus 22:13. Also, we have instructions concerning the vows of widows and divorced women in Numbers 30:9–16. In Deuteronomy 22:13–21 we have the procedure that was to be followed in case a man married a woman whom he accused as not being a virgin or if, perhaps, she was found not to be a virgin. The rest of the chapter has further rules regulating the marriage relationship.

In Deuteronomy 22:22 we read: "If a man be found lying with a woman married to an husband, then they shall both of them die, both the man that lay with the woman, and the woman: so shalt thou put away evil from Israel." Observe how carefully exempted from punishment is the innocent party, the husband of the wife who lies with another man.

The same was true in the case of a virgin girl who was betrothed or engaged to a husband even as the Virgin Mary was to Joseph. If a man found her in the city and lay with her, who was to be punished? Only the virgin who went astray and the man with whom she went. They were to die by being stoned, but not the innocent man to whom the virgin was engaged (Deut. 22:23–24).

For further proof of God's benevolent consideration for the innocent party in the conjugal relationship, we read: "But if a man find a betrothed damsel in the field, and the man force her (observe that she does not consent to this rape), and lie with her: then the man only that lay with her shall die. But unto the damsel thou shalt do nothing; there is in the damsel no sin worthy of death: for as when a man riseth against his neighbor, and slayeth him, even so is this matter. For he found her in the field, and the betrothed damsel cried, and there was none to save her" (Deut. 22:25–27).

Having Relations With a Virgin Should Lead to Marrying Her

In Deuteronomy 22:28 and 29 we are told about the obligation a man is found under to marry a virgin he had relations with. "If a man find a damsel that is virgin, which is not betrothed, and lay hold on her, and lie with her, and they be found; then the man that lay with her shall give unto the damsel's father fifty shekels of silver, and she shall be his wife; because he hath humbled her, he may not put her away all his days." Again evident is God's compensation with obligatory marriage by the man to the girl he forced, since such a girl would then stand no chance of marriage and would remain in an unprotected state in the Jewish society.

*Christ Did Not Change God's Concern for the Innocent Party
in Divorce*

All throughout the law the Lord did not abrogate His
protection and consideration of the innocent party in marriage.
God's moral character has not changed in this. Jesus Christ, if
anything, provides stricter rules in making the law complete or
fulfilling it.

Actually in Numbers 5:11–31 we have the prescribed
method of how a wife was to be tested to determine whether or
not she had been with another man. Further references as to Old
Testament rules on the subject are to be found in Isaiah 50:1,
Jeremiah 3:1 and Ezekiel 44:22.

Capital Punishment for Adultery Decreed but Not Applied

From all of the above Old Testament passages it is evident
that although capital punishment was supposed to be inflicted in
case of marital unfaithfulness or fornication, yet we have no
specific historical evidence that such punishment was actually
inflicted. In late Jewish practice the penalties were merely
divorce with the wife's forfeiture of her dowry which had been
given by the bridegroom and his family if she was proven not to
be a virgin. There is not, according to Lightfoot, an example of a
wife punished for adultery with death.[1]

The New Testament and the Innocent Party in Divorce

The New Testament bears out the same effect. In His
references to the subject in Matthew 5:32, etc., the Lord Jesus
clearly speaks of the husband's obligation to give his dismissed
wife a bill of divorcement. The basic reason given for Joseph's
decision to put away his betrothed wife privily without making
her a public show is that he was a just man. As Hastings
says: "The weightiest evidence on the other side is derived from
the narrative of the woman taken in adultery (John 8:3–11).
From the reference to stoning, it might be inferred that her status
was that of a betrothed woman, and the implication of the
narrative seems to be that there was but a step between her and
death. It is, however, to be remembered that Jesus was
surrounded by enemies who labored to entangle Him in His
talk—especially to bring Him into collision with Moses, and the

plot in this instance doubtless was to put Him in the dilemma of either declaring for the revival of a practice which had already become obsolete, or of giving His sanction to the apparent infraction of the law which the substitution of divorce involved.[2]

At all events, the reply of Jesus supported the abrogation of the law until judges were found who themselves were innocent as tried by His own heart-searching test. On the contrary, the prophetical writings imply that there was widespread guilt and widespread immunity. The story of Hosea implies the post-nuptial fall of the prophet's wife. It would follow from this that in the 8th century B.C., the law not only did not inflict capital punishment, but did not even, as later, insist on divorce. In spite of the legal enactments then, it may be assumed that death was not actually inflicted, and that it was deemed that the husband was sufficiently protected by his right of divorce; the woman sufficiently punished by loss of status and property, while the adulterer might be punished in damages" (ibid, p. 273).

[1]James Hasting's *Dictionary of the Bible,* T. & T. Clark, 1904, vol. III, p. 273.

[2]Art. "Adultery," *Kitto Bible Cyclopedia.*

12

DIVORCE IN CHRIST'S
SERMON ON THE MOUNT

Matthew 5:27–32

The first occurrence of divorce in Christ's teaching is in the Sermon on the Mount. Unfortunately, most writers on the subject of divorce isolate Matthew 5:31 and 32 from its context, thus compounding the difficulties encountered in understanding what Christ really taught.

Christ's Relationship With the Law

The teaching of the Lord Jesus on divorce ought to be examined with Matthew 5:17 when He delineates His relationship with the law and prophets. "Think not that I am come to destroy the law, or the prophets: I am not come to destroy, but to fulfill." Actually, the Greek word *katalusai* (destroy) could be better translated "abrogate, to render invalid." Therefore, what the law and the prophets said is not cancelled out by Christ, but fulfilled. The expression "the law and the prophets" refers to the entire Old Testament, the Pentateuch and the Prophets. For this reason the subject of marriage, divorce and remarriage cannot be studied only from the New Testament. An acquaintance with the teaching of the Old Testament on the subject is a must. Therefore, in case you started reading this treatise at this point, please go back and study our previous chapters dealing with the Old Testament.

The Law Became Necessary Because of Man's Sin

These Old Testament Scriptures containing God's rules for man's life were necessary because of man's sinfulness, but man could not live up to them. For this reason the Lord Jesus Christ came so that in Him God's desire for man may be realized.

Through His virtue and our acceptance of His substitutionary death, the keeping of the whole law is imputed to us. But that does not mean that the provisions of the law concerning our behavior are abrogated. Rather, they are validated. They are made complete in Christ. He completes them. It is as if God had a glass partly filled with His revelation, and then Christ came and filled it to the brim. This is made clear in Matthew 5:17–20.

The Law Regulates Our Relationship With Others

These rules of life in the Old Testament are important primarily in the realm of our relationship with God and others. This is why the Lord speaks first about the sanctity of another's life. To kill another person is forbidden in the Decalogue. But Jesus refines this law. Sin is not merely overt killing, but what ultimately leads to murder—anger! The Lord wants us to nip the evil in its inception.

Observe that the Lord states in Matthew 5:21, "Ye have heard that it was said." Those to whom Christ was speaking knew what God had said in the Old Testament.

Christ Refines the Provisions of the Old Testament

Then in verse 27 He uses the same expression: "Ye have heard that it was said." And He carries the commandment one step further by speaking of a man who looks on a woman to desire her when he shouldn't as having actually committed fornication against her. This is Christ's refinement of the Old Testament, not the abrogation of it.

Fidelity to One's Spouse Involves an Instinctive Sense of Right

But when we come down to verse 31, He does not repeat the expression, "Ye have heard that it was said," but simply, "It was said."

Because this involves an instinctive, natural knowledge of the impropriety of the act He is about to elaborate upon, He does not say "Ye have heard that . . ." but simply "It was said." It is not necessary to hear it to know that it is wrong to flirt and ultimately have a relationship with a woman other than your wife. In a case of murder, another person is involved. But in looking at a woman to desire her, knowing she belongs to some other man or does not and cannot belong to you, you involve just yourself. You may commit adultery against a woman just by the desire in your heart without in any way externalizing that desire into an overt action. Most likely she would not know it and neither would her husband if she were a married woman.

The Wandering Eye and Adultery Against Another Woman

Observe carefully Matthew 5:28 before you go on to verses 31 and 32. "But I say unto you that whosoever (anyone) seeing a woman for the purpose of desiring her, has already committed adultery against her in his heart" (Author's translation). It is unfortunate that the translations in the Authorized Version and even in the more recent New International Version say, "he has committed adultery *with* her already." This implies consent on the part of the woman which is not the case at all. The Greek verb is in the active voice *emoicheusen,* "committed adultery," with an accusative *auteen,* "her," which makes it a transitive verb. It is "he committed adultery *against* her," or, if we could coin an active transitive verb in English, we would say, "he adultered her." This is without her consent or knowledge of it at all. As we read in Gerhard Kittel's *Theological Dictionary of the New Testament:* "With accusative (*auteen*) of adultery *against* a woman (Matt. 5:28)."

This in reality is equivalent to mental or heart rape. In actual rape, a woman could not be held guilty for what a man does to her. She is overpowered. As Peter says, "Having eyes full of adultery, and that cannot cease from sin" (II Peter 2:14).

Interestingly enough, the Greek text of Matthew 5:28 does not say, as the Authorized Version has it, "That whosoever looketh on a woman," but "whosoever keeps on looking on a woman."[1]

The sin of lustful desire develops through the wandering eye, continually looking at a woman. Take that eye off the forbidden woman, says our Lord, and when you come down to it any woman other than the one you can legitimately love and marry is a forbidden woman, even as the tree was forbidden in the case of Adam and Eve. In spite of the fact that they could have anything else in the whole world to their full satisfaction, their lustful eyes fell on the one forbidden tree. It is better to pluck out the eye, our Lord says, than have sin be the victor.

The Lord is really explaining the commandment He referred to in verse 27, "Do not commit adultery," or in the English verb we have coined for this translation, "Don't adulter." It is *moicheuseis,* the restrictive word referring to illicit relations with a married woman.

[1]*Ho blepoon,* "the looking one," in the present participle active.

13

THE CAUSE AND RESULT
OF
LUSTFUL LONGING

Matthew 5:31 to 32 cannot be separated from its context, for in these verses the Lord quite clearly implies that he who keeps on looking lustfully upon a woman he cannot have may end up in divorce.

The Lord didn't have to say, "Ye have heard it said," in this instance, and it is the only time in this context of the Sermon on the Mount that He leaves out "Ye have heard it said." (See Matthew 5:21, 27, 31, 33, 38, 43.) It is as if our Lord wanted to emphasize its intrinsic evil. A man doesn't have to be told that this is evil. He knows it is. *"It was said . . ."* Period! Whether one has heard it or not does not make any difference. When a man is found divorcing his wife as a result of that lustful look he kept casting upon that other woman, nobody needs to inform him that such a thing is wrong. A person knows it instinctively and is responsible for the evil. No criminal can stand before a judge and say, "I did it, but I didn't know it was wrong." No judge will let a man escape just through pleading ignorance of the law as long as there is a law regulating moral or immoral action. Verses 31 and 32 cannot be taken separately and examined apart from the preceding message in verses 27 to 30 and yet arrive at their correct meaning.

When the Lord in Matthew 5:31 says, "Whosoever shall put away his wife," whom did He mean by the word "whosoever"? Actually, the Greek relative pronoun *hos* means "he who." He is speaking about the man He has just finished describing in verses 27 to 30. It's the man with the wandering eye who keeps on looking lustfully upon a married woman. Then he desires her and he commits adultery against her, first in his heart. Of course, he is not satisfied with just that. He then wants to have her no matter what. Never mind if she is a married woman, he finally begins to reason, she can get a divorce from her husband. But how about me, the one whose eye has been enthralled with her? I am also married. Well, I can divorce my wife too. I'll have it made.

His wife knows nothing about this lust affair at its start. I don't call it a love affair, because really it is not. Love is based on the spiritual relationship of a man and a woman before any relationship of the flesh. They who are spiritually joined together become one flesh that never separates. But they who are attracted only by the physical appearance constantly live in the temptation of seeing someone else who may be more attractive. The possibility of steadfastness in a marriage that is based on looks and mere sexual satisfaction is very small indeed compared to the spiritual relationship based on *agape* love that seeks not self-satisfaction primarily, but meeting the need of one's partner. The satisfaction of usefulness in life in meeting the need of another is far greater than the satisfaction of selfish procurement.

The man the Lord Jesus describes in Matthew 5:27 to 30 just cannot dismiss his wife at pleasure. He has an obligation to her. He must give her "divorce papers." Actually, the Greek text of verse 31 literally translated says: "He who if he dismisses the wife, his own, let him give her a bill of divorcement." In the Greek the word is *apostasion,* meaning the socially acceptable document that she needs having been dismissed by him.

"If he dismisses her," the law in Deuteronomy 24:1 declares, then he ought to show her, the victim of his crime, the basic consideration of giving her a bill of divorcement. He must not just send her away, but must think of her future. Why should she suffer, in addition to the trauma of sending her away, the stigma of nobody knowing what the circumstances of her separation are?

In the Lord's reiteration of the Old Testament's defense of the innocent party, we must not read into it His condoning in any way divorce itself, which would involve the sin which causes it. One has to remember what the Lord declared in Malachi 2:15 and 16 when speaking symbolically of Israel being separated from Himself: "Therefore take heed to your spirit, and let none deal treacherously against the wife of his youth. For the Lord, the God of Israel, saith that he hateth putting away." This refers to the dismissing by a guilty spouse of his innocent party. Of course, the Lord hates the committing of a crime by anybody against an innocent party, especially when the perpetrator of the crime is one's own spouse.

In all this discussion of our Lord's reference to the law of Moses, we must never forget what He said when He began to make mention of the Mosaic law. In Matthew 5:17 we hear Him saying: "Think not that I am come to destroy the law, or the prophets: I am not come to destroy, but to fulfill." He came to become the fulfillment of the law and to add to it. His complement of the law is expressed by His words: "but I say unto you" (Matt. 5:2, 20, 22, 28, 32, 34, 39, 44). He did not cancel the law that demanded that the husband who dismisses his wife for any reason other than fornication grant her a bill of divorcement. He added that the only justifiable reason for dismissing one's wife is fornication. The law also implied this as we have seen, but did not state it as explicitly as the Lord Jesus did.

14

WHAT DOES IT MEAN "TO COMMIT ADULTERY" AGAINST ANOTHER?

For the person who is unable to read the New Testament in Greek, it may be a help to know when the verb *moicheuoo*, "to commit adultery," is used in its active form in a variety of tenses.

The Active Form of the Greek Verb, Moicheuoo

Matthew 5:27 – "Thou shalt not commit adultery," or "Thou shalt not adulter." [1]

Matthew 5:28 – "Whosoever looketh on a woman to lust after her hath committed *(emoicheusen)* adultery with (against) her already in his heart."

Matthew 19:18 – "He (the rich young ruler) said unto him (Jesus), Which (commandment)? Jesus said, Thou shalt do no murder; thou shalt not commit adultery." [2]

Mark 10:19 – "Thou knowest the commandments, Do not commit adultery." [3]

Luke 16:18 – "Whosoever putteth away his wife and marrieth another, committeth adultery." [4]

Luke 18:20 – "Thou knowest the commandments, Do not commit adultery. . . ." [5]

Romans 2:22 – "Thou that sayest a man should not commit adultery, dost thou commit adultery?" [6,7]

Romans 13:9 – "For this, Thou shalt not commit adultery. . . ." [8]

James 2:11 – "For he that said, Do not commit adultery,[9] said also, Do not kill. Now if thou commit no adultery,[10] yet if thou kill, thou art become a trangressor of the law."

Revelation 2:22 – "Behold, I will cast her into a bed, and them that commit adultery[11] with her into great tribulation except they repent of their deeds."

[1]*Ou moicheuseis,* future indicative.

[2]*Ou moicheuseis,* future indicative.

[3]*Mee moicheusees,* first aorist subjunctive.

[4]*Moicheuei,* present indicative meaning "continuously is in a state of adultery."

[5]*Me moicheusees,* first aorist subjunctive, referring to any particular time in the future.

[6]*Me moicheuein,* present infinite.

[7]*Moicheueis,* present indicative, meaning "Do you commit adultery on a continuous basis?"

[8]*Ou moicheuseis,* future indicative meaning, "Thou shalt not commit adultery at any particular time in the future."

[9]*Mee mooicheusees,* first aorist subjunctive meaning, "Do not commit adultery at any particular time in the future."

[10]*Ou moicheuseis,* future indicative, referring to a particular future time.

[11]*Tous moicheuontas,* accusative plural masculine participle present, meaning "those who are continuously adultering or committing adultery."

15

WHAT DOES IT MEAN TO COMMIT ADULTERY AGAINST ONESELF OR HAVE ADULTERY COMMITTED AGAINST ONESELF BY ANOTHER?

The middle voice is used when the action reverts on oneself. The passive voice is used when an action is committed by someone else upon another. The form of the middle and passive voices is the same, *moicheuomai,* but the determination whether the meaning is middle or passive is made by the understanding of the context.

Let us look at the passages in the New Testament where *moicheuomai* is used:

Matthew 5:32 – "But I say unto you, that whosoever shall put away his wife, saving for the cause of fornication, causeth her to commit adultery." [1] Since this involves the innocent wife divorced by her licentious husband, it does not involve her in committing adultery. [2] This innocent woman does not commit adultery against herself; she is adultered against. Someone else commits adultery against her. She is made to be considered or stigmatized as an adulteress since her husband dismisses her without giving her a bill of divorcement. [3] She is not yet remarried. Therefore, the presumption of this adultery being committed by her against herself or by a new husband is totally unwarranted. [4]

Matthew 5:32b – "And whosoever shall marry her that is divorced committeth adultery." [5] The determination whether this middle or passive form of *moichaomai* has a middle or passive meaning depends on who this "dismissed woman" whom he marries is. She cannot be a woman dismissed by her husband due to her sexual infidelity. If that was the reason for her dismissal, according to the Old Testament provisions in

Leviticus 20:10 and Deuteronomy 22:22, she deserved death and not a bill of divorcement. The man committing adultery also deserved death. Such a bill of divorcement was only to be granted, according to Deuteronomy 24:1–4, to a wife dismissed for reasons other than infidelity so that she could remarry without the stigma of being considered an adulteress. Therefore, "the dismissed one," the *apolelumeneen,* must refer to the innocent wife unjustifiably dismissed by her first husband. She bears upon herself the stigma of an adulteress because her first husband did not give her a divorce. The necessity of giving such a divorce is what Jesus taught in saying, "Let him (the licentious husband) give her (the innocent wife) a writing of divorcement." It is not due to the remarriage of such an innocent divorceè bearing the stigma of a dismissed wife without a divorce that she is considered an adulteress. When, therefore, a man who was never married or who himself is the innocent party of a divorce, marries such a woman, he himself, by virtue of that action, commits adultery against himself. He does so by virtue of his choice to marry such a woman. In that regard the meaning of *moichatai* is middle. But it can also be said to have a passive meaning in that she, bearing the unjustified stigma of adultery, brings upon him the same stigma. But since the choice of marrying such a woman is entirely his, implied in the active verb *gameesee,* "if he shall marry her," the weight of the meaning of *moichatai* is middle — he, the innocent man, marrying an innocent woman dismissed by her husband, takes upon himself the stigma of her undeserved adultery.

The meaning of *moichatai,* therefore, in Matthew 5:32b and 19:9b, referring to the man who marries an unjustifiably dismissed wife is primarily "causes adultery upon himself" by virtue of marrying her. This is made clear by the voice of the verb in Luke 16:18b: "And whosoever marrieth her that is put away from her husband committeth adultery." [6] It is not she who commits adultery, but he, and this by virtue of his marriage to a woman stigmatized by having been dismissed by her husband. He now bears the consequences of her former husband's action. It was his choice, and as a result, the verb is used in the active voice, present indicative, *moicheuei,* to indicate that responsibility more indirectly implied by the middle meaning of the middle-passive form *moichatai.* [7]

Matthew 19:9 – "And I say unto you, Whosoever shall put

away his wife, except it be for fornication, and shall marry another, committeth adultery." [8] This must definitely be taken as in the middle voice. This man commits adultery upon himself by not merely dismissing his innocent wife, but by also marrying another woman for whom he lusted. He is totally responsible for his sin of adultery.

"And whoso marrieth her which is put away doth commit adultery." [9] The thing that we must determine here is whether the meaning of the verb *moichatai* is middle or passive. The form allows either usage and the meaning must be determined by the contextual exegesis. Since the participle, dismissed (woman), *apolelumeneen,* as in Matthew 5:32b, refers not to the guilty but to the innocent wife and should be translated, "the dismissed one" (the unjustifiably dismissed one), the one who marries her marries one who is stigmatized or considered an adulteress, not by virtue of her remarriage to a new husband who has either never been married or is the innocent party in a divorce, but by virtue of the unjustifiable dismissal by her first husband. She was not in reality an adulteress, but by virtue of what her husband did to her, she is made to appear as one in the sight of others since she was not given a bill of divorcement to clear her of presumed guilt as the Old Testament prescribed and Christ confirmed. She did not, however, have to have a bill of divorcement in order to remarry. A certificate of divorce then was not an official document necessary for a second marriage as today. It was simply a certification of innocence which if issued by a guilty husband declared a wife innocent. Whether, however, the wife had such a certificate or not, she could marry anyway. If she had it, she did not cause any guilt upon her new husband. But if she did not, then the new husband marrying her took upon himself the false guilt of adultery. Since, therefore, a man in good standing marries a woman unjustifiably dismissed by her licentious husband, he bears upon himself the social stigma of committing adultery against himself. Therefore, we must ascribe middle meaning to the verb *moichatai,* here as in Matthew 5:32b, rendering it "causes adultery upon himself" for the rest of his life. The woman *moichatai,* is "adultered" against by virtue of her unjustifiable dismissal and the new husband *moichatai,* is "adultered" for the rest of his life by virtue of his marriage to one who bears the social stigma of dismissal because of her first husband's arbitrary dismissal for any reason other than her own sexual infidelity.

Mark 10:11 – "And he saith unto them, Whosoever shall put away his wife, and marry another, committeth adultery against her." [10] Here the licentious guilty man, if he dismisses his wife unjustifiably and he marries another, causes adultery forever against the new woman he marries. It is the new wife who becomes the recipient of his guilt of adultery. Mark here designates the object, *ep auteen,* "against her," to give the passive form of *maichatai* also passive meaning. The licentious husband causes adultery to be committed against his new wife. In Matthew 5:32b the verb *moichatai* does not have an explicit object and therefore can be interpreted first as having a middle meaning, "he commits adultery against himself," and also as clearly stated in Mark 10:11, as having passive meaning, "causes adultery to be committed against the woman he marries."

Mark 10:12 – "And if a woman shall put away her husband, and be married to another, she committeth adultery." [11] This concerns a woman who unjustifiably dismissed her husband and is married to another man. The passive form of *moichatai* in this instance can be taken as having first middle meaning. She brings the stigma of adultery upon herself since she is married to another man other than her innocent husband. Secondly, it can have passive meaning in that she causes her new husband to suffer adultery by virtue of what she has done.

John 8:4 – "They say unto him, Master, this woman was taken in adultery,[12] in the very act." This present participle refers to the very time when she was alleged to have been caught. At the time she was being "adultered." Adultery was committed against her and with her. She was not raped, however. She participated in the desire and act of adultery. The meaning is also middle: "She was bringing adultery against herself." This is why the Lord said to her, "Neither do I condemn thee: go, and sin no more" (John 8:11). This meant that she participated in the sin of adultery.

[1] *Moichasthai,* TR; *moicheutheenai,* UBS.

[2] Therefore, we preclude the form *moichasthai,* the present infinitive of *moichaomai,* being in the middle voice.

[3] The United Bible Society Text has this infinitive in the first

aorist infinitive passive, *moicheutheenai,* not allowing it to be mistaken as being in the middle voice. It definitely refers to adultery committed against her, the innocent woman, by her licentious husband.

[4]The definite passive mood of *moicheutheenai* (UBS) carries weight to be placed on taking the Textus Receptus reading to be passive in meaning although the form can be either middle or passive.

[5]*Moichatai,* third person singular present indicative of *moichaomai* meaning "commits adultery the rest of his life."

[6]*Moicheuei,* third person singular active indicative present. The verb *moichaomai* has been taken by some to be a deponent verb, an active verb with a middle or passive ending, *omai,* but with active meaning. Even if this were to be conceded, according to the Greek lexicographer D. Demetrakos (Vol. I p. 785) deponent verbs may also have passive meaning. And we add that if this is so, they may also have middle meaning (*The Great Lexicon of the Greek Language,* D. Demetrakos, 9 Volumes, Athens, 1949). See also: *A Grammar of the Greek New Testament in the Light of Historical Research,* pp. 332-333; 811-813; 817; *A Grammar of the Greek Language* by William Edward Jelf, Oxford, (1861 Vol. II, p. 18, 26-27).

[7]As A.T. Robertson says: "The active voice is usually transitive. . . . The voice does not deal primarily with the transitive idea. That belongs rather to the verb itself apart from voice . . . . The active voice represents the subject (in this case the man who marries the dismissed wife) as merely acting" (p. 331). Thus *moicheuei* and *moichatai* indicate the same transitive action.

[8]*Moichatai,* third person singular present indicative of *moichaomai.*

[9]*Moichatai,* third person singular present indicative of *moichaomai.*

[10]*Moichatai,* third person singular present indicative of *moichaomai* meaning, "causes adultery against her" (*ep auteen,* actually "upon or against her").

[11]*Moichatai,* third person singular present indicative of *moichaomai.*

[12]*Moicheuomenee,* nominative singular feminine participle, present middle or passive.

16

WHY DOES THE LORD JESUS REPEAT THE OLD TESTAMENT PROVISION THAT AN ADULTERER MUST GIVE HIS DISMISSED WIFE A DIVORCE DOCUMENT?

"It hath been said, Whosoever shall put away his wife, let him give her a writing of divorcement." Matthew 5:31

The word *apostasion*, "bill of divorcement," occurs only three times in the New Testament—in Matthew 5:31, 19:7 and Mark 10:4. It is derived from the preposition *apo*, "from," and the verb *histeemi*, "to stand." It means a document that entitles a person, in this case the wife, to stand afar off, implying cessation of the marital responsibility. In Matthew 19:7 and Mark 10:4 it is spoken of as *biblion apostasiou*, "a small book of divorcement or estrangement."

Now we must go to the Old Testament to find the purpose of what is called a "bill of divorcement," which takes us back to Deuteronomy 24, verses 1–4: "When a man hath taken a wife, and married her, and it come to pass that she find no favor in his eyes, because he hath found some uncleanness in her: then let him write her a bill of divorcement, and give it in her hand, and send her out of his house.

"And when she is departed out of his house, she may go and be another man's wife.

"And if the latter husband hate her, and write her a bill of divorcement, and giveth it in her hand, and sendeth her out of his house; or if the latter husband die, which took her to be his wife;

"Her former husband, which sent her away, may not take her again to be his wife, after that she is defiled; for that is abomination before the Lord: and thou shalt not cause the land to sin, which the Lord thy God giveth thee for an inheritance."

Here, as in the case of Matthew 5:31, we have a hypothesis. *If* a man for a stated reason decides to divorce his wife, he had better give her a bill of divorcement. The law and Christ had consideration for the wife who is put away. God as a just God is always against the guilty and protects the innocent. She is entitled to a divorce certificate.

"I Dismiss You Because I Don't Love You Anymore."

The law does not in any way argue that this excuse for dismissing one's marital partner is a valid reason which has God's approval. Maybe this is the reason why the basis for the dismissal is so vague. "When a man hath taken a wife, and married her and it come to pass that she find no favor in his eyes...." This is the same as saying: "If he does not like her anymore." This "something" he does not like can be anything. Simply the man can say, "I don't like your looks any more. You don't sexually satisfy me any more, or I really never loved you; therefore, I am dismissing you." It is exactly what is happening today. It's not something new. Call it incompatibility or whatever you will.

In no way can these verses be interpreted as God's command or encouragement for men to put away their wives when they don't like them any more. This is not the point at all. The point is only what is their duty toward the wives whom they are dismissing, and in no way can it be construed that God condones such action.

Nor does it say that one must dismiss his wife when she finds no favor in his eyes any more or when he has found some unclean thing in her, no matter what that is. Really, it is not important to find out what this unclean thing is, but it does not refer to sexual immorality on the part of the wife as we shall deal with later in this book. The implication is that it is not a valid reason for divorce.

17

DID JESUS CONDONE DIVORCE OR WAS HIS CONCERN FOR THE INNOCENT PARTY?

"It has been said whosoever shall put away his wife, let him give her a writing of divorcement." Matthew 5:31

In the New Testament the sinful state of adultery is declared to be utterly inconsistent with the Christian standing to the extent that it entails exclusion from the eternal Kingdom. St. Paul says in I Corinthians 6:9, "Know ye not that the unrighteous shall not inherit the kingdom of God? Be not deceived: neither fornicators, nor idolaters, not adulterers, nor effeminate, nor abusers of themselves with mankind" (homosexuals and lesbians).

Deuteronomy 24:1 Refers to Divorce for Reasons Other Than Adultery

The Lord Jesus, realizing how oppressed women were in the Old Testament, speaks of their rights in Matthew 5:31 and 32. Why should the man have the audacity to put away his wife for no fault of her own and then not give her a divorce which clears her of guilt in the breakup of the marriage? This is the Lord Jesus' concern in Matthew 5:31: "He, who, if he dismisses his wife, let him give her a bill of divorcement." This man really would not be obligated to give her such a bill of divorcement if she were put away for a valid reason such as adultery on her part. In Deuteronomy 24:1, if the "finding no favor in his (her husband's) eyes, because of some uncleanness" was really adultery, then the law would prescribe death by stoning as in the other passages in spite of the fact that such stoning was not actually practiced. Nevertheless, it was prescribed at other times for adultery which is not the case in Deuteronomy 24:1, and we can, therefore, conclude that this verse refers to the toleration of divorce for reasons other than adultery.

If a man decided to divorce his wife he had to do the following:

1. Write her a bill of divorcement;

2. Give it to her in her hand;

3. Send her out of his house.

Now, what could the woman divorced by her husband for no valid reason other than adultery do? This was prescribed in verse 2: She was free to marry another man.

If she was divorced by her second husband or he died, she was not permitted to go back to her first husband.

Her first husband, according to verse 4, could not remarry her for that would be an abomination to the Lord. Why would it be an abomination? Because she would have been the wife of another man.

Clearly, the Lord Jesus in Matthew 5:31 was referring to this provision in Deuteronomy 24:1 to 4 about the necessity of a husband who divorces his wife for any reason other than her own infidelity to give her divorce papers. Evidently it was common for a man to dismiss his wife in those days without valid reason and contrary to God's original law of marrying for life. Neither the God of the Old Testament nor Jesus Christ in any way condoned this practice of men to put away their wives for reasons other than the wife's infidelity no more than He condoned murder just because He made laws governing its punishment. It was man's choice in his sinful state. And that sinful state had to be regulated for the protection of the innocent woman who was dismissed unjustly by her husband. At least, the law said, give her a divorce.

A Divorce Certificate Gave the Right to Remarry to the Innocent Party

The divorce certificate was for the purpose of being able to remarry. In Deuteronomy 24:1 to 4, this is very clear. When the husband dismissed his wife and gave her a divorce, she was then permitted to remarry without the stigma of adultery. Verse 2 says, "And when she is departed out of his house, she may go

76

and be another man's wife." And if her second husband died, she could not go back to her first one. But after the dismissal by her first husband she could remarry if she wanted to. Nothing hindered her.

In Matthew 5:32, our Lord contrasted His attitude with the practice manifested in the Old Testament. The Lord agreed with the Old Testament prescription that a bill of divorcement should be given to the wife, unjustly divorced, enabling her to remarry. But Christ did not leave the matter there.

He castigated the evil of divorcing one's wife for no valid reason. Giving her a divorce mitigated the evil somewhat only as far as the innocent woman was concerned because that gave her the possibility of remarriage.

The Lord says why dismiss your wife at all if there is no real reason for it. "But I say unto you." The Lord here asserts His superiority above the law or anything that was said before. What was said was good and valid. Justice should be rendered to a wife unjustly dismissed. He in no way implies that no divorce certificate should be given to her. The Lord does not violate man's free choice to sin, but He does show His interest on behalf of the innocent victim of sin. That same interest of the law He upholds.

Jesus Was Speaking to His Disciples

The words of Jesus, "But I say unto you," did not stop man from divorcing his wife for unjustified causes. Nevertheless, Christ calls it a sin and says that man should live on a higher level if he truly wants to be a disciple of His. We must not lose sight of the fact that the Lord here in the Sermon on the Mount is speaking to His disciples and not to unbelievers (Matthew 5:1–2, 13). The Jews of the Old Testament felt satisfied in giving a divorce, but you, my disciples, asserted the Lord Jesus, are not Jews living in Old Testament times but in the new economy of My indwelling your heart. How can you as My followers think only of the consequences of your sin on the life of your partner and not on the sinfulness of your very act. Jesus was anxious for His disciples not to simply mitigate the consequences of evil but to avoid the evil altogether. As He said concerning murder, not only don't kill, but don't get angry. Don't only avoid actual adultery, but also visual adultery. It is best not to put your wife

77

away at all for any reason other than her infidelity, but if you do put her away when she does not deserve it, at least give her a bill of divorcement.

18

HOW TO AVOID DESIRING
ANOTHER WIFE OR HUSBAND

*"But I say unto you, That **whosoever** shall put away his wife...."*
Matthew 5:32

The Lord goes on to give the hypothetical case for the second time. Unfortunately, the translation of the Authorized Version does not make this supposition clear. It says, "That whosoever shall put away his wife, saving for the cause of fornication, causeth her to commit adultery: and whosoever shall marry her that is divorced committeth adultery." In both instances where we have "whosoever" in Greek, we have two Greek words meaning "whosoever if." [1] Who is "whosoever"? Of course anyone, no matter who that may be. But the relative pronoun *hos*, "whosoever," must be taken also in relation to its context. Verses 28 to 30 speak of what leads to divorce: "But I say unto you, that whosoever looketh on a woman to lust after her hath committed adultery with her (or against her to be more accurate) already in his heart." Such a lustful individual is the most likely one to commit physical adultery by divorcing his wife and marrying the one he lusts after.

Very interestingly, the Greek word in Matthew 5:28 translated "whosoever" is not the same as that in verses 31 and 32 (TR). In Matthew 5:28 we have the pronoun *pas* which means "everyone, anyone, no matter who." There are no exceptions. No one can say, "Because I am what I am or because I belong to a special class, I can look with license upon a woman and desire her." In verses 31 and 32 in the Textus Receptus, we have the relative pronoun *hos,* "whosoever," which in this context can be taken as a little more definitive. And in spite of the fact that it is somewhat removed from the *pas* of verse 28, exegetically because of the sequence in which they occur, it relates him who divorces his wife to the one who flirts with another while married. So what the Lord says in verses 31 and 32 could have some connection with the licentious person of verse 28. In reality, exegetically, verses 29 and 30 could be bracketed as constituting a parenthetical statement as to how a person can avoid becoming an adulterer. If one reads it that way, it becomes quite obvious. That person spoken of in verse 28 who lusts after another woman and dismisses his wife must give her a bill of divorcement. The general context obligates us to exclude the possibility that the Lord is here speaking of dismissing one's wife because she deserves it. What the Old Testament teaches affirms this.

And then the Lord narrows down the divine precept: But I tell you something better yet—he ought not to divorce her unless there is some moral justification. It is as if the Lord were giving us a new commandment, "Don't dismiss your wife but for moral reasons." And even then, this is not required. Be redemptive, not punitive, in all your relationships, and above all in your marital relationship. This is the teaching of the entire Sermon on the Mount.

Didn't the same Lord say in John 13:34 "A new commandment I give unto you, that you love one another"? That word "new" in Greek is *kaineen* meaning "qualitatively new, of a better quality." And in Matthew 5:28–32 He says in essence, that you who keep looking at other women are most likely to divorce your wife for no moral infidelity on her part. You will surely find some excuse such as they did in the Old Testament. And in order to put away their wives they were simply content to grant a divorce, but here is something better. Don't look at another woman, don't pet another woman with your hand (Matthew 5:30) and you won't be tempted to put away your wife for any petty excuse. Only for reasons of fornication or adultery on her part would you be justified in divorcing her.

[1]In the Textus Receptus, *hos an* and *hos ean.* In the UBS in verse 31 we have *hos an* and in verse 32, *pas hos apoluoon,* "whosoever the dismissing one."

19

THE BACKGROUND OF SEXUAL IMMORALITY AGAINST WHICH CHRIST AND THE APOSTLES SPOKE

Fornication is a sexual vice which was common before the time of Moses, being grossly prevalent in Egypt, as shown in Genesis 39:7 and the evidence of the monuments. It was also prevalent in Babylonia. (Rawlinson, *Ancient Monarchies,* iii. 30)

The Ten Commandments considered marriage inviolable for the preservation of the community life of the people of Israel (Ex. 20:13, 14; Deut. 5:17, 18). But adultery in the flesh as distinguished from adultery in the heart, spoken by the Lord Jesus, was possible only if there was carnal intercourse between a married man and a married or betrothed Israelitess (Lev. 20:10; Deut. 22:22ff).

Prostitution, a heinous crime (Josephus Antiquities IV viii. 9), was not tolerated by the Sinaitical code, being an abomination in the sight of God (Lev. 19:29, Deut. 23:17, 18). The price derived from prostitution could not be accepted in the sanctuary (Micah 1:7), and death by stoning was the penalty for an unmarried woman who had concealed her crime (Deut. 22:20, 21). It would seem from the term "strange woman" in Proverbs 2:16, that harlots were procured from foreigners. A harlot's vile methods and their terrible effects are severely portrayed in Proverbs 2:16–19; 5:3–6 and 7:5–27, and arouse the displeasure of God (Jeremiah 5:7 and Amos 2:7; 7:17).

A man was under obligation to avoid all non-marital intercourse in which case it was called fornication. By virtue of practice, however, unconditional fidelity was demanded only of the woman who in marriage became the possession of her husband. The adulterer and the guilty woman, if caught in the act, were to be both punished by death (Deut. 22:22), since the covenant with the Holy God demanded the sorting out of everything evil from within Israel. The actual prescribed punishment, however, was usually stoning (Deut. 22:22, Ezek. 16:40).

Punishment was, nevertheless, more lenient against a slave (Lev. 19:20ff), and more severe against a priest's daughter (burning, Lev. 21:9). In the Mishnah, strangling was the penalty for adultery. If there was suspicion against a wife, the husband could demand that she be purified from it by the ceremony of bitter water (Num. 5:16ff), but the husband was not forced to take steps against her (Matt. 1:19).

Marital infidelity was common then even as it is today. The adulterer violates the law of God and also attacks the rights of God before Whom his marriage was concluded. Philo describes adultery as the greatest of crimes (Decal. 121).

The Mishnah represents the body of Jewish law transmitted orally as against Mikra which denotes the law transmitted by written documents (Scripture). More specifically, the term "Mishna" denotes the collection of oral laws compiled by Rabbi Judah, the Prince (born in the year 135 of the Christian Era). The Mishnah and Talmud give more precise legal definitions of the act and the punishment. So far as possible, they seek to evade the issue of the death penalty. Only adultery with an Israelitess was to be punished. There was no penalty for intercourse with the wife of a non-Israelite. Only the wife, who was set apart for her husband alone by the ceremony of qiddusin (betrothal), and not the husband, who had behind him the ancient right of polygamy, was exposed to the full threat of the penalties.

Roman Law in Regard to Marital Infidelity

The death penalty was done away with in the Roman period 40 years before the destruction of Jerusalem. Later, whipping was mentioned as a penalty. The husband was simply forced to divorce an adulterous wife who forfeited the money assigned her under the marriage contract and was not permitted to marry her lover. Divorce was sufficient protection against any adulterous wife.

This was the prevailing background of the practice which

our Lord spoke concerning adultery and divorce. A mark of the ancient view of marriage is that unconditional fidelity was demanded *of a wife only*. The married man was not forbidden to have intercourse with an unmarried woman. For instance, Demosthenes in his Or. 59, 122 (Stob. ecl. IV 497, 15ff) writes: "We have the companions *(hetairas)* for the sake of pleasure, and the concubines for the daily ministration of the body, and the wives for bringing forth legitimate children."

In Roman law, the husband had the one-sided right of private revenge against the guilty wife even to putting to death, whereas the wife must accept the adultery of her husband. Only the increasing moral disintegration of the imperial period led to legal measures by the state. The law, however, was not followed by an improvement of the situation. Divorces became very common. Women counted the years not by the chiefs of state (consuls) but by the number of their husbands. The infidelity of wives became almost an accepted fact.

New Testament Concept of Adultery—Christ's Teaching

In the New Testament, an intensifying of the concept of adultery becomes apparent. The right of a man to sexual freedom is denied. Like the wife, the husband is under an obligation of fidelity. The wife is exalted to the same dignity as the husband. Marriage is a life-long fellowship of partners, and to such a degree that Christ likens the Church to His bride. On this ground, our Lord rejects the understanding of the Law by the Jews concerning divorce of the wife under legal form of a bill of divorcement (Deut. 24:1). From Christ's point of view, adultery does not consist merely in physical intercourse with a strange woman be she married or unmarried; it is present already in the desire which negates fidelity (Matt. 5:28). In distinction from the scribes, who as interpreters of the Law gave definitions and relativized the divine commandment by assimilating it to the actualities of life, our Lord tried to make men realize how absolute is the divine requirement.

Apostolic Teaching

The apostolic preaching and message concerning marital infidelity was against the degeneration of sexual morality in the Hellenistic world which regarded offenses in this sphere as quite natural (I Cor. 5:2). The apostles made it clear to the churches that the full marital fidelity of both spouses is an unconditional divine command (I Cor. 5:1ff; 6:9). Adultery is not just a matter of civil law (Rom. 7:3). It is to be judged in accordance with the holy will of God (I Cor. 6:9ff; I Thess. 4:3). Women are fellow-heirs of the kingdom of God and are thus worthy of the same honor as men (I Pet. 3:7). According to the absolute judgment of Paul, adultery excludes one from God's kingdom (I Cor. 6:9). Marital fidelity is to be maintained intact (Heb. 13:4), even though there are no human witnesses. The omniscient God is the judge of the adulterer. The apostolic prohibition of adultery is not confined to the negative avoidance of the sinful act. It finds its true fulfillment only in the love of spouses who are joined together by God. Warnings by Paul against adultery are rare because he usually issues sexual admonitions in terms of the broader term, *porneia*, "fornication." Impulsive and uncontrolled desire is sinful even in the lustful glance (II Pet 2:14).[1]

The Shepherd of Hermas (Mand. IV.1.6) lays down the rule that adultery demands separation or divorce (*apolusatoo auteen*), because, by continuing to live with his wife after she has been convicted of guilt, the husband becomes "an accomplice in her adultery." On the other hand, he is equally insistent that the man thus wronged must not marry another lest he cut his guilty partner off from the hope of repentance, and lest he involve himself likewise in the sin of adultery.

Such excesses were very common among the heathen in the time of the apostles (I Cor. 5:1, 9, 10; 6:9, Gal. 5:19, Eph. 5:3). Terms for this vice in the Old Testament are frequently used in a symbolical sense as in the case of the apostate chosen nation being represented as a harlot or adulteress (Isa. 1:21, Jer. 2:20, Ezek. 16, Hosea 1:2; 3:1). Idolatry itself is designated as a sexual sin (Jer. 3:8, 9, Ezek. 16:26, 29; 23:37). Apostolic teachings, even as Jesus' teaching on the subject, were comple-mentary to that of the Old Testament. Fornication is a type of unholy alliances in the book of Revelation, especially in chapters 17, 18, and 19.

[1]See articles on adultery in *Dictionary of the Bible,* Hastings, under "Crimes"; Vol. I pp. 520-521; *Theological Dictionary of The New Testament* by G. Kittel, Vol. 4, pp. 729–735.

20

CULTIC PROSTITUTION IN THE NON-BIBLICAL AND BIBLICAL WORLD

A distinction must be made between cultic and secular prostitution, and in cultic prostitution a further difference must be made between the single act and the permanent state. This will help solve some of the statements of Paul through which he excludes whoremongers and/or fornicators from God's kingdom. Such were guilty not of a single act of fornication, but were living in a permanent state of fornication. Such Scriptures are I Corinthians 6:9–10, "Know ye not that the unrighteous shall not inherit the kingdom of God? Be not deceived: neither *fornicators,* nor *idolaters,* nor *adulterers,* nor effeminate (male prostitutes), nor abusers of themselves with mankind (homosexual offenders), nor thieves, nor covetous, nor drunkards, nor revilers, nor extortioners, shall inherit the kingdom of God."

Another such pronouncement is found in Ephesians 5:5: "For this ye know, that no whoremonger *(pornos),* nor unclean person, nor covetous man who is an idolater, hath any inheritance in the kingdom of Christ and of God." The word "whoremongers" here must include adulterers.

Another important Scripture concerning God's inevitable judgment upon those in the state of adultery and fornication is Hebrews 13:4: "Marriage is honorable in all; and the bed undefiled: but whoremongers *(pornoi)* and adulterers *(moichoi)* God will judge." And when it comes to the final exclusion from heaven, the words of Revelation 22:15 are most solemn: "For without are dogs, and sorcerers, and whoremongers *(pornoi)* and murderers, and idolaters, and whosoever loveth and maketh a lie." Here, again, whoremongers must include adulterers.

The Lord, however, welcomed repentant harlots into His kingdom. This is always so with the Saviour, but there must be repentance and forsaking of sin. To the woman who was brought to the Lord accused of adultery, the Lord said, "Neither do I condemn thee: go, and sin no more" (John 8:11). To live in a state of fornication which includes adultery excludes one from God's kingdom.

The Permanent State of Fornication

Now the question is: Does a person who willfully enters a state of adultery by dismissing his wife without a scripturally acceptable cause fall into the category of an adulterer and fornicator as if in a permanent state? This is so important that it will demand our very serious and detailed examination later on in this study. All we are now trying to establish is the meanings of the two terms, adultery and fornication.

On Greek soil, sacral prostitution was generally rejected. It found, however, an entry in Corinth and Athens, probably through the trading connections of these cities with the Orient. In Corinth, especially, the temple of Aphrodite on Acrocorinth with its 1000 prostitute priestesses (*hierodoulai*) was famous. In these Greek temples, for instance, they had the "holy slaves" or *hierodoulai* who gave their bodies to prostitution and the payment received accrued to the goddess to which the temple was dedicated. This type of prostitiution was widespread in Asia Minor in cults of mother deities. It was found also in Syria and Egypt.

I have witnessed this practice in India even today. There are temple prostitutes who constitute a caste. They are organized into unions.

In the history of Israel we find such temple prostitution penetrating Judaism through the Canaanitic cults such as Baal and Astarte.

The Corinthian penetration by cultic fornication explains the constant reference by Paul to this evil in his Corinthian epistles. In the New Testament the word-group of *porneia,* "fornication," occurs 55 times. *Porneia,* "fornication" as a noun alone, accounts for 25 times. Of these, Paul employs their use 21 times and 15 of these are in I and II Corinthians. In Revelation it is used 19 times. From this frequency we can easily realize that the question of fornication comes up for discussion particularly in the confrontation with the Greek world and in the context of the final judgment. The inclusive meaning of it is what caused the Lord Jesus to use it as giving the right for an innocent marriage partner to legitimately dismiss his or her spouse.

Prostitution in the Greek World

Prostitutes and brothels were unknown in the Homeric age. Masters could keep a concubine (*pallakee*) or have casual intercourse with female slaves who were mostly carried off during war. Prostitution arose with increased prosperity and commerce. Solon, the famous lawmaker, in his laws tried to protect marriage and to prevent sexual excess. He forbade the giving up of daughters, or sisters, to prostitution if they had not already fallen into it. Among state revenues was that derived from prostitution (*pornikon telos*), which was collected by publicans (collectors) of prostitutes, i.e. prostitution agents (*pornoteloonai*). In antiquity a constant source of prostitution was slavery, which made people mere chattels. Female slaves were at the mercy of their masters' lusts. As time passed the professional "friend," *hetera*, became a common figure in Greek society. A crisis developed in marriage. Even as early as Herodotus (484–410 B.C.) *hetaira*, "friend,"—we would call her the predecessor of "girl friend"—was the euphemism for a woman who granted casual sexual intercourse for money.

The Main Cause of Prostitution in Greek Society

The main cause of prostitution was the Greek view of life which regarded sexual intercourse as just as natural, necessary, and justifiable as eating and drinking. Sexual abstinence was regarded as more harmful than moderate free intercourse. Only civil marriage was protected by law and custom. Even the married man was permitted extra-marital intercourse as he pleased so long as he did not violate a civil marriage. On the other hand, *all extra-marital intercourse was forbidden to the wife*. Towards the practical exercise of free sexual relations, the judgment of the Greeks was very tolerant. Only excess and overindulgence were censured. On the other hand, to visit a brothel was regarded as scandalous. This ambivalence of outlook was characteristic of antiquity.

Plato tried to solve the problem by compromise. Intercourse

with harlots was permissible so long as it took place in secret and caused no offense. With complete injustice to the wife, who was kept at home, a man sought with the "girl friend" what he could not find in his wife. But the circle of eminent "girl friends" was probably small. Most of them were sought only for reasons of sensual desire.

Sparta and the Doric branch maintained sexual discipline more strongly than Athens, Corinth, and the Ionic sphere. It was here, however, that homosexuality began to spread and then covered the whole of Greece and was practiced rather than censured even by notable figures. Lesbianism was much less common. In a fateful way, both opened the door to unnatural perversion.

Fornication in the Old Testament

In the Septuagint the verb *porneuoo,* "to fornicate," occurs 16 times and the stronger word, *ekporneuoo,* "to live very licentiously," 36 times. *Porneia* in the Old Testament is "whoredom" and it is used also to figuratively refer to "unfaithfulness to God," which would be equated more to adultery since man is presented as God's rightful possession. Fornication may in some circumstances involve adultery (Sir. 23:33).

The older historical books show that the harlot was a familiar figure in national life (Tamar, Gen. 38:15; Rahab, Josh. 2:1; etc.)

Fornication or fornicate refers only to the woman. Extra-marital intercourse on the part of a man did not come under the concept and was not forbidden so long as he did not take the wife of a fellow countryman. This significant distinction is probably grounded in the unequivocal patriarchalism of the Old Testament, and it is a result of the unambiguously patriarchal stamp on the view of revelation and religion in Israel. The influence of the matriarchal nature religion of Canaan with its religious interpretation of unrestricted sex shattered the strict custom of Israel. On the high places, secular and sacral prostitution went hand in hand (Jer. 3:2). On the basis of their understanding of God and man, the prophets combatted both as strenuously as they could (Jer. 5:7, Amos 2:7, etc.). From that time onward, any religious justification of extra-marital intercourse became impossible. The later provisions of the Law developed in part out of this prophetic attack. (See also I Kings 14:24.) According to Deuteronomy 22:21, the licentiousness of a betrothed woman is to be punished by stoning on the ground that she thereby commits a serious offense which threatens the whole people and that she has made her father's house into a house of whoredom.

Fornication in Later Judaism

The use of *porneia,* "fornication," gradually broadened. In the first instance, *porneia* is mostly harlotry, extra-marital intercourse. However, it often means adultery. In Sir. 23:23 we read *en porneia emocheuthee,* "in fornication she was adultered" or was subjected to adultery. Potiphar's wife says of Joseph *eis porneian me ephelkusato,* "unto fornication he attracted me." *Porneia* is also incest (I Cor. 5:1). It can also be unnatural vice, sodomy, or unlawful marriages. *Porneia,* "fornication," then comes to mean sexual intercourse in general without more precise definition.

Fornication and the New Testament

The New Testament unconditionally repudiates all extra-marital and unnatural intercourse. The Lord Jesus declares the prohibitions of the Old Testament and the legalistic practice of later Judaism as inadequate. He introduces His concept of the marital relationship. The wife is no longer man's chattel, but a partner of equal dignity before both man and God.

Harlots and the Gospels

The Gospels presuppose that there were harlots in Palestine and that their profession was in direct opposition to the righteousness required for the kingdom of God.

In Matthew 21:31 the Lord Jesus, to accent the contrast between the unwillingness of the sons to go to work in the field and the willingness of the despised of the earth to follow Him, said, "Verily I say unto you, That the publicans and the *harlots* go into the kingdom of God before you." The elder brother in the parable of the prodigal son said to his father, "But as soon as this thy son was come, which hath devoured thy living with *harlots,* thou hast killed for him the fatted calf" (Luke 15:30).

The incident which occurred in the house of Simon the

Pharisee in Luke 7:36–50 with a harlot who had been forgiven indicates that a number of these harlots must have repented as a result of John the Baptist's and Jesus' preaching.

The Lord Jesus taught that it was not only the physical act that was sinful but also the thoughts of sexual licentiousness which dwell in the heart and rise up thence to defile the whole man. In Matthew 15:19 we read the words of our Lord: "For out of the heart proceed evil thoughts, murders, *adulteries, fornications,* thefts, false witness, blasphemies."

21

WHAT IS FORNICATION— *PORNEIA?*

There are primarily two Greek words referring to sexual immorality. The one is *moicheia* from the verb *moicheuoo* meaning "to commit adultery." The noun *moicheia* is the violation of the marriage of another (Gen. 39:10).

In Matthew 5:32 our Lord for the first time introduces a second Greek word, *porneia,* referring generally to sexual immorality. In verses 27 and 28 He used the verb *moicheuoo* which refers specifically to the sexual immorality of at least one of the two partners being married.

The word *porneia* in Greek, meaning "fornication," is a much broader term referring to all kinds of sexual impropriety including adultery. *Pornee* was the name for "harlot for hire or prostitute." The word comes from the verb *perneemi* which means "to sell," especially of slaves. Harlots were usually bought slaves. *Pornos* is the masculine meaning "whoremonger," one who has intercourse with prostitutes, and specifically one who lets himself be abused for money, "male prostitution." *Porneia,* the act of fornication, is rare in classical Greek. *Moicheuoo,* "to adulter," is narrower than *porneuoo* and refers solely to adultery. Demosthenes (Or. 19, 200) considers homosexuality as fornication. The verb *porneuoo* is transitive and means to prostitute. It is used passively of a woman (*porneuomai*) meaning "to prostitute oneself," "to become a harlot."[1]

The introduction of this new word, *porneia,* has become a bone of contention. There are those who claim that the word refers only to sexual relations prior to marriage.

No one claims that the two terms, *moicheia,* "adultery," and *porneia,* "fornication," are synonymous. All lexicographers of the Greek language and the Church Fathers state that *moicheia* is a specific term that is included in *porneia.* The term *porneia* is far more inclusive than *moicheia.* Otherwise why does it occur one time after the other in Matthew 15:19: "For out of the heart proceed evil thoughts, murders, adulteries, *(moicheiai),* fornications, *(porneiai),* thefts, false witness, blasphemies"?

In Mark 7:21 the same statement occurs: "For from within, out of the heart of men, proceed evil thoughts, adulteries, fornications, murders." This is what the Textus Receptus has and consequently the King James Version. But the UBS text has only fornications, which under no stretch of the imagination would exclude adulteries.

Another Scripture where the two terms occur together is Hebrews 13:4: "Marriage is honorable in all, and the bed undefiled: but whoremongers *(pornous)* and adulterers *(moichous)* God will judge." The Apostle wanted to make sure that no one could say, "I cannot be punished as morally sinful since I am married." If those who claim that *porneia* refers only to sexual sin prior to marriage are correct, then a married person cannot *porneuei,* "commit fornication," since fornication is a sin that only the unmarried can perpetrate. That would have been the inevitable effect if the apostle said only whoremongers *(pornous)* God will judge. As there are those who today say concerning Matthew 5:32 that "saving for the cause of fornication" means exclusively the sins of sex prior to marriage and not after, the same people could say that if God were to judge only the *pornoi,* "fornicators," rendered "whoremongers" in Hebrews 13:4, the *moichoi,* "adulterers," would be excluded. This is the reason why God did not use only the term *pornoi,* but also *moichoi,* in Hebrews 13:4. The judgment of God would have included all who commit sex sins before and after marriage regardless of whether the Apostle had simply stated *pornoi,* the general term. But he was not permitted to do so by the Holy Spirit who is the real author of the Bible and Who caused him to include *moichoi,* "adulterers," lest anybody would think that the married sex sinners were to escape God's judgment. If there were today, Bible interpreters who attribute to fornication *(porneia)* the restrictive sense of the sinful sex of the unmarried only, why couldn't there be those who would claim that God was going to punish only those who sexually sinned in singleness, if Hebrews 13:4 stated that God would judge only *pornous,* "fornicators or whoremongers."

Fornicators and Adulterers Are Cited Together Again in I Corinthians 6:9

Paul in I Corinthians 6:9 refers to both fornicators and adulterers together when it comes to God's punitive action in not letting them inherit the kingdom of God: "Know ye not that the unrighteous shall not inherit the kingdom of God? Be not deceived: neither *fornicators,* nor idolaters, nor *adulterers,* nor effeminate nor abusers of themselves with mankind."

This was for exactly the same reason as we explained in the case of Hebrews 13:4. God did not want anyone to think that since only fornicators were mentioned, the adulterers would not be included.

[1]The intransitive active *(porneuoo)* has passive meaning, "to commit fornication." The compound verb *ekporneuoo (ek,* "from," and *porneuoo)* is a stronger form of *porneuoo* meaning "to live very licentiously."

93

22

CAN THE WORD "FORNICATION," *PORNEIA IN MATTHEW 5:32 AND 19:9, POSSIBLY MEAN "RELATIONS BEFORE MARRIAGE"?*

There are those who claim that when the Lord used the word "fornication," *porneia* in Greek, in Matthew 5:32 and 19:9 as the only valid reason for one to dismiss his or her spouse, it did not refer to sexual infidelity after the spouse's marriage, but before. If a man married a woman and then found that she was not a virgin, only then could he dismiss his wife.

First of all, we must resort to reputable lexicographers to find out whether the word *porneia*, "fornication," is the general term for sexual immorality of all kind including *moicheia*, "adultery," which refers to sexual immorality involving at least one married person.

I. Let us take John Parkhurst. His excellent etymological *Greek and English Lexicon to the New Testament* (London, 1769) under *"Porneia"* has the following:

"1. It denotes in general whoredom, i.e., any commerce of the sexes out of lawful marriage. (See II Cor. 12:21; Eph. 5:3; Col. 3:5; I Thess. 4:3. Compare Acts 15:20, 29; 21:25; I Cor. 6:13, 18.)
"2. Simple fornication between two unmarried persons, as distinguished both from *moicheia*, 'adultery,' and *aselgeia*, 'lasciviousness of other kinds' (Mark 7:21); as distinguished from both these, and also from *akatharsia*, 'uncleanness,' (Gal. 5:19).
"3. Whoredom in a married woman, adultery (Matt. 5:32, 19:9).
"4. It is applied to incestuous whoredom (I Cor. 5:1).

95

"5. It may include *all kinds of lewdness* (Rom. 1:29).

"The Apostle comprehends absolutely all kinds of uncleanness under the name of *porneia.* (Compare I Cor. 7:2; I Thess. 4:3 and following verses.)

"6. It denotes the communication of Christians in idolatrous worship which was a violation of the marriage between God or Christ and His Church, and was often accompanied with bodily prostitution (Rev. 2:21; 14:8; 17:2, 4; 18:3; 19:2)."

II. *The Vocabulary of the Greek Testament,* illustrated from *The Papyri* and other non-literary sources by Moulton and Milligan, Eerdman's:

"*Porneia,* which is rare in classical Greek, originally meant 'prostitution, fornication', but came to be applied to *unlawful sexual intercourse generally.* It was a wider term than *moicheia,* 'adultery', embracing the idea of 'barter, traffic in sexual vice,' though in the Old Testament there was a tendency to assimilate in some respects the two terms."

III. *Theological Dictionary of the New Testament* by Gerhard Kittel: Article by Hauck/Schulz (Vol. VI, pp 579-595)

"*Porneia,* 'whoredom.' Fornication may in some circumstances involve adultery.

"Later Judaism shows us how the use of *porneia,* etc. gradually broadened as compared with the original usage. In the first instance *porneia* is mostly 'harlotry, extra–marital intercourse,' Ab., 2, 8, often with adultery . . . Potiphar's wife says of Joseph, 'unto fornication he attracted me'; the 'incest' . . . *porneia* can also be 'unnatural vice.'

"*Porneia* can then come to mean sexual intercourse in general without more precise definition.

"*Porneuoo,* 'to commit fornication', is materially *moicheuoo,* 'to commit adultery.'

"Bigamy is also branded as fornication (*Damascus Document* 4:20 [7:1]).

"In later Rabbinical usage, the Hebrew word applies not merely to all extra-marital intercourse but also to intercourse in marriages which run contrary to Rabbinical decisions." (Transliterations provided by author).

Referring to Matthew 5:32 and 19:9, we have this statement:

"In both verses *porneia* refers to extra-marital intercourse on the part of the wife, which in practice is adultery (cf. Sir. 23:23): *en porneia eimoicheuthee,* 'in fornication he suffered adultery'.

"The drift of the clauses, then, is not that the Christian husband, should his wife be unfaithful, is permitted to divorce her, but that if he is legally forced to do this, he should not be open to criticism if by her conduct his wife has made the continuation of the marriage quite impossible.

"The Post Apostolic Fathers—Though *porneia,* 'fornication', (or *porneuoo,* 'to commit fornication') is distinguished materially from *moicheuoo,* 'commit adultery' on the one side (Herm. m., 8, 3; Did., 5, 1; 2, 2; Barn., 19,4), on the other *moicheuoo* is *porneuoo* (to commit adultery is to commit fornication [Herm. m., 4, 1, 5])."

IV. *A Greek-English Lexicon of the New Testament* and other early Christian literature by Walter Bauer translated by Arndt and Gingrich:

"*Porneia,* prostitution, unchastity, fornication *of every kind* of unlawful sexual intercourse. . . . Differentiated from *moicheia* (adultery). . . .On the other hand *moicheia,* 'adultery', appears as *porneia,* 'fornication,' (cf. Sir. 23:23) Hm 4, 1, 5. Of the sexual unfaithfulness of a married woman, (Matt. 5:32; 19:9; I Cor. 7:2)."

V. *The Great Lexicon of the Greek Language* by D. Demetrakou (from Greek to Greek), Athens:

"*Porneia,* the sexual intercourse of a man with a woman; intercourse of a married or unmarried man with an unmarried woman giving her body for bodily gain for pay, for bodily pleasure, for friendship."

VI. A *Patristic Greek Lexicon* edited by G.W.H. Lampe, (Oxford, 1965):

" 1. *Porneia,* fornication, unchastity, sexual impurity
" 2. *Porneia,* illicit intercourse in general
" 3. Specifically, prostitution
" 4. Linked with adultery, but distinct from *moicheia* . . .

and *porneia* and *androphonia,* "killing of men" (Just. Dial. 93.1). . . . linked with adultery as ground of divorce after which remarriage is allowable . . . marital infidelity not *porneia* but *moicheia,* (Chrysostom hom. in I Cor. 7:2 (3.198C); distinction defined *porneia* on the one hand . . . the fulfillment of the desire of one on another without defrauding, (trans. i.e., on a single woman); *moicheia* on the other hand the coveting and injustice against another (i.e., on a married woman) Gregory Nyss, ep. can. 4 (M. 45. 228C).

" 5. Of illicit intercourse committed by married people, hence incl., or identified with, adultery;

a. by either party, Bas. Moral. 73.1 (2.308A; M31.849D);
b. by married man (who by custom is not divorced by his wife . . .) with unmarried woman . . .; with married woman
c. by married woman
d. in opinion of some rigorists all *porneia* is really *moicheia* since only permissible union is in marriage.

" 6. Of marriages contracted without permission by those who are not of free condition;

a. by girls under parental authority
b. by slave women

" 7. Of illicit union with heathens
" 8. Of polygamy
" 9. Ref. Matthew 19:9 and Matthew 5:32 interpreted as adultery . . . as prostitution by married woman . . .
"10. Unchastity, lewdness
"11. Metaphorically of sin and rebellion against God, especially of idolatry."

As for the verb *porneuoo,* this same *Patristic Lexicon* lists the following meanings:

"1. fornicate
"2. linked with, but distinct from *moicheuoo* in catechetical instruction
"3. Refers to illicit intercourse committed by married people, hence, = commit adultery
"4. Of a woman who presumes her husband's death and remarries

98

"5. Of those marrying irregularly
"6. Distinct from polygamous marrying of patriarchs
"7. Behave unchastely; of lewd behavior in general
"8. Metaphorically be unfaithful to God; apostasize."

The above overwhelming lexical evidence of the word *porneia* as referring to many other sexual immoralities including *moicheia*, "adultery" ought to put to silence once and for all those who claim that the word *porneia* used by our Lord in Matthew 5:32 and 19:9 referred not to the sexual deviation of the married husband but to one of three things, namely:

1. Illegal marriages
2. Incestuous marriages
3. Sodomite marriages.[1]

That *porneia* includes the above and every conceivable sexual deviation there is absolutely no doubt. But it also includes *adultery,* which has a special name, *moicheia,* as many other of the sins also have special definitive names by a single word such as "sodomy" or "sodomites" (I Kings 14:24; 15:12; 22:46; II Kings 23:7); *arsenokoitai,* "abusers of themselves with mankind, or homosexuals" (I Cor. 6:9, I Tim. 1:10); *malakoi,* "effeminate" (I Cor. 6:9).

Why single out three particular meanings of *porneia* and exclude a common one, sexual infidelity within marriage?

The handbook referred to is incorrect in our opinion in stating that the view that the word *porneia* does not include *moicheia* caused the church fathers to refuse to accept the exception clause of Matthew 5:32 and 19:9 as grounds for divorce. Such a claim cannot be substantiated as demonstrated by the *Patristic* (Church Fathers) *Lexicon.*

Furthermore, may we present one more incontrovertible argument that the Lord Jesus could not have been referring to illegal, sodomite, or incestuous marriages with the exception clauses.

Jesus' treatise has no clue at all as pertaining to retrospection after marriage. It would be somewhat incomprehensible for Jesus to tell His disciples that it is important to look backwards to see whether the wife a person has already married is really what she ought to have been once the marriage was consummated. That ought to have been done before even the betrothal, which for all practical purposes was binding upon the spouses although the sexual union did not begin until after the betrothal festivities and the wedding-night procession of the bridegroom's party to the bride.

From the whole tenor of the passages, the Lord was concerned about the breaking up of the marriage for the sin of lusting after another woman while one is married, and not about digging into the past of the person to whom a commitment was already made in betrothal and marriage. The Lord is not challenging the exercise of the memory of the man but of the proper focusing of the right eye and the proper use of the right hand. (See Matthew 5:27–32).

In our opinion there is no logical, grammatical, linguistic or exegetical ground at all in the position proferred that fornication in Matthew 5:32 and 19:9 refers to immorality prior to marriage. It refers to immorality after marriage.

When we come to I Corinthians 5:1 in the case of the young man who had sexual relations with his mother or stepmother, we note that Paul calls this unfortunate sin *porneia,* yet it involved a married woman, the young man's mother or stepmother. If *porneia* excludes *moicheia,* Paul should have called it *moicheia.* But it involved an unmarried and a married person. Therefore by strict definition, for the young man it was fornication, *porneia,* and for the mother it was adultery, *moicheia.* But Paul is more correct by calling it by its more general name, fornication, *porneia,* because it includes both the sexual sin of an unmarried and a married person.

The reason that the Lord in Matthew 5:32 and 19:9 says except for fornication, or "saving for the cause of fornication" and "except it be for fornication," was that the new woman this married man was going to marry may have been unmarried or married. How could the Lord preclude the woman for whom this married man would lust as being exclusively another married woman? Only in that eventuality could the Lord correctly have said "except for the cause of *adultery",* instead of *fornication.*

[1]See *Rebuilder's Guide,* Institute of Basic Youth Conflicts, 1982.

23

DOES AN ACT OF ADULTERY OR FORNICATION EXCLUDE AN INDIVIDUAL FROM THE KINGDOM OF GOD?

There are two words in the New Testament that refer to illicit sexuality, *porneia,* "fornication," which is the general term referring to illicit sex before or after marriage by either a married or unmarried person. And the second word is *moicheia,* "adultery," referring principally to illicit sex by a member of a married couple.

There are some very serious pronouncements in the New Testament as to the ultimate fate, as far as their eternal destiny is concerned, of those who are guilty of such sexual sins. Take, for instance, I Corinthians 6:9 and 10 which says: "Know ye not that the unrighteous shall not inherit the kingdom of God? Be not deceived: neither *fornicators,* nor idolaters, nor *adulterers,* nor effeminate, nor abusers of themselves with mankind ... shall inherit the kingdom of God."

Did the Apostle Paul mean that those who committed a single act of fornication or adultery shall not inherit the kingdom of God?

The answer to this question is whether the one who is designated *pornos* or *moichos,* "a fornicator or an adulterer," whether male or female, is a person who simply at one time in his life committed fornication or adultery, or is it an unsaved person whose mode of life is that of constant fornication and adultery?

Who Is a Fornicator or an Adulterer?

In the New Testament, we must differentiate between the designation of a person as a fornicator or an adulterer and one who commits an act of fornication or an act of adultery. We are never told in the New Testament that a person who has committed a sexual sin at one or more times in his life will be excluded from the kingdom of heaven. Fornication and adultery must be taken as other sins for which there is always forgiveness with God once there is repentance and the forsaking of the sin in which a person is involved.

The Sins of the Unsaved and the Sins of the Saved

We must differentiate between one who sins because he is an unsaved sinner, and therefore his acts of sinfulness are the natural outcome of his being an unredeemed sinner, and one who sins in contraposition to the fact that he is a redeemed sinner. And we do find such a differentiation in the New Testament.

It is interesting to note the Scriptures in the New Testament which refer to those sinners, particularly fornicators and adulterers, who will not enter the kingdom of heaven. Let us look at I Corinthians 5:9 first. "I wrote unto you in an epistle not to company with fornicators."

This epistle to which Paul is referring here, and also the one in II Corinthians 7:8, are not available to the Christian community today. However, it is obvious that Paul had written a similar admonition as this one not to associate with fornicators. The Corinthians must have taken this in its absolute sense and never had anything to do with anybody who at any time committed an act of fornication. Can you imagine how restricted a Christian's company would be if he or she avoided everyone who at any time committed an act of fornication? Not, of course, that there are not those who have never committed acts of fornication, but there would have been very few in Corinth which was the center of fornication. And the Christians that were living at the time were those who had come out of hedonism and Jewish background, which were so lenient toward acts of fornication. So probably Paul is writing to these Corinthians for the second time, and now he expresses to them his admonition that this avoidance that he was recommending should be only toward those who were practicing fornicators and not those who at some time in the past had committed one or more acts of fornication.

To qualify this Paul goes on to say in the 10th verse: "Yet not altogether with the fornicators of this world." The expression

102

pantoos, "not altogether," means "generally." Don't mix the two groups, those sinners who have never been saved and don't claim salvation, and those who claim salvation but live in continuous sin. He didn't want them to have fellowship with practicing fornicators who did not embrace the Gospel, for they could lead the believers astray. That is the first general principle. Here is what Paul says: "I wrote to you in the epistle not to keep company with fornicators" (Author's translation). Then he goes on to explain the general statement he had given in a previous epistle apparently lost to us.

Verse 10: "Yet not *generally* (without due differentiation) with the fornicators of this world or with the covetous, or extortioners, or with idolaters; for then must ye needs go out of the world."

In other words, the world is full of such sinners. If you were to avoid them altogether, you would need to get out of this sinful world which, however, you are supposed to win to Christ. Such people are within God's grace to save.

And then in verse 11 he makes the distinction between those who are unsaved and those who are thought of as brothers and sisters in Christ, but they live in sin which is contrary to the Christian character.

"But now I have written unto you not to keep company, if any man that is called a brother be a fornicator, or covetous, or an idolater, or a railer, or a drunkard, or an extortioner; with such an one no not to eat." What he is saying here is: 1. No one who calls himself a Christian and lives in continuous sin, including fornication, is truly saved. 2. It is more dangerous to keep company with such pseudo-Christians because others would get the idea that Christianity permits sin as a matter of course instead of strict sanctity. 3. It is dangerous for any true believer to be intimately mixed with a spurious believer. The "keeping company" of verses 9 and 10 becomes "eating together" in verse 11 when it comes to the so-called believer.

Paul includes these fornicators with other sinners whose evil expresses itself in other forms of sin besides fornication such as covetousness, extortion, idolatry, and so on. Paul is saying here that if the Corinthian Christians were to avoid sinners entirely, they would have to depart from this world because this is a world of sinners.

And then in the 11th verse Paul makes it clear that it is

impossible for a true brother in Christ to also be such a sinner as he mentioned in verse 10. If he is a fornicator, or covetous, or idolater, or railer, or drunkard, or extortioner in his nature, he cannot at the same time be a brother in Christ.

The distinction in I Corinthians 5:9 to 11 is between unsaved sinners and so-called believers who are sinners.

People Sin When They Are Unrighteous, and They Are Unrighteous Because They Have Never Been Saved

I Corinthians 6:9: "Know ye not that the unrighteous shall not inherit the kingdom of God? Be not deceived: neither fornicators, nor idolaters, nor adulterers, nor effeminate, nor abusers of themselves with mankind. . . ."

All these sinners that Paul mentions he includes in the group of "the unrighteous." It is very clear in the Scriptures, of course, that the unrighteous shall not inherit the kingdom of God. These are people who have never by faith received Jesus Christ as their Saviour so that they would be justified before God and made righteous in and through Christ since that is the only way they can become righteous. The form of their unrighteousness may manifest itself in fornication, idolatry, adultery, being effeminate or homosexual. Again, this Scripture refers to those who have never tasted the grace of God and who live in the constant practice of their unrighteousness, manifesting itself predominantly in one or the other propensities of sin. It is interesting to note, however, that four of these sins are related to sex.

Natural Sins Which Spring From One's Unsaved Natural State

Ephesians 5:5: "For this ye know, that no whoremonger, (*pornos*, "fornicator"), nor unclean person, nor covetous man, who is an idolater, hath any inheritance in the kingdom of Christ and of God."

Here, also, we have reference to people who live in sin because they are sinful in their nature and have never been born again. They are not going to be refused into the kingdom of Christ and of God because they at one time may have committed an act of adultery or fornication, nor because at any time they were idolaters, or are covetous. They are what they are because of their sinful nature.

104

Once a Fornicator Is Saved, He Is No Longer Counted as a Fornicator

I Timothy 1:10: "For whoremongers *(pornois),* for them that defile themselves with mankind (homosexuals), for men-stealers, for liars, for perjured persons, and if there be any other thing that is contrary to sound doctrine."

If you go back to the 9th verse, you will find that the Apostle Paul is saying that the law was not enacted for the righteous, but for the lawless and disobedient, for the ungodly and for sinners. And then in verses 12 and 13, Paul goes on to say that he himself was previously sinful by nature. Although he does not say he was a fornicator himself, yet he enumerates other sinful propensities that indicated that he was unrighteous: "I, who was before a blasphemer, and a persecutor, and injurious: but I obtained mercy, because I did it ignorantly in unbelief."

A sinner is a sinner, no matter how his sinfulness is manifested overtly. In the case of Paul, he was a persecutor and a blasphemer. His testimony, however, is given in verse 14: "And the grace of our Lord was exceeding abundant with faith and love which is in Christ Jesus." The same grace can save a fornicator, and adulterer, and a homosexual, and once God's grace comes into him in response to repentance and forsaking of his sin, he is no more counted as a fornicator or an adulterer or a homosexual, for his salvation implies not only the cessation of the practice of a particular sin, but also the abhorrence of it.

The True Believer and Fornication

The true believer should be characterized by a holy life, separated from evil and attached to Christ. No sin is so abhorrent as the sin of fornication from which Paul desired the Christians to abstain. In I Thessalonians 4:3 and 4, he says: "For this is the will of God, even your sanctification, *that ye should abstain* from fornication: That every one of you should know how to possess his vessel in sanctification (holy living), and honor." And then in verse 7 he says, "For God hath not called us unto uncleanness, but unto holiness."

This should be the goal of every Christian. As Peter says, "Dearly beloved, I beseech you as strangers and pilgrims, abstain from fleshly lusts (which includes fornication), which

105

war against the soul."

Did Paul mean by "fornication" only the sexual sin before marriage as some mistakenly claim? No. It is sexual sin before *and* after marriage.

When a person in unbelief has engaged in fornication, such sin as well as every other sin is forgiven by Christ providing the sinner's repentance is genuine. Let us never forget the meaning of forgive. It is the Greek verb *aphieemi,* which means "to remove from oneself." It does not mean to declare someone guiltless and permit him to continue unabated in his sin. It means to remove the guilt of sin because of the sinner's acceptance of the payment Christ made for his sin through His blood on the cross. The sinner is then justified. But also simultaneously the sinner is made just, that is, his nature changes. From that moment on, he ceases to be an unsaved sinner pursuing sin, but he is a saved sinner pursuing holiness. Nevertheless, sin pursues him, and it is possible for sin of any kind, including fornication, to trip him and cause him to fall prey to it. Is he, at that time, disinherited from God's kingdom?

The example Paul gives us in I Corinthians 5 of a young member of the Corinthian Church is very illuminating. His sin is called *porneia,* "fornication" (verse 1). He had sexual relations with his own mother or stepmother. We don't know whether the husband of this woman was alive or divorced from his wife, the mother or stepmother of this young man. The concern of Paul, however, being only for the young man indicates that neither the mother or father were Christians.

Paul argues for the necessity of the expulsion by the local congregation of the young member because of his fornication. In no place in I Corinthians 5 is this particular young man called *pornos,* "a fornicator." In verses 9 to 11 Paul speaks of *pornos* (singular), "*a* fornicator," or *pornoi* (plural), "fornicators," but only as referring to the fornicators of this world, evidently unsaved people (verses 9 and 10) and to the so-called brother who being a *pornos,* "fornicator," cannot be a true believer. Evidently this term is ascribed to sexual sinfulness for anyone married or unmarried. For the young man it was actually fornication and for the stepmother adultery.

He had fallen into the sin of fornication from which he repented and was restored to the fellowship of the Corinthian

106

Church as is evident from II Corinthians 2:7 when Paul, speaking of him, says, "So that contrariwise ye ought rather to forgive him, and comfort him, lest perhaps such a one should be swallowed up with overmuch sorrow." Apparently the Corinthians did not want to receive such a notorious backslider into their fellowship. That is why Paul continues to say to them, "Wherefore I beseech you that ye would confirm your love toward him."

Practicing Fornicators Categorized With Practicing Liars

Revelation 21:8: "But the fearful, and unbelieving, and the abominable, and murderers, and whoremongers *(pornois)*, and sorcerers, and idolaters, and all liars, shall have their part in the lake which burneth with fire and brimstone: which is the second death."

If this referred to all people who at any time lied in their lives, there would be absolutely no one to enter heaven. And yet the liars are placed on an equal level as far as deserving this final punishment of God with the fornicators or whoremongers. They will be cast into the lake of fire not because they lied or committed an act of fornication, but because they were sinners or unbelieving and such sins are the natural expression of their unregenerate nature.

Revelation 22:15: "For without are dogs, and sorcerers, and whoremongers *(pornoi)*, and murderers, and idolaters, and whosoever loveth and maketh a lie."

This is the same as saying that all sinners are going to be punished, not because they commit these particular sins, but because they are sinners. They do not have a right to the tree of life as the previous verse states.

The Term "Adulterer" Indicates a State of Unredeemed Sinfulness

The designation *moichos*, "adulterer,"[1] occurs only three times in the New Testament as follows:

Luke 18:11: "The Pharisee stood and prayed thus with himself, God, I thank thee, that I am not as other men are, extortioners, unjust, adulterers *(moichoi)*, or even as this publican."

This Pharisee wanted to exclude himself from the company

107

of such people because it was well taught and well known that such could not inherit the kingdom of God because they were sinners. Of course, he himself was worse than these even if he was not a fornicator because he was a self-righteous braggard.

I Corinthians 6:9 combines fornicators and adulterers together as not entering the kingdom of God. Also Hebrews 13:4 refers to adulterers with fornicators as being judged by God.

Consequently, we can conclude that adultery and fornication are states of being and indicate unredeemed sinfulness. It is not because of fornication or adultery that they are going to be refused admission into the kingdom of God, but because of their unrepentant sinfulness.

Relevant to our discussion, however, in regard to exclusion from the kingdom of God is Galatians 5:16 to 21. Verse 21 says: "Envyings, murders, drunkenness, revelings, and such like: of the which I tell you before, as I have also told you in time past, that they which do such things shall not inherit the kingdom of God." We find among these "lusts of the flesh" adultery and fornication (verse 19). This designation, "lusts of the flesh," comes to the same denominator as these people being called adulterers and fornicators because of the expression that we find in verse 21, "that they which do such things shall not inherit the kingdom of God." In Greek[2] the present participle active denotes that, among other things, committing adultery and fornication is a way of life of these people, and it is not something that they may have fallen into regrettably and from which they may have repented.

Although we do not conclude that everyone who has fallen into sexual sin will be excluded from the kingdom of heaven, since even this sin is covered by the blood of Christ when one repents and turns from it, the truly born-again child of God will never presume upon His grace.

Even among those who call themselves Christians, there are some who live under the mistaken philosophy that God is such a loving God that He will forgive any sin committed and therefore the Christian is free to sin. It might be wise at this point to bring to the forefront again the awesome Scripture found in Hebrews 10:26–31:

"For if we sin wilfully after that we have

received the knowledge of the truth, there remaineth no more sacrifice for sins, But a certain fearful looking for of judgement and fiery indignation, which shall devour the adversaries. He that despised Moses' Law died without mercy under two or three witnesses: Of how much sorer punishment, suppose ye, shall he be thought worthy, who hath trodden under foot the Son of God, and hath counted the blood of the covenant, wherewith he was sanctified, an unholy thing, and hath done despite unto the Spirit of grace? For we know him that hath said, Vengeance belongeth unto me, I will recompense, saith the Lord. And again, the Lord shall judge his people. It is a fearful thing to fall into the hands of the living God."

[1]The substantive *moicheia,* "adultery," is found three times in the New Testament, that is in Matt. 15:19; Mark 7:21 and John 8:3, none of which is relevant to our discussion that they who commit such sins will not enter into the kingdom of God or heaven.

[2]"*Hoi . . . prassontes,*" nominative plural masculine present participle active of *prasso,* "to do," usually an evil thing, as opposed to *poieoo* "to do with a good connotation."

24

MAY AN INNOCENT WIFE DISMISSED BY HER HUSBAND BE CONSIDERED AN ADULTERESS?

"But I say unto you, that whosoever shall put away his wife, save for the cause of fornication, causeth her to commit adultery; and whosoever shall marry her that is divorced committeth adultery." Matthew 5:32

The most controversial part of Christ's teaching in regard to divorce are the three words which conclude the Greek text of Matthew 5:32, namely *poiei auteen moichasthai* (Textus Receptus) or *moicheutheenai* (ABS Text).

The Authorized Version and many other translations render it "causeth her to commit adultery." This expression in Greek consists of a verb *poiei,* "makes."[1] In this instance of Matthew 5:32b it means "to cause" as rendered by the Authorized Version.

A Licentious Husband Dismisses His Wife Unjustifiably

Now we must find out who is the subject of this verb. Who causes what? There is no doubt whatsoever that the Lord refers to the person, the licentious husband, no matter who he is, who dismisses his wife for cause other than fornication which refers, as we have seen, to any sexual deviation from that of marriage which permits relations only with his wife.

We must point out here that there is a difference in the verb *apoluoo* in the first part of Matthew 5:32 between the Textus Receptus from which the Authorized Version or King James Version is translated and the newest United Bible Society Greek Text. The Textus Receptus says:

Hos an apolusee teen gunaika autou, which literally translated is: "He who if he dismisses the wife of his." The verb occurs in the aorist subjunctive, *apolusee,* which refers to a

111

specific act performed at a specific time. The verb does not imply continuity. This licentious husband, after continuously looking upon and caressing another woman, decides at a certain time to dismiss his own wife. (See Matt. 5:28–30.) That he dismisses his own wife for a reason other than fornication, which reason cannot be valid at all, there is no doubt.

The relative pronoun *hos,* "he who," is used in the Textus Receptus and the pronoun *pas,* "whosoever," is used in the UBS Text. The relative pronoun is followed by the particle *an,* meaning "if," making it a hypothesis which takes the verb *apoluoo* in the subjunctive *apolusee.* In the UBS Text *pas,* "whosoever," is followed by the present participial noun *ho apoluoon,* "the dismissing," which in it implies the ease with which a wife was put away by a husband. Essentially the two expressions mean the same. We prefer the Textus Receptus because the aorist subjunctive *apolusee,* "if he dismisses," agrees with the aorist subjunctive of the verb *apoluoo* which precedes it in verse 31 in the clause, "Whosoever shall put away his wife." This in Greek is *hos an apolusee teen gunaikai autou,* "he who if he dismisses the wife his." Apparently a copyist decided to change the aorist subjunctive *apolusee* occurring for the second time in Matthew 5:32a to avoid repetition. But I believe that repetition here lends itself to a better exegesis as it provides continuity of thought and action.

–*"It* was said:

"He who (*hos*) if he dismisses (*apolusee*) his wife, let him give her a bill of divorcement."

–*"But* I say to you:

"That he who (*hos*) if he dismisses his wife saving but for the cause of fornication." (This is how the Textus Receptus has it.)

The UBS has it: "That whosoever" (*pas*), the same pronoun found in Matthew 5:28: "But I say to you whosoever (*pas*) who keeps on looking at a woman to lust after her already committed adultery with (or better against) her in his heart."

If we take the UBS reading: "Whosoever the one dismissing (*pas apoluoon*) his wife saving for the cause of fornication," it reverts it to a principle rather than a historical action. "Whosoever does such a thing," i.e., dismisses his wife for any reason other than fornication.

The Principal Verb Is "Causes," *Poiei*

In either case the principal verb in the first clause of Matthew 5:32a is neither the subjunctive, *an apolusee* (TR-"if he dismisses"), nor the participial noun, *ho apoluoon* (UBS-"the one dismissing"), but the verb *poiei*, "causes," to which the previous can only be a dependent clause. As the very word "subjunctive" (*hupotaktikee*) suggests, that is a word which is under another action or state. Webster defines subjunctive as a verbal form "designating or pertaining to that mood of, or verb representing, the devoted action or state not as fact, but as contingent." The principal action verb in Matthew 5:32a is *poiei*, "makes, causes." This action of causing adultery is contingent upon such a man dismissing his wife. This contingency is better expressed with the subjunctive *hos an apolusee*, "he who if he dismisses," placing the action of the dismissal at a particular, historical time context. In the future, having done this and it being consummated, this is the present continuous effect of it, *poiei*, "causes." He "causes" her to be declared an adulteress.

Dismissal Causes Permanent Harm on the Unjustifiably Dismissed Wife

The verb is *poiee* in the present indicative making it durative, continuous. If a man dismisses his wife, the Lord Jesus says, he performs a particular act in a historical context. He dismisses his wife at a certain distinct time. The dismissing is a one-time act; but the consequence of that one historical act is forever, expressed with *poiei*, the one dismissing "causes forever" the wife he dismisses to be stigmatized as an adulteress. That stigma that he brings on his wife as a result of the dismissing can never be eliminated. One sinful action on a person's part places forever the burden of a stigmatized life on a non-guilty individual, and God will surely hold the person perpetrating such an act accountable.

The Action of the Husband Passes on to the Wife

A verb can be transitive or intransitive. The action of a transitive verb passes on to another. This verb *poiei* is in the active voice. This verb is also transitive.[2] The result of the action

113

passes from the subject to another. The object of *poiei*, "causes" in this instance, can only be *auteen*, "her," referring to the innocent woman dismissed by her husband.[3]

The Unjustifiably Dismissed Wife Does Not Commit Adultery

Now when the translators render the infinitive *moichasthai* (TR) or *moicheutheenai* (UBS) as meaning "to commit adultery," they make the dismissed woman the subject of her own adultery. They say "she commits adultery." Nothing could be more removed from reality. How can an innocent woman unjustifiably dismissed by her husband commit adultery if to this moment she did not do anything wrong? Many presuppose her adultery as being the result of her remarriage, but remarriage has not yet been brought into this discussion. She has just been dismissed. That was a crime perpetrated against her, not by her. What has misled the translators is the occurrence of the accusative of the object *auteen*, "her," in the clause "he causes her" with the infinitive *moichasthai* or *moicheutheenai*.[4] The subject of the infinitive *moichasthai* or *moicheutheenai*, "to commit adultery," is not the dismissed wife. Therefore, the infinitive could not be translated as "she commits adultery." She does nothing of the sort. She has suffered the trauma of being dismissed without a valid reason. She was the *victim* of the crime, not the criminal. Isn't it a gross mistake for us to make someone who is the victim of a crime the very criminal who committed it. God never holds the victim of a crime as deserving of further suffering.[5]

The conclusion we arrive at is as follows:

The subject of the verb *poiee*, "causes," is the licentious husband who dismisses his wife for a cause other than fornication.

The direct object is the accusative *auteen*, "her," the innocent wife.

The infinitive *moichasthai* or *moicheutheenai* does not have as subject the innocent dismissed wife, but the licentious husband who divorced her. What is it that he causes to be done to her? To be adultered or be stigmatized as an adulterer. Thus the infinitve acts as the indirect object qualifying the accusative *auteen*, "her," the innocent wife.[6]

Conclusion: The clause with the main verb *poiei*, "he causes," must be translated "he causes her to be stigmatized or accused or considered as an adulteress."

114

[1]Third person singular of the verb *poieoo,* "to make, to endue a person or thing with a certain quality or qualities" as in Matthew 3:3, 4:19; 5:36, etc.

[2]A.T. Robertson, *A Grammar of the Greek New Testament,* p. 331.

[3]A.T. Robertson says on page 471 of his grammar: "The most common accusative is when it is the object of a transitive verb." *Auteen,* "her," is in the accusative case.

And another great grammarian of the Greek language, William Edward Jelf (Oxford, London, 1861) writes: "The infinitive as the object stands as the accusative after the verb; and, generally speaking, signifies that to which the verbal notion supplies the particular point in or on which it develops itself or takes effect, or operates" (pg. 361 para. 663 3[b]).

[4]That great grammarian of the Greek New Testament, A.T. Robertson, sheds light on the reason for this mistranslation. He says on page 489 of his grammar:
"The accusative with the infinitive. The grammarians generally speak of the accusative as the subject of the infinitive. I confess that to me this seems a grammatical misnomer."
I confess the same. In this case Robertson's conclusion would be the same as mine.

[5]Grammarian William Edward Jelf writes:
"Without the article the infinitive is used as object after verbs or adjectives which express or imply the notion of ability, efficacy, power, prosperity, capacity, causing or their contraries as . . . *poieoo,* 'make or cause' " (Wm. Edward Jelf, *A Grammar of The Greek Language,* John Henry and James Parker, Oxford and London, 1861, pp. 368-370).
Also, A.T. Robertson comments on this: "The infinitive clause in indirect discourse does correspond to a finite clause in English, and a clause with *hoti* (that) and the indicative (which here is *poiei,* 'cause') may often be used as well as the infinitive clause. But it is not technically scientific to read back into the Greek infinitive clause (here *poiee auteen moichasthai)* the syntax of English, not even of the *hoti* 'that', clause in Greek. Besides, not only is the infinitive a verbal adjective (the participle) but being non-finite (in-finitive) like the participle (partaking of both verb and noun), it can have no subject in the

115

grammatical sense. *No one thinks of calling the accusative the 'subject' of the participle."*

Then Robertson gives as an illustration Matthew 16:28: "Till they see the Son of man coming in his kingdom." He points out that here the accusative *ton huion,* "the Son," is the object of "they see," *idoosin,* and the participle "coming" *erchomenon,* is descriptive of "the Son," *ton huion.*

[6]A.T. Robertson says on page 490 of his grammar, "When the infinitive is used with the accusative, it indicates the agent who has to do with the action by the accusative since the infinitive can have no subject in the technical sense."

Grammarian William Edward Jelf writes: "Verbs which denote a motion of the will; the infinitive denotes the aim, or the result. Whereof, or that whereon or wherein the verbal notion rests or operates: it stands as the equivalent accusative as is clear from it being always possible to insert a demonstrative in the accusative to which the infinitive would then stand in opposition" (p. 368, para. 664 A[1]).

25

WHAT WAS THE TEACHING
OF JESUS IN MATTHEW 5:32?

"But I say unto you, That whosoever shall put away his wife, saving for the cause of fornication, causeth her to commit adultery: and whosoever shall marry her that is divorced committeth adultery." Matthew 5:32

The first thing the Lord taught is that no man and, by application of the same principle (Mark 10:12), no woman may put away or divorce his or her spouse for any reason other than fornication. "But I say unto you that he who, if he send or put away his wife except for reason of fornication. . . ." Let us take this part of the Lord's saying first and interpret it.

Why Did Christ Use the Word "Fornication," **Porneia,** *Instead of Adultery?*

The reason the Lord is using the more general word *porneia,* "fornication," here instead of the more restrictive one, *moicheia,* "adultery," since a married man is involved, is to make the prohibition per se more comprehensive.

If a married person has sexual relationships with a married woman or an unmarried one, for him it is in either instance *moicheia,* "adultery," because he is a married man. But for the woman with whom he has relations, if she is unmarried, it is fornication.

The Spouse of an Unfaithful Partner Is Given the Option of Dismissing Him or Her

The Lord wanted also to give the liberty of optional permission to a spouse to divorce a partner who may be guilty of any illicit sexual relationship. He does not distinguish between a man or woman, but promulgates a principle which would also cover homosexuality or incest as we have seen the word "fornication" to include.

When a spouse detects and proves that his or her partner has deviated sexually in any way, then that spouse has the right if he or she so chooses, to divorce the guilty party. The innocent spouse is in no way under command or obligation to dismiss the sinning partner. There is liberty of action. The innocent party is free to dissolve the marriage partnership without committing sin. Of course, he or she can exercise forgiveness in order to win the erring partner into a life of chastity once again.

The emphasis of the Lord is not placed on the fact that the innocent partner has the right to put away the guilty spouse for reason of sexual deviation, but that he does not have the right to put away his wife for any reason other than fornication. This is the only basis of divorce as taught in Matthew 5:32, thus eliminating any other reason for it. The Lord emphasizes the exception in order to make clear the rule. One cannot tell his marriage partner that he doesn't love her anymore and therefore wants a divorce. That is forbidden. A married person *may* seek a divorce and not sin if the partner is a fornicator. This teaching of Christ, however, has to be studied and complemented with other more explicit and explanatory pronouncements by the apostles and our Lord on other occasions. These we shall study later.

Our Lord teaches that if a man should divorce his wife for any reason, he must not consider the effect of the action upon himself only, but the effect it has upon her.

A Licentious Person Exercises Immorality by Looking and Touching

The Lord is definitely speaking of the same person He discussed from verse 27 on. "You heard that it was said by them of old time, Thou shalt not commit adultery." This referred to the physical act of adultery. "But I say unto you, That whosoever looketh on a woman to lust after her hath committed adultery *against* her already in his heart."

The Authorized Version says, "he hath committed adultery *with* her." The translation "with" is absolutely wrong. A man may look upon a woman to sexually desire her and thus commit adultery against her without her ever knowing about it.

In this case under discussion, however, the looks and the

caresses lead to the actual desire to divorce. If this was meant to convey the notion of committing adultery *with* her, the Greek expression would have been *emoicheusen met autees,* and not *emucheusen auteen.* The man commits adultery in his own heart first. He does not cause the woman to sin unless he entices her to have illicit sexual relations with him. It is he, therefore, and he alone who, in the first instance, makes himself an adulterer. The woman may be totally innocent and pure in mind while the man indulges his lustful fantasies.

Is the Woman for Whom a Man Lusts a Sinner?

Now this woman who is the victim of the lustful one's imagination may be married or single. It makes no difference. He is still an adulterer toward or against her. If the woman consciously has encouraged it or participates in making the sin of sight and touch the sin of active participation, then she becomes a fornicator. If she is married, she becomes an adulterer. Our Lord in a few words covered a lot of eventualities.

In this connection, please refer to Revelation 2:22 where we have "and them that commit adultery *with her*" (*met autees*). Guilt here is ascribed not only to the man who commits adultery, but also to Jezebel, who actually is the one who lures the sinner to sin.

Christ's Basic Teaching Is Preventive Ethics

In reality, the Lord is not talking basically about the eventuality of dismissing one's wife because of fornication, *porneia.* What the Lord is basically talking about is that person described in verses 28 to 30 who himself is an adulterer by looking at and touching another woman, no matter who she is. This important truth, however, may not be too clear as one reads this passage in the English translation.

Just How Serious Is the Sin of Immorality?

And then the Lord interjects two seemingly unrelated verses:

"And if thy right eye offend thee, pluck it out, and cast it from thee for it is profitable for thee that one of thy members should perish, and not that thy whole body should be cast into hell.

"And if thy right hand offend thee, cut it off, and cast it from thee: for it is profitable for thee that one of thy members should perish, and not that thy whole body should be cast into hell" (Matt. 5:29, 30).

Are these verses really unrelated? Did our Lord deviate from His discourse? Not at all. Has He not been speaking about the eye leading one into sin? And after the lust of the eye follows the action of the hand. Why the right hand? Perhaps because most people are right handed and it is this which initiates the physical action. Our Lord is telling us to nip the evil in the bud no matter what the cost and no matter how important it may seem to us. He is trying to impress upon us just how very serious is this sin.

How Is Adultery Committed "Against" His Wife?

As previously mentioned, there are two Greek pronouns used in this context: the pronoun *pas* in verse 28 and the relative pronoun *hos* in verses 31 and 32 used three times in the Textus Receptus and only twice in the ABS text. The three instances of the relative pronoun *hos,* meaning "he who," must relate in this context to the person demonstrated in the first instance by *pas,* "whosoever" or "anyone," who keeps looking upon "another woman" and caresses her. It is as if our Lord were saying, "Eyes and hands off any woman who is not your wife." Of course the same applies to any wife in regard to another man other than her husband.

The last *hos* introduces the second clause of verse 32, "and whosoever (*hos*) shall marry her that is divorced committeth adultery." Observe that the conjunction "and" (*kai*) precedes this last *hos* and therefore introduces another hypothesis dependent on the previous hypothesis. The first supposition is: "If anyone puts away his wife, saving for the cause of fornication, he causes her to commit adultery."

The second supposition which depends on the first is: "*And* whosoever shall marry her that is divorced committeth adultery."

The above is what the King James Version says taken from the Textus Receptus. But the UBS text here in Matthew 5:32, instead of *hos,* "whosoever," has *pas ho apoluoon,* which means "anyone, the dismissing one." This we discussed previously in Chapter 18.

If we should take the UBS text as correct, we must point out that there is agreement between *pas ho blepoon,* "anyone, the one continuously looking upon a woman to lust after her" of verse 28 and *pas ho apoluoon,* "anyone, the dismissing one" of verse 32a. Both are present participles, *ho blepoon* and *ho apoluoon,* preceded by *pas,* "anyone, each one, no matter who he may be." Anyone looking and anyone dismissing or divorcing is what we have in verses 28a and 32a. Both participles are in the present indicative, *ho blepoon,* "the one looking," and *ho apoluoon,* "the one dismissing." This is indicative more of a principle of character instead of merely a single act of behavior.

The "whosoever" of "he who," *hos* of verse 31 in the clause "Whosoever shall put away his wife," must have some exegetical connection to *pas,* "anyone, no matter who," of verse 28, "whosoever looketh on a woman."

Verse 31 refers to the person who lusts after another woman and dismisses his wife unwarrantedly, not for the reason of immorality, thus causing adultery to be committed against her. This is especially so if he does not give her a bill of divorcement which would clear her of guilt. By his action she was stigmatized in her community since the only legitimate reason for a Jewish man to dismiss his wife was fornication, i.e., immorality on her part. And if immorality was proven as having been committed by a wife, her proscribed punishment was death by stoning (Lev. 20:10; Deut. 22:22), although more commonly, she was cast out without the benefit of a divorce. The only way to compensate the innocent dismissed wife for the evil done against her was to give her a certificate of divorce so that she would be free to remarry. If her husband did not give her this, then she bore the stigma of an adulteress who should have been put to death, but was spared execution. Although she was not stoned, she was dismissed as a wife bearing the trauma, the stigma, of a harlot. Without a bill of divorcement, she then must bear the disgrace of an implied adulteress or a harlot whom few men would want to marry.

26

DOES AN INNOCENT MAN WHO MARRIES AN UNJUSTIFIABLY DISMISSED WOMAN COMMIT ADULTERY?

". . . causeth her to commit adultery: and whosoever shall marry her that is divorced committeth adultery." Matthew 5:32b

In the latter portion of this verse, the Lord turns His attention to the man who marries a wife who was unjustifiably dismissed by her previous husband. If her first husband did not give her a bill of divorcement, he allowed the stigma of adultery to be assumed by her. It therefore compounded the sin of a licentious husband when dismissing an innocent wife not to give her a bill of divorcement declaring her innocent of any guilt on her part. By doing so, he would have taken the blame for the dismissal upon himself. And the question is, how many such husbands would be honest enough to do so? Christ's concern was for the victim of the crime of fornication who was destined to bear the guilt of her licentious husband all her life. Also, whoever would marry such a dismissed woman took upon himself the unjustifiable guilt of adultery by marrying an adulteress. As commentator R.C.H. Lenski correctly says: "This man as little 'commits adultery' as the woman 'commits adultery.' Neither 'commits' anything; both have had something committed upon them. The man who marries this woman thereby shares her position."

Bearing the Stigma of Divorce

The verb *moichatai,* "committeth adultery," in Matthew

5:32b should then be exegetically translated as "is stigmatized as adulterous." The verb *moichatai* is in the present durative tense, passive or middle voice, which indicates the constant stigma which both the dismissed woman and the man who marries her must bear. It is not because either of them has done anything wrong, but it is the result of the sin of the woman's original husband.

The verb *moichatai* is in the third person singular middle-passive form referring only to the person who decided to marry such a dismissed, innocent wife. Her first husband committed adultery against her by stigmatizing her as an adulteress since he did not give her a divorce. And now her present husband, in deciding to marry her appears to commit adultery against himself by marrying a supposedly licentious woman although he or she has done nothing wrong. In such a case, *moichatai* can be taken as having middle voice, meaning that the action reverts to and affects himself.

Observe that the verb in the second clause of verse 32 does not qualify the object of the apparent adultery. It does not have an object at all. It says, "And whosoever, if he shall marry a dismissed one (an innocent one bearing the stigma of her husband's action who dismissed her without giving her a bill of divorcement) commits (or better 'causes') adultery first against himself." It does not say what the previous clause (Matt. 5:32a) said, "makes her to be stigmatized with adultery," or causes adultery against her, i.e., his innocent wife. She is the object of her husbands' crime. She is the one who suffers because of what he has done. Mark 10:11, corresponding with Matthew 5:32 and referring to the marriage of a dismissed, innocent wife, says that such a husband *moichatai ep' auteen,* "commits adultery against her." But Matthew 5:32b in the case of the man who marries this dismissed, innocent wife, simply says *moichatai* without an object. Therefore, the object has to be understood first as being himself, in which case the passive verb takes middle voice meaning. But it can also have as its object the dismissed, innocent wife he married, as Mark 10:11 very explicitly declares. He brings this "cultural" stigma upon her although she does not deserve it. If such a woman were not married again, the stigma would be assumed as less than if she were to be married again. Her presumed stigma is then accentuated simply because her former husband did not give her

124

a bill of divorcement declaring her innocent. Had her first husband not behaved so unjustly against her, she would not have had to bear even the possibility of this unjustified stigma.

Matthew 5:32b is a statement which has been greatly misunderstood because of the erroneous translation. The Authorized Version translates it "and whosoever shall marry her that is divorced committeth adultery." How can this be since, though she is dismissed by her first husband, yet she is the innocent party?

This translation as we have it in the Authorized Version, "committeth adultery," cannot be correct for the following reasons:

1. She is made to be guilty of adultery in spite of the fact that she never did anything wrong. She has innocently suffered separation from her husband because most probably he saw, touched, and finally had sexual relations with another woman. The wife has been victimized. One trauma is enough—to be dismissed for reason other than adultery on her part. How on earth can the Lord of justice who never attributes guilt to the innocent consider her to have committed adultery herself? This is impossible.

2. Matthew 5:32a does not deal with her remarriage. The second statement in verse 32b only does. Here are the two statements in a paraphrase of what the Lord really said from our exegesis thus far:

a. "But I say unto you that he who (hos–the married man who lusts after another woman) if he dismisses his wife for any reason other than fornication or adultery (on her part), causes her to be considered as an adulteress." That latter statement has been wrongly expressed as "causes her to commit adultery." A discussion of this based on Greek grammar was given in Chapter 24 of this book. Further elucidation will follow.

b. The second statement of verse 32 is "And whosoever ("he who," hos) marries a dismissed but innocent woman, presumes upon himself the guilt of adultery and also upon the innocent dismissed woman he marries."

Let us now examine what the first licentious man does to the innocent wife he dismisses. The Authorized Version says: "He causes her to commit adultery," or more accurately, to be stigmatized as an adulteress. It is definitely wrong to translate

125

this as "causes her to commit adultery," without explaining what it really means.

The Greek text says, *poiei auteen moichasthai* (Textus Receptus), or *moiheutheenai* (UBS, 1966) which more accurately should be rendered as "makes her to be adultered against," if we could coin such a term, or "causes adultery to be committed against her." The subject is the licentious man, the guilty husband who puts away his wife for no valid reason. The only valid reason could have been if she had committed fornication, or adultery to be more specific. But she hasn't, and yet her husband dismisses her without giving her a bill of divorcement which would be tantamount to an absolution certificate as far as her guilt in the case is concerned.

Let Us Withhold Stones

Now, since the Lord Jesus permits divorce only on the basis of the sexual sin of one's partner, when a man puts away his wife and gives no explanation, or she gives no explanation, it will be assumed that the separation is because she has done something morally wrong. Therefore, putting her away involves placing on her the automatic stigma of her being considered an immoral woman. Who is the person who when upon divorcing his or her spouse, does not like to give the impression that the other person is the guilty party? She is divorced! Therefore, she must have done something wrong, is usually the public assumption; otherwise, her husband would not have divorced her. That is how public opinion usually runs. Thus, the meaning here is that an innocent woman who has been dismissed automatically suffers the stigma of being an adulteress by virtue of having been put away no matter whether she did something wrong or not.

How careful we must be not to throw stones at any divorced person simply because that person is divorced. Let us not add vinegar to an open wound. The trauma for an innocent divorced woman or man is enough to bear, let alone branding that person an adulteress or an adulterer!

The Woman Cannot Return to Her Former Husband

The verb in this expression of Matthew 5:32 is *poiei*, "makes" or "does." What does he do? He puts out his wife once and for all. This is not an act that one can come back and undo. It

126

is one of those sins that once performed has no redress. The guilty party will live with it for the rest of his life and his partner will, too. You recall that Deuteronomy 24:1–4 forbade the return of the divorced wife to her former husband even if her second husband were to divorce her or die. First of all, *poiei,* "does, makes, or causes," is in the active voice which means, he, the licentious husband, *is fully responsible for the act.* Secondly, it involves the doing once and for all. Thirdly, it involves the producing and bringing forth of something which, being produced, *has an independent existence of its own. The man cannot alter the new situation he creates.* (Trench)

The verb *poiei,* "makes, does, or causes," forms a whole with the infinitive *moichasthai* (TR), "to cause adultery against her." He, the divorcing husband, is the cause of what is happening to her. The infinitive *moichasthai* is the passive infinitive of *moichaomai.* As Lenski says: "the agent of this passive must be the subject *poiei,* 'does or causes.' " It is not the woman who is dismissed who commits adultery, but the man who dismisses her for no valid reason. He makes her to suffer from the stigma of being thought of as an adulteress simply because he, her husband, divorced her. It is equivalent to saying: "Her husband causes adultery to be committed against her." This is the only possible exegetically valid translation of this statement of our Lord.

27

THE INNOCENT WOMAN HAS ADULTERY COMMITTED AGAINST HER

". . . causeth her to commit adultery: and whosoever shall marry her that is divorced committeth adultery."

Matthew 5:32b

John Murray, Professor of Systematic Theology at West-minster Theological Seminary of Philadelphia, in his excellent treatise on this subject writes:

"The evil of putting away (for any other reason than that of adultery) is viewed from the standpoint of what it entails for the woman divorced. The man makes her to be an adulteress. If we are to give passive force to the inifinitive in this clause it could be rendered, 'he makes her to suffer adultery.' "[1]

After John Murray wrote that, he went on to state in a footnote: "The passive of the verb *moicheuoo* occurs very infrequently in Biblical Greek." Yet, the Textus Receptus from which the Authorized King James Version is translated has the word in the passive. It is *moichasthai*. It is not active. The newer United Bible Society Greek text has it *moicheutheenai* which is also passive, first aorist infinitive. Thus, both Greek texts use the passive voice. In the latter part of Matthew 5:32: "and whosoever shall marry her that is dismissed is made adulterous," the verb is *moichatai* which is again passive from *moicheuomai*. In Matthew 19:9, it is used twice in the passive—*moichatai*. The translation of this verse should actually be: "And I say to you, that he who dismisses his wife except for fornication, and marries another, (*moichatai*) *is made adulterous* and he who marries a dismissed woman *is made adulterous*." The verb *moichatai* is the passive form of the verb *moichaomai* or *moicheuomai*. And again in Mark 10:11 and 12 it is used twice in the passive voice *moichatai*: "Whosoever shall release his

129

wife and marry another is made adulterous in regard to her; and if she, having dismissed her husband, and shall marry another, she is made adulterous (*moichatai*)."

The active verb *moicheuoo* occurs in Matthew 5:27, 28; 19:18, Mark 10:19, Luke 16:18; 18:20, John 8:4, Romans 2:22; 13:9, James 2:11, Revelation 2:22.

We believe that John Murray is unjustified by arbitrarily refusing to accept the verb *moichasthai* or *moicheutheenai* (infinitives) as is in its passive form, simply because as he states: "In addition to this verse, the only instances in the New Testament are Matthew 19:9 and John 8:4."

But there are others. The verb *moicheuomai* in the passive form occurs six times: namely, twice in Matthew 5:32, once in Matthew 19:10, twice in Mark 10:11, 12, and once in John 8:4. Aren't these instances enough? It is inconceivable that anyone should reject the voice of the verb, changing it from passive to active simply because it occurs only six times in the New Testament. Such licenses cannot be taken with Greek grammar, especially when proper exegesis makes it mandatory to take the verb as its form demands in the passive. The only license we have is to allow the middle voice sense if the exegesis warrants it since the form of the passive and the middle are the same. *Moichatai*, therefore, must be translated "is made to suffer adultery."

J.H. Thayer in his *Greek English Lexicon of the New Testament* says that when the passive is used of the wife it means "to suffer adultery, to be debauched." He does, however, concede that the translation of Matthew 5:32 may be "he makes her to commit adultery." He writes: "In Matthew 5:32, therefore, it is not impossible to regard *moicheutheenai* (he takes the United Bible Society Greek text instead of the Textus Receptus, which has *moichasthai*) as having an active meaning, namely to 'commit adultery.' In this case the clause would be rendered, 'he makes her to commit adultery, . . . Let the sense be active or passive, the woman is conceived of as entering into adulterous relations. *Moichatai* is present indicative middle. Any attempt to remove from the word the notion of active participation in the sin of adultery is entirely indefensible."

It is my conclusion that in view of the indefensibility of the resulting exegesis, if *moichasthai* and *moicheutheenai* is taken as active, which it is not, Murray's position must be considered as indefensible. The verbs are in the passive. It is true, of course, that the form of the middle and the passive voices are the same, but the passive or middle are not to be considered active. Nor can *moichaomai* be considered a deponent verb. As A.T. Robertson says: "The name 'deponent' is very unsatisfactory. It is used to mean the laying aside of the active form in the case of verbs that have no active voice (such as *poreuomai,* passive in form but active in meaning: 'to go' [Author's comment]). But these verbs in most cases never had an active voice."[2] *Moichaomai,* which never occurs in the New Testament in its passive form, however, has an active form *moichaoo* or *moicheuoo.* Therefore, *moicheuomai* cannot be considered as active in meaning particularly in Matthew 5:32.

John Murray has an acceptable exegesis for Matthew 5:32. He could strengthen his point, however, by attributing passive meaning to the passive verb. He writes, "Admittedly, this phrase, 'to suffer adultery' (*moichatai*—on the part of the dismissed wife [Author's parenthesis]) is a difficult one. It should be apparent that the wife does not become an adulteress simply by being divorced. She is contemplated as illegitimately divorced on the part of her wanton husband. She is the victim of his unlawful action, and her station could not therefore in justice be viewed as one of adultery. Indeed, she is viewed as innocent of adultery in the act of divorce, and so the act of divorce of which she is not the agent cannot of itself make her an adulteress" (pp. 23–24).

Murray translates *poiei auteen moichasthai* or *moicheutheenai* "makes her to suffer adultery" and implicates some responsibility for the wife who is put away. Such implication of the innocent wife is wrong. Lenski's exegesis which does not place any guilt on the innocent dismissed wife is much more preferable. Murray does not connect verses 31 and 32 as we have done with verses 28 and 30, which we must if we are going to attribute guilt to the husband only and innocence to the wife. Nor can we take this statement to imply that the innocent wife's adultery comes into the picture on her remarriage. Why should she be considered an adulteress when she remarries since she did absolutely nothing wrong and is innocent since her husband dismissed her for no reason of unfaithfulness on her part?

A brilliant linguistic scholar friend of mine working in Guatemala with the Wycliff Translators, Ray Elliott, shared with me a very worthwhile paper corroborating what I have tried to say in regard to the translation of this phrase that came out of the mouth of our Lord which has been so greatly misunderstood.

Elliott states: "In verse 32, one way of describing the Greek grammatical structure in English terminology would be to say that there is a single verb, *poiei,* 'he makes, he causes,' and an object of that verb which consists of two words *auteen moicheutheenai* (UBS text or *moichasthai,* TR [Author's parenthesis]), which express what it is 'he causes.' As was the case in 5:28, there is no obvious way to translate these words in 5:32 into English while retaining the same grammatical structure that is used in Greek. One way to express the meaning in English would be to say *'he causes her to be adultered'*—but that is not good English, even though it reflects the actual Greek structure better than any English translation I am aware of.

"Turning now to the contexts of the two verses:

"Both verses occur in the 'Sermon on the Mount' in which Jesus is distinguishing between common human attitudes and those which He considers to be appropriate in relation to the kingdom of heaven. He has already pointed out, for example, in the passage beginning with 5:21, that *anger can be an attitudinal equivalent to murder,* even if no bodily harm has been done to the object of the anger. The damage done, of course, involves the relationship between two people, and both suffer as a result of a wrong relationship in which unreconciled anger is a factor. Though the 'victim' may not be aware of the anger, the angry person is in fact in the grip of a murderous attitude.

"In much the same way, Jesus in Matthew 5:28 indicates that an inappropriate attitude toward one of the opposite sex can be the occasion of the mental equivalent of adultery—whether the 'victim' is aware of it or not. A man who looks at a woman with an attitude of sexual desire has already 'adultered' her in his heart, even if she is unaware of his desire and has done nothing to provoke or encourage it. To say 'adultered' does not make good English but it reflects the Greek structure and emphasizes for the English reader the fact that it is specifically *his* action, not necessarily hers nor jointly with her. The phrase does not imply that there is any guilt or participation on her part. It is worth our while to notice specifically here that no *physical* contact has taken place. All the action, so to speak, is 'in his heart.'

132

"Turning now to verse 32, Jesus refers to the case of a man and his wife. He specifies that the woman has not been guilty of sexual sin, but her husband divorces her. Jesus says that when he divorces such a wife, a man *poiei auteen moicheutheenai* (or *moichasthai*) 'causes her to be adultered,' a phrase which specifies sin on the husband's part but implies none at all for the wife. *She* has not committed adultery nor become an adulteress—the Greek construction does not allow such a meaning. The passive form of the infinitive indicates something done *against* her, not *by* her.

"Once this fact is clear, another puzzle is resolved—one which should have demanded solution long, long ago. Jesus has just specified in verse 32 that the woman in this case has not been guilty of sexual sin. How could it be, then, that (as all English versions I know of would require) guilt for sexual sin attaches *to her* simply on the basis of the fact that her husband divorced her? Well, as a matter of fact, it doesn't; Jesus never said any such thing! Any translation which implies or states that 'she becomes an adulteress' or that 'he causes her to commit adultery' is a mistranslation. Sexual sin is not attributed to her by the Greek text, either as a precondition to the divorce or as a consequence of it.

"Thus, there remains no necessity for attempting to explain—or explain away—what is otherwise a very strange and uncharacteristic statement by Jesus: *Her husband divorced her and that made her an adulteress!* God forgive us for putting such words into the mouth of our Lord!

"A few translators have tried to make sense of the divorced-wife-as-adulteress situation created by misreading the Greek by bringing into the first part of the verse something from a separate statement in the latter part of it. Since the end of the verse speaks of remarriage of a divorced woman, perhaps (it was surmised) *it could be implied that remarriage would make the woman an adulteress.* So some translations have gone that route, making the first part of the verse read somewhat as follows: 'The man who divorces his wife when she has not been guilty of sexual sin causes her to commit adultery if she remarries.' Whether or not that statement is *true* is not my point here; my point is that this is not what Jesus is saying in the first part of verse 32.

"Correctly read, then, Matthew 5:32 makes two rather straightforward statements: (1) The man who divorces his wife

133

when she is not guilty of sexual sin causes adultery on his part; and (2) the man who marries a woman who has been divorced commits adultery."

In this second statement, I disagree with my friend Elliott as I have already explained the meaning of the second statement being "and whosoever marries a dismissed wife, stigmatizes himself and her as adulterous."

Elliott continues: "Note one further point about the situation underlying the context of verse 32. As was the case in verse 28, so it is here: In neither verse is *physical* sexual contact a factor. *In both verse 28 and verse 32 it is mental activity on the part of the man.* Not even in the latter case is it physical sexual activity in focus, for the husband causes adultery by divorcing his wife. *Thus divorce, at least in God's sight, would seem to constitute adultery in this case.* The wife is the 'injured party' or 'victim' in the divorce, which is mental or spiritual adultery on the part of the man. He is unfaithful to God, to her, and to himself in not maintaining the marriage bond which he promised would be lifelong."

[1]*Divorce,* The committee on Christian Education, The Orthodox Presbyterian Church, P. 21.

[2]pp. 811–812, *A Grammar of the Greek New Testament,* A.T. Robertson.

28

MARRYING A DISMISSED WOMAN

"*. . . and whosoever shall marry her that is divorced committeth adultery.*" Matthew 5:32b

It is evident from verses 28 to 30 that the licentious man dismissed his wife for no legitimate reason. He sinfully lusted after another.

The second part of verse 32 deals with the action of a man in marrying an innocent, dismissed wife. "And he, who if he marries a dismissed woman, is adultered." He takes upon himself her stigma of adultery which she has already suffered whether she remarries or not.

Who is the person who marries? It cannot refer to the same licentious person who dismisses his wife. The two *hos,* "he who," stand in a series connected with *kai,* "and," which distinguishes the two persons as distinct. It is another person who proceeds to marry an unjustly dismissed wife of another man.

Who does he marry? The Greek text has the participial noun *apolelumeneen,* "a dismissed woman or wife." The word "woman" or "wife" is understood in view of the fact that *apolelumeneen* is feminine. There is no definite article in front of the participial noun. Therefore, it cannot possibly refer to *only* the wife put away by the licentious husband for any reason less than fornication or adultery. Rather, the participle refers to *any* woman thus dismissed by her husband.

All throughout this context and those of Matthew 19, Mark 10 and Luke 16:18, the verb *apoluoo,* as we see in our detailed examination of the texts, refers to the putting away of an innocent partner by a guilty husband without giving the dismissed partner a certificate of divorcement as had been demanded in Deuteronomy and by the Lord Jesus. All the emphasis of the Lord was on the partial redress that such an unjust spouse owes his innocent partner: namely, to grant a bill of divorcement which would take guilt away from the innocent party and enable her to remarry if she so wishes.

A person who marries such a dismissed woman brings upon himself a stigma of adultery since she is considered an adulteress due to her unjust dismissal. He now shares in that stigma. Thus the verb *moichatai* in the passive voice has the meaning again that "he suffers adultery or takes upon himself the stigma of adultery," and as far as she is concerned, she has already begun suffering the stigma from the moment her first husband unjustly put her away.

The Undeserved Burden Is for Life

The verb that is used in this clause of Matthew 5:32b is *moichatai* from *moichaoomai.* This is in the present durative tense. He continuously causes her to be adultered. The verb *gameesee,* "shall marry her," in the clause "and whosoever shall marry her that is divorced committeth adultery," is in the aorist subjunctive. The marrying he does once, but the stigma of adultery he will suffer is for his whole life.

The conclusions we reach are:

1. One cannot divorce his wife or husband for any reason other than fornication, and this only if he chooses to do so. It is not a command.

2. If he or she does dismiss a spouse for reason other than fornication, there must be a divorce issued which enables the innocent party to honorably remarry.

3. One can legitimately dismiss one's spouse for engaging in sexual sin.

4. In looking at a woman or caressing her with sexual desire, adultery has already been committed against her, and at the same time, against the perpetrator's own wife.

5. In marrying an innocent, dismissed wife, one must be ready to carry for life the unjustified false stigma of adultery she has already been suffering when her first husband dismissed her unjustly. She, however, does not in herself commit an act of adultery by remarrying. Her first husband brought upon her the stigma of being considered an adulteress although she was not.

Thus an exegetical paraphrase of Matthew 5:32 and 33 is as follows:

"And it was said, If a licentious person dismisses his own

136

wife, let him give her a bill of divorcement (so she can remarry). But I say unto you that he who (the licentious person who lusts after another woman, married, divorced, or unmarried) dismisses his own wife but for the reason of fornication (sexual infidelity on her part) causes adultery against her (makes her appear as if she were put away because of her sexual infidelity), and he who marries a thus dismissed woman assumes upon himself the stigma of adultery which she has borne from the moment her husband unjustifiably dismissed her without giving her a divorce."

after another woman, married, divorced, or unmarried) dismisses his own wife but for the reason of fornication (sexual infidelity on her part) causes adultery against her (makes her appear as if she were put away because of her sexual infidelity), and he who marries a thus dismissed woman assumes upon himself the stigma of adultery which she has borne from the moment her husband unjustifiably dismissed her without giving her a divorce."

29

THE PHARISEES QUESTION JESUS WHETHER IT IS PERMISSIBLE TO PUT AWAY ONE'S WIFE

"The Pharisees also came unto him, and saying unto him, is it lawful for a man to put away his wife for every cause?" Matthew 19:3

In the first two verses of Matthew 19, we find the Lord Jesus in Perea having just come from Galilee with His disciples on His way to Jerusalem. Great multitudes had followed him, and He healed many there.

Verse 3 says: "The Pharisees also came unto him (testing) him, and saying unto him, Is it lawful for a man to put away his wife for every cause?"

These Pharisees knew they were posing a difficult and controversial question. In the same manner as Satan tried to tempt Jesus, so did these Pharisees. They were not motivated by a sincere desire to find out the solution to the problem of divorce, but rather wanted to entrap Jesus to answer in such a way that they could then accuse and discredit Him as not in agreement with the Mosaic law. The Lord knew their malicious motive but did not hesitate to answer knowing that His answer would clarify the perplexing problem of divorce for the people of His time and ours. Without these answers, the teaching we would have on this subject would be sketchy and limited at best.

The Pharisees Questioning Jesus on Divorce: "Is It Permissible for a Man to Dismiss His Wife for Every Reason?"

In spite of the Pharisees' evil motivation, what was the basic question?

"Is it permitted for man to dismiss his own wife for every reason?"

Actually, the word *exesti* translated "is it lawful" does not strictly mean that. It is an impersonal verb derived from *ex* which means "out" and the verb *eimi* which means "to be." Is it to be far removed from us, something that we should carefully avoid? If it is the law that regulates what we can or cannot do, then the word could be translated "is it lawful." But if it refers rather to our estimate of what is right or wrong, then the translation should be "is it permitted." I believe originally these Pharisees may have desired Jesus to speak out as to whether it is right or wrong for a man to dismiss his wife for any reason. They were not really interested in Jesus' interpretation of the law but in His concept of what was the right thing to do in such a matter. Later on, after they heard His thoughts on divorce and found them unpalatable, they made an appeal to Moses' law in order to support their desired view on divorce.

What is right to the Lord Jesus is more important than what is legal. He showed this in His previous teaching on divorce in Matthew 5. The law, He said, states: "Do not commit adultery." The law, however, will never punish anyone who commits adultery by merely looking or touching a woman to lustfully desire her. The law steps in only when a guilty person involves another person, harming him physically or psychologically. The Lord, however, condemns the person whose crime does not harm or involve another in its initial stage at least. Thus, what is right may be different from what is lawful. It is the Christian's duty to avoid not only what is illegal, but what is not morally right. If the Lord only explained what is contrary to the law of Moses, it would have little effect upon Christians who are not under the law, but under grace.

Therefore, I prefer to translate the question "Is it permitted or permissible for a man to divorce his own wife for every reason?" It is wrong for me to do that which God, in His creation, never meant me to do, or not to do that which He meant me to do. That is inherent good and evil. If I do the wrong thing, then God has to legislate laws regulating the punishment of evil. That is the difference between what is right and what is lawful. According to Jesus, sin is not mere deviation from certain laws but from God's original purpose for man. The law which is enacted consequent to sin is to make sin more apparent and obvious. That is why Paul says in Romans 5:20: "The law entered (squeezed through), that the offence might abound."

140

30

FINDING ANY EXCUSE FOR DISMISSING ONE'S WIFE

". . . .Is it lawful for a man to put away his wife for every cause?" Matthew 19:3

The word that is used for "put away" in Matthew 19:3 is *apolusai.* It is derived from the preposition *apo,* "from," and the verb *luoo,* which means "to loose" or "to free." In its basic form it may mean to loose from prison, the opening of a thing that is closed, the destruction of foundations and walls, to release someone from his fetter, etc. The compound *apoluoo,* means "to set someone free from one's self, to release, to set free." It implies a previous bond, a relationship which binds two persons together and then releases them. A woman belongs to a particular man and a man belongs to a particular woman. That is marriage. When one of these persons is released from the other, that is putting away or dismissing, *apoluein.* Dismissing one's marital partner in its basic idea entails the freedom that ensues for the individual who is released, and naturally also for that person who releases his or her partner. It implies the idea of releasing someone, not really for his or her sake, but for the consequent releasing of oneself.

Interestingly, another derivative of the verb *luoo* is *kataluoo,* with the intensive preposition *kata,* "down," and *luoo,* "loose." It means to set it down and to let it alone, to remove it from being up on the surface, to make it inapplicable to the times. That is translated as "destroy" in such passages as Matthew 5:17: "Think not that I am come to destroy the law, or the prophets. I am not come to destroy, but to fulfill." The word "destroy" is *kataluoo (katalusai).*

Therefore, *apoluoo,* "remove, release, dismiss," is to set someone formerly bound to a person away from him or her as totally unrelated. This is the word that is used of Joseph's desire to "put away" Mary when he realized that she was pregnant before he had any relations with her (Matt. 1:19). The word is also used in Matthew 5:31 and 32 translated "put away."

The Pharisees Recognized Monogamous Marriage

The Pharisees recognized monogamous marriage in their question to the Lord Jesus: "Is it permissible for man to divorce his very own wife?" There was to be only one wife to one husband.

It is interesting that there is the pronoun *autou,* "his own," which strengthens the belief among them that in spite of all the polygamous practices to which they were exposed, yet they were upholding the monogamous marriage. Each man had his very own wife. She was his possession.

The question posed is, Does he have the inherent God-given right to release her for any reason?

What Were the Prevalent Ideas About Dismissing One's Marital Partner?

First, there was the provision of the Mosaic law in Deuteronomy 24:1-4. One could divorce his wife if she found no favor in his eyes because he had found some uncleanness in her. Because of the ambiguity of what these reasons for dismissing one's wife were, there were various interpretations as to what was this unclean thing, or as the Septuagint has it, *ascheemon pragma,* "shameful or uncomely thing." Actually the Greek word means "without shape," *(a-scheema),* therefore ugly, without figure. There were two main schools of interpretation in regard to this.

The Interpretations of Two Rabbis, Shammai and Hillel, as to What Constituted Valid Reason for Dismissing One's Wife

There was the school of Shammai who interpreted Deuteronomy 24:1-4 as follows: "The man is not to release his wife unless he has found something indecent in her." He did not in any way clarify what was "indecent" in the wife. So he allowed one's own interpretation of indecency.

Another Jewish leader, Hillel, however, did not allow people to interpret this provision but gave his own liberal interpretation saying that if the wife burned the food in cooking or whatever, it could be considered the indecent thing which would permit the husband to dismiss his wife.

Rabbi Akiba, according to Lenski, referring especially to the expression, "that she find no favor in his eyes," permitted her release when the husband found a better looking woman.

Shammai, nevertheless, was stricter than Hillel. Of course, the Pharisees preferred the laxity of Hillel in marriage so that when they decided to change their wife, any reason would suffice.

An Endeavor to Justify Dismissing a Marital Partner

Interestingly, the Greek expression in Matthew 19:3 is *kata pasan aitian*. The preposition *kata* means "according" or "against," as for instance in the verb *kateegoreoo* from *kata*, "against," and *agoreuoo*, "to speak," thus giving us the phrase "to speak against or to accuse." What they wanted was to have something, no matter what, which they could blame and thus justify the action of divorce. They did not want to be found or be accused of doing something wrong when dismissing their wives. And after all, who is the person who is willing to accept the blame himself for the wrong he does? Isn't this all too common among fallen human nature? Didn't Adam blame Eve and also God Himself: "The woman whom thou gavest to be with me, she gave me of the tree, and I did eat" (Gen. 3:12)? So the actual question of the Pharisees was: "Can't we always find some excuse for divorcing our wives?" Of course it can be found, but whether it is a valid and legitimate excuse is another matter.

31

THREE GREEK VERBS MEANING "TO DISMISS"

In the Greek New Testament there are three verbs which are used to refer to what we call "divorce."

1. *Apoluoo* meaning "to set loose from oneself." This word is used throughout the Synoptic Gospels: Matthew 1:19; 5:31, Mark 10:2, 4, Luke 16:18.

2. *Aphienai* (infinitive), *aphieemi* (present indicative). This is made up of the preposition *apo* meaning "from" and the verb *hieemi* meaning "to send." The compound verb therefore means "to send from me, to separate."

Interestingly, this is the commonly used word in the New Testament to express remission or forgiveness of sin. It is causing the sin to separate from the individual. It is not disregarding sin, but removing it so that it is no more a part of the individual. In the same manner it is used of divorce as a separating process; i.e., a man sends his spouse away from him; therefore, he frees her from any responsibility toward him, but at the same time frees himself of any obligation or responsibility he has to her.

This word standing for "sending away from" or "dismissing or putting away" is used in I Corinthians 7:11, 12, and 13.

In Matthew 22:25 it has the meaning of "leaving" a wife, at death, to another.

3. *Choorizeen*, (infinitive) for *choorizoo* means "to separate, depart," or "to terminate a marriage union" as in I Corinthians 7:10, 11, and 15. It refers to what the initiator of the action does to himself.

All three words convey the same basic principle: dismissing or separation from oneself, a sending away from oneself, a setting loose or freeing from oneself.

145

32

THE PHARISEES WANTED DIVORCE TO BE THEIR PRIVILEGE FOR ANY REASON WHATSOEVER

"Is it lawful for a man to put away his wife for every cause?" Matthew 19:3

The contractual agreement to live together as man and wife was being broken in the Mosaic period and thereafter, even in the time of Christ's earthly ministry. When the Pharisees asked the Lord the question whether it was permissible to dismiss one's marital partner, they did not thereby seek the condemnation of the custom, but an excuse for what they were practicing so flippantly.

The Lord had already spoken on this matter to His disciples and the multitudes who followed, and undoubtedly many Pharisees were among them. That teaching was part of His Sermon on the Mount delivered on the Mount of the Beatitudes in Galilee (Matt. 5:27-32). In that passage the Lord declared that divorce was permitted by Him only for one reason, and that was fornication which included adultery.

Apparently they were not willing to accept His precept on the subject and wanted to argue the point. They would rather have an excuse that would permit them to dismiss their wives for any reason, as they evidently had been doing.

"Is it permissible for man to dismiss his own wife for every reason?" The two last words must be explained from the Greek text. "Every" is *pasan* which refers not only to the individual reason, one of many, but all of them put together. Actually it could be rendered "any and all" reasons. The Pharisees wanted divorce to be their privilege for whatever reason or reasons. The word translated "reason" is *aitia* which actually refers to a charge, a ground for complaint or accusation without necessarily having proof or substantiation for it. As Trench says, *"Aitia* is an accusation, but whether false or true the word does not attempt to anticipate; and thus it could be applied, indeed it was applied, to the accusation made against the Lord of Glory Himself (Matt. 27:37)."

Thus what the Pharisees were after was license to dismiss their wives for any unsubstantiated accusation against them. They ought to have known that there was no way that the Lord Jesus would agree with them on that.

Pharisaic Entrapment

What were they really after? I believe it was basically the entrapment of the Lord Jesus. Had He declared Himself against divorce, they reasoned, He would be most unpopular with the majority of the people who were already practicing it so flagrantly and irresponsibly. But weren't they really attempting to justify their evil actions? Isn't the same attitude prevalent today—who wants to hear what the Lord Jesus really teaches about divorce? Rather, we want Him to agree with what we desire to do or else we attempt to twist the Scriptures to agree with our wishes. We proceed to do what we want, what is popular, and justify that action, but still vehemently declare that we are His faithful followers.

The Pharisees wanted to alienate Jesus from His followers by forcing Him to elaborate on an unpopular position although He had already declared His stand on the subject in Matthew 5:32 and 33.

These Pharisees thought that they would be able to depreciate the Lord Jesus in the eyes of the faithful Jews who were followers of the Mosaic law if they could only cause Him to declare Himself in opposition to some of its provisions. This is the reason, as a preface to His specific teaching about what the Old Testament taught and what His earthly mission was, the Lord emphatically stressed that He had not come to destroy but to fulfill (Matt. 5:17-20). They knew that Moses' law in Deuteronomy permitted divorce. Had Christ not declared that He had come to fulfill and not to destroy the law?

At least they knew they would set Him in opposition to some of the people who were followers of Shammai, the conservative, if He liberalized the cause of divorce, or against the followers of Hillel, the liberal, if He tightened the reins a bit. These

Pharisees knew that on this subject of divorce, He could not say anything that would please them all. Don't the enemies of Christ always try to play the same trick on us who love Him? Let's determine we can't please them all.

There is no doubt, as we have already examined it, that the provision of the Mosaic law on the subject, and especially Deuteronomy 24:1-4, was not too clear as to the causes enabling men to divorce their wives. Where clarity is missing, there is confusion and a multiplicity of interpretations.

33

MARRIAGE IS GOD'S DOING AND MUST BE CONDUCTED ACCORDING TO HIS INSTRUCTIONS

"... he which made them at the beginning made them male and female. And said, For this cause shall a man leave father and mother, and shall cleave to his wife; and they twain shall be one flesh? Wherefore they are no more twain, but one flesh. What therefore God hath joined together, let no man put asunder." Matthew 19:4-6

Jesus' answer to the question of the Pharisees as to whether it was permissible to divorce one's wife for any reason was a masterpiece as were all of His answers.

Jesus' Appeal to the Scriptures

The first thing the Lord did was to appeal to their knowledge of the Scriptures: "Have ye not read . . . " It was as if He were emphasizing that on important matters such as marriage we should not decide independently according to our own convenience and desire. We cannot do as we want. Since it is God who made us what we are—man and woman—we must also adhere to His rules if such union is to produce the intended purposes.

When a manufacturer makes a car, he knows best how to make it operate efficiently so that it may yield the expected results. The operator of the automobile does not and cannot decide whether or not he wants to use gasoline or diesel, or what size tires or fan belt he wants to buy.

But we have tried to operate our married lives and our conjugal relationships as though we were the ones who made man and woman. God is the One who instituted marriage and He is the only One who knows how it can bring the best results and be preserved. Our disregard of God's rules for a happy

151

marriage is the reason for its collapse.

God's Rules for Successful Marriage

The first is the recognition of monogamy—one man and one woman—not two or more women to one man or vice versa. In reality, in the Greek text it says *arsen*, "male," and *theelu*, "female." He created Adam and Eve with their special and complementary characteristics for procreation and mutual care and satisfaction. As someone said, He did not create Adam and Bob nor Eve and Mary. Homosexuality is *not* God's doing. It is man's perversion and sinfulness. Two men or two women cannot have children which was God's method of perpetuating the human race, nor do they complement each other as two of the opposite sex do.

The Lord intimated to the Pharisees in His answer that what they were doing in the matter of marriage and divorce was not because they were ignorant of God's requirements, but because they deliberately ignored them or disobeyed them. The deteriorated state of marriage could not be blamed on God, as if He, as man's maker, had neglected to give the Manufacturer's instructions of operation. He gave the necessary instructions, but man could not make marriage operate properly because of his neglect of the directives. Who has not experienced buying a toy or some piece of equipment unassembled? We attempt to put it together—without bothering to read the instructions. Finally losing our patience, we say, All the parts aren't here; there is something missing, and we take it back to the store. All the parts were there, however, but we did not bother to read the instructions for assembling the product. We can't blame anybody else but ourselves. As the saying goes, "When all else fails, read the instructions."

Similarly, if marriage has not worked among men according to God's design, it is man who has failed. He has not read and followed the Creator's instructions.

Originally God made one man, Adam, and one woman, out of the man's side. Adam could not divorce his wife and take another, for there was no other to take. It was an inseparable union. If he were to put away his wife, he would be tearing asunder a piece of himself. If we truly believed that our spouse was part of our flesh, one flesh with us, we would never think of

152

mutilating our body, would we? Such action can only produce pain and scars for both members of the marriage.

34

ONE MAN, ONE WOMAN FOR LIFE

". . . made them male and female." Matthew 19:4

The Lord Jesus speaks of man's marriage as unique in His work of creation. He said it is not permissible for man to put away his wife because of the special manner in which God created man and woman.

Animals don't marry. They mate. And for the most part, they mate without life attachment. The rest of the higher creation was made male and female, but no specific mention of the union between one male and one female is made regarding them. Man's purpose of union is not mere procreation as the case is with the other creatures, but companionship and fulfillment that the animals know nothing about. It was never said of any of the other creatures what was said of man: "So God created man in his own image, in the image of God created he him, male and female created he them" (Gen. 1:27). They were made each one by the direct act of God. He first made Adam and then Eve by taking one of Adam's ribs. But by the institution of marriage, God made the two "one." And the two having become one cannot by God be made two again. That is the original, fundamental law of marriage.

God's Law of Marriage Irreversible

The verb used in Christ's answer to the Pharisees is *poieesas,* "made." It's in the aorist tense referring to a once and for all action of God. That procedure, as far as His creative activity is concerned, is finished. It is never to be changed by Him. There is no other way whereby man can procreate, and that must be only within the bond of marriage. Of course, the Apostle Paul later tells us that it is possible to be single and happy. But it is not possible for one man to marry more than one woman or vice versa or to be "married" to one or more of the same sex and fulfill God's purpose of marriage.

155

The Pharisees, in asking the question about divorce, were referring to Deuteronomy and the law instituted by Moses. The Lord in answering them put things in their proper perspective. The law was to regulate man's behavior at that time, and especially the Jewish community in their fallen state. Had man not disobeyed God, perhaps the law would not have been given because it would have been unnecessary. Isn't that the function of the law today? It is necessary to preserve society and to protect one man from the sinful behavior of another. Sin necessitated the law. But from the beginning, the Lord said, it was not so.

It is interesting to note that the word *ap archees,* "from beginning," in Matthew 19:4 does not have the definite article before it. This makes it absolute as referring to the origin of everything. When God created all things, when He made man, He meant one wife for one man in an indissoluble union established by Him. The permission for man to dismiss his wife was not God's original provision for man, but it was God's legislation to police and regulate a situation that was directly a consequence of man's sin and disobedience. God did not make it so from the beginning when He created one woman for one man to spend their lives together.

The Motive of the Pharisees' Questioning Was to Tempt Jesus

Jesus knew that the Pharisees were tempting, or testing, Him. Usually He did not bother with people whose motives were such that instead of a genuine desire to know, they were intent on trapping Him. He only responded positively to the ones acknowledging His divinity. Because, however, the subject was and is so important, He decided to elaborate in spite of the wrong motivation of their questioning. (See the narrative in Mark 10:2.)

Jesus Explains Moses' Law on Dismissing One's Marital Partner

In His answer He referred directly to Moses as the law-giver. Since He was speaking to Jews, He acknowledged Moses as their law-giver in their particular time and for their particular people to accomplish God's second best for them in view of Adam's sin. He said: "What did Moses command *you?*" (Mark

156

10:3). That was a commandment to regulate their particular behavior in the matter. They started to divorce as a consequence of sin, and thus the law was given to regulate and control their sinful lives.

For the Christian, however, it is Christ within who should regulate his life. His purpose is to restore man to freedom of action through an intrinsic conformity to the Lord Jesus. In this life, because of the restrictiveness of the body in which our spirit dwells and the sinfulness of our environment, it is impossible for us to reach His goal for us as it was in the beginning. But in the consummation of the age this full restoration will become a reality.

35

HOW TO TREAT PARENTS
WHEN ONE MARRIES

"For this cause shall a man leave father and mother, and shall cleave to his wife. . . ." Matthew 19:5

The Lord distinctly elucidated what was God's original marriage institution.

He said that man should leave father and mother and should cleave to his own wife (Matt. 19:5; Mark 10:7). It is interesting that in both narratives the Lord says, "For this cause or reason." He stresses that in order that this union in marriage may be accomplished, it is necessary for the man and the woman to leave their parents. The verb used here is *kataleipoo*[1] which, when referring to people, means to leave someone behind when one departs from a place.

The solidarity of marriage depends, our Lord explicitly stated, on the separate habitation of the newlyweds from their parental home. This is another demonstration of Jesus' equal treatment of man and woman. If the newlyweds were to stay with one set of parents, the wife's or the husband's, the others would necessarily be discriminated against. It is therefore better to leave behind both sets of parents. He was indirectly stressing the fact that the child-parent relationship changes when a child marries. But in contrast, the relationship between husband and wife is non-ending, for life.

Matthew Henry says: "A man's children are pieces of himself, but his wife is himself. As the conjugal union is closer than that between parents and children, so it is in a manner equivalent to that between one member and another in the natural body. As this is a reason why husbands should love their wives, so it is a reason why they should not put away their wives; for no man ever yet hated his own flesh, or cut it off, but nourishes and cherishes it, and does all he can to preserve it."

No Reckless Abandonment of Parental Families

This, of course, does not imply reckless abandonment of a child's duties toward his or her parents, but the recognition that when a child marries, his first fidelity is to his or her spouse. The parents should not interfere and the newlyweds should not show undue dependence upon and attachment to the parents. That such leads to divorce is the implication of Christ's teaching. The spouse comes first in all human relationships. The parents and child or children are not one flesh as is the spouse. They are not to have a relationship either in duration or kind as that of one's spouse. Understand this and the chance of a divorce is lessened.

[1]From the intensive *kata* and *leipoo*, "leave behind."

36

MARRIAGE IS MUTAL ATTACHMENT OF HUSBAND AND WIFE

". . . For this cause shall a man leave father and mother, and shall cleave to his wife . . . ." Matthew 19:5

The Lord Jesus in His reply to the questioning Pharisees concerning divorce said further (Matt. 19:5b) that not only should the newlyweds leave their parents and cleave to each other, but also that *"they shall be one flesh."*

It is interesting to note that the Greek verb used in both Matthew 19:5 and Mark 10:7 is the basic verb *kolleetheesetai*, which means "he shall be glued to his wife." In Mark 10:7 it uses the compound verb *proskolleetheesetai (pros,* "unto" and *kolleetheesetai,* "shall be glued"), which means "he shall be glued unto her." This cannot be passive but middle voice. He shall not be glued to his wife by anybody else, but by himself.[1]

Not One-Sided but Mutual Attachment of Husband and Wife

In Matthew 19:5 in the expression, "For this cause shall *a man* . . . cleave to his wife," the word *anthroopos* is used.

One of the reasons, I believe, that the Lord used *anthroopos,* the generic word for "man" which may refer to either man or woman, and not the specific word *aneer* which would refer to the male partner only, is because this gluing process in marriage is not a one-sided action. It is not the duty of the male only to glue himself to his wife, but it is also the duty of the wife, the female, to glue herself to her husband.

Of course, in the process of gluing something, we have a bonding together, a joining of two items into one which cannot be then separated.

To whom will this man be glued? To his own wife. Not two or

161

more wives but only to one and that one must be his very own wife. The expression in Greek is *tee gunaiki autou,* "to the woman, his very own." Not simply to one at a time, but to his very own for a lifetime. That one is expressed by the singular, *gunaiki,* "woman," in the dative.

In this verse the word for husband is *anthroopos,* the generic word for "male man," or simply "man." As far as "husband" is concerned, it could have been rendered with the more specific word for "husband," *andri (aneer* in the nominative). *Anthroopos,* "male man," is used to indicate the pre-marital status. A male should forsake his father and mother and glue himself to his own wife, or to his own woman.

[1]It is to be remembered that the form of the passive and the middle voices are identical and the context decides which they are. The middle voice indicates that the action is self-imposed, while the passive voice indicates that the action is imposed by one other than self.

37

IF IN MARRIAGE THE TWO BODIES DO NOT BECOME ONE FLESH, THEY CAN EASILY BE PUT APART

"Wherefore they are no more twain, But one flesh. . . ."
Matthew 19:6

"And the two shall be into one flesh." Again we must notice the expression *hoi duo,* "the *two,*" one man and one woman, becoming something which they were not before marriage. Such a status in marriage is unique among all relationships and applies only to humans. Although the mating of male and female is also the means of reproduction in the animal world, such a relationship of commitment is not usual among them. Generally speaking, among animals there is no permanent relationship such as among humans.

Two human beings were originally created from one. God first created Adam, a male. He took one of his ribs and created a wife for him (Gen. 2:21-25). She was flesh of his flesh. This ought not be forgotten. If the Lord wanted Adam to have two women to see which one he would like better, He would have taken two ribs and made two women. Or if the Lord wanted Adam to have more wives than one, He would have originally arranged it so.

As Two Emerged From One, Two Become One in Marriage

As two emerged out of one, so in marriage through God's creative power, two human beings, a man and a woman, become "one flesh." The Greek word for "flesh" is *sarx.* It is the only instance that two human individuals are said to become one flesh. A mother gives birth to a child. It is flesh from her flesh and yet the two, mother and child, are not said to be one flesh. One flesh refers to that special relationship spoken of by the Apostle Paul in I Corinthians 7:4: "The wife hath not power of her own body (that is *sooma* which refers to flesh, her physical body), but the husband: and likewise also the husband hath not power of his own body, (again, *sooma)* but the wife." The word translated "power" in Greek is *exousia,* meaning "authority." Here reference is made to that marital, conjugal, physical relationship whereby the wife's body is the husband's and the husband's is the wife's. Therefore when one divorces, he is actually tearing his one flesh into two. That is why divorce is so traumatic and ought not to be taken lightly.

There can be no superiority of the one over the other. There must be no sexual prevalence of the husband over the wife. There must be equality in the two sexes, in the claim of a husband over his wife and vice versa. There is subjection of the wife to the husband but not in the flesh as far as sex is concerned. There is in certain other respects such as the spiritual and emotional relationships of husband and wife, but sexually a wife is to have equal power over her husband as the husband over his wife.

The Fleshly Life

Flesh is synonymous with body. Look for instance at I Corinthians 6:15: "Know ye not that your bodies are the members of Christ? Shall I, then, take the members of Christ, and make them the members of a harlot? God forbid." That word "harlot" in Greek is *pornee,* actually meaning "fornicator," a woman who may be unmarried or married but engages in illicit sex. This harlot refers to absolutely anyone other than a man's own wife and not merely to a professional prostitute.

Paul is speaking to the Christian here and referring particularly to self-imposed discipline inasfar as his body is concerned. Note carefully verse 9 of I Corinthians 6: "Know ye not that the unrighteous shall not inherit the kingdom of God?"

And who are the unrighteous? Those who do not permit God to exercise His right of ownership upon them which is due to the fact that He not only created them, but also in the Lord Jesus Christ redeemed them from the slavery of sin into which they had sold themselves.

And then Paul goes on to say: "Be not deceived: neither fornicators, *(pornoi),* nor idolaters, nor adulterers *(moichoi),* nor effeminate (soft ones or male prostitutes), nor abusers of themselves with mankind (homosexuals—those who being male lie with males or by extension, those who are women lie with women), . . . shall inherit the kingdom of God."[1]

And then Paul goes on in I Corinthians 6:10: "Nor thieves, nor covetous (those who always want more because their fellowmen have more), nor drunkards, nor revilers (those who constantly are ridiculing others), nor extortioners (those who are grasping to get all they can), shall inherit the kingdom of God."

That is the state of the unrighteous whose bodies are not acknowledged as God's rightful possession. But the moment that one believes on the Lord Jesus Christ and appropriates His righteousness and acknowledges God's rightful ownership of him, then his body is not his own; it's God's.

How Should the Christian Live?

See what Paul now says in I Corinthians 6:11: "And such *were* some of you: but ye are washed, but ye are sanctified, but ye are justified in the name of the Lord Jesus, and by the Spirit of our God."

The moment one believes and is born again, life is completely changed; otherwise the profession of faith is but a farce—it means nothing. If one continues in the same sins and habits as before claiming to be saved, he is just deceiving himself. Either a person is saved and sanctified, i.e., living a life owned by God, or he is not. A person cannot claim to live in the straight way (Matt. 7:13 and 14) and live like everybody does who is on the "broad way." A "narrow-gate" profession necessitates a "narrow way" life. Today we have too many so-called Christians having what they self-deceptively think is a good time in the broad way. Christians yield to the dictates of Satan while with their mouths they claim to be God's children. That was the state of the Church in Corinth—it is the state of the church today. We have too much churchianity that lets us live undisturbedly on the level of the world. Divorce is simply the consequence of our way of life. We marry without completely and unreservedly becoming "one flesh" and refuse to live absolutely in a one-spouse relationship, all inclusive as far as our own spouse is concerned and all exclusive, ceasing to look at anybody else lustfully or even thinking of anyone else.

The translation of the following verses of I Corinthians 6 can be misleading. Verse 12 reads in the translation: "All things are lawful unto me, but all things are not expedient." The word "lawful" in Greek is *exestin,* which means "they lie within my power to do," but that does not mean that they lie within God's law as enjoying God's approval. An example of that is the forbidden fruit in the Garden of Eden. It was within man's reach to take and eat, but not within God's approval.

Sinful men, judges, or parliamentarians who make societal laws may make fornication, adultery, drunkenness, homosexuality or even murder anybody's inherent right, but the results are disastrous inasfar as man's temporary earthly and eternal heavenly well-being are concerned. We are sick because we have chosen to live the way we have been living. The only way to be liberated is by turning over our bodies to God in Christ.

[1]The A.V. translation is rather confusing by translating the latter part of verse 9 as "nor effeminate, nor abusers of themselves with mankind." The Greek text has it *malakoi,* (effeminate), "soft ones" or "men prostitutes." The last word is *arsenokoitai* (periphrastically translated as "nor abusers of themselves with mankind," which means homosexuals), or in the singular *arsenokoitees,* those who lie with an *arsen,* "male," presupposing of course he is writing to males and by extension, to females lying with females, i.e., lesbians.

166

38

THE MOSAIC LAW AND THE DISSOLUTION OF MARRIAGE

"They say unto him, why did Moses then command to give a writing of divorcement, and to put her away? He said unto them, Moses because of the hardness of your hearts suffered you to put away your wives: but from the beginning it was not so." Matthew 19:7-8

What did Moses really permit inasfar as the dissolution of the marital relationship was concerned?

The text in Matthew 19:8 says that Moses *permitted* them, or *suffered* them as the King James version has it, to dismiss their wives. But from the beginning it did not take place that way. In their questioning, however, the Pharisees did not use the verb "permitted," but the word "commanded." The Pharisees' question was: "Why did Moses then *command* to give a writing of divorcement, and to put her away?"

Was it really a command? No, said the Lord, it was not a command; Moses gave but mere permission to put away one's wife. The command pertained to the obligation of the dismissing one to give the innocent, dismissed wife a bill of divorcement declaring her innocence in this manner. Even if a person found justification for dismissing his wife, he was not under legal obligation through Moses to put away his wife. He could do so, but he didn't have to.

The whole passage in Deuteronomy 24:1 to 4, which we have already examined, demanded not that a man divorce his wife for certain stated reasons, but that if he decided to divorce her, he ought to at least give her a bill of divorcement. And this was so that she might have the right of remarriage. Otherwise, she could not remarry without giving to her new husband the presumed guilt of adultery falsely assumed from her first husband.

Moses, under God's revelation and even like Christ later on, stands for the defense of the innocent party. The reason for the wife "finding no favor in his eyes, because he hath found some uncleanness in her," was not infidelity on her part. If that were so, the prescribed punishment would have been death by stoning and not granting a bill of divorcement which would enable her to remarry. Moses therefore did not *command* divorce, but provided protection for the wife by stating that if a person unjustifiably wanted to dismiss his wife, he ought to give her a bill of divorcement. Divorce was tolerated, permitted, the Lord said, but not *commanded,* and even that toleration was due to the hardness of their hearts.

Note the Lord's answer in Matthew 19:8: "Moses, because of the hardness of your hearts, permitted you to put away your wives, but from the beginning it was not so."

The Recognition by Christ of the Relationship of the Pharisees of His Day to Moses

What arrests our attention is that the Lord acknowledged the connection existing at that particular time between Moses and the Pharisees: "Moses, because of the hardness of *your hearts. . . .*" But these Pharisees were not alive when Moses instituted this law. How could it then be for the hardness of *their* hearts? The Lord Jesus confirms, as Paul does so eloquently in his epistle to the Romans and elsewhere, the inherited guilt we all bear for the sins of our forefathers. "Wherefore, as by one man sin entered into the world, and death by sin, and so death passed upon all men, for all have sinned . . . Nevertheless, death reigned from Adam to Moses, even over them that had not sinned after the similitude of Adam's transgression . . ." (Rom. 5:12, 14). In other words, our Lord holds these Pharisees responsible for the enactment of the law about divorce just as much as the Jews of Moses' day. You are no different, He implies. If Moses lived today he would have found it necessary to enact the same law.

Mankind Has Always Been Hardhearted

"For the hardness of *your* hearts," the Lord said to these Pharisees, not for the hardness of *their* hearts. In other words, don't blame God for permitting divorce in contradistinction to what He originally meant marriage to be when He created man and woman. *He* did not harden men's hearts; *Mankind* permitted them to become hard through the disobedience of Adam and Eve.

What the Lord actually implies is not merely guilt by association, but actual sin on their part. Jesus condemned them as having a hard heart which was not only the case with their progenitors, but with them, too, in their disobedience to God. Ever since, the consequences of this disobedience, which in the case of marriage is its dismal dissolution or at best, its less than utopian happiness, must be suffered by all humanity.

What Is Hardness of Heart?

This word *skleerokardia,* "hardness of heart," occurs in the two passages on divorce, Matthew 19:8 and Mark 10:5. Also in Mark 16:14 we find this word: "Afterward he appeared unto the eleven as they sat (eating), and upbraided them with their unbelief and *hardness of heart,* because they believed not those who had seen him after he had risen." Hardness of heart in this verse is identified with unbelief. So is divorce. It is the direct consequence of the breaking down of the relationship between man and God.

Since that relationship is restored through Christ, in that new relationship marriage should also be restored to its first state—one man for one woman for life. But, nevertheless, as we shall see, because of the continuance of our existence in a sinful body in a sinful environment, even for the hardness of the believer in Christ, God permits, *not* commands, the dissolution of marriage. As Moses had to regulate the dissolution of marriage in his day to protect the innocent party, so does Christ for His followers. He already made His pronouncement in Matthew 5:27-32 and now confirms in dialogue what He had declared in precept.

The command of Moses as well as of Christ was that once a man chose to dismiss his wife, not under divine obligation but rather in opposition to God's commands, he ought to give her a bill of divorcement. Since she was innocent (for an immoral wife was to be stoned), she ought to be declared so officially so she could remarry if she so chose. Otherwise, the bill of divorcement had no real value for the dismissed wife.

Therefore, the first answer of our Lord to the Pharisees in Matthew 19:8 and Mark 10:5 was that divorce was permitted by Moses because of man's original fall and man's continuing in sin and disobedience.

"Moses, because of the hardness of your hearts, permitted you to put away your wives . . ." (Matt. 19:8).

"For the hardness of your heart he (Moses) wrote you this precept" (Mark 10:5). This precept was what the Pharisees mentioned in verse 4: "And they said, Moses permitted (a man) to write a bill of divorcement, and to put her away."

In the Greek the verb *epetrepsen,* "permitted," refers to two things: writing a bill of divorcement which is the first action; and then secondly follows the dismissing of one's wife. But actually that which is second is the primary thing that is permitted. "Moses permitted to put away one's wife" as per the understanding of Deuteronomy 24:1 to 4. He did not command that one had to put away his spouse. Once, however, this decision was made by the individual to dismiss one's wife, then he was obligated to give her a bill of divorcement. Therefore, when the Lord replied to the Pharisees in Mark 10:5, He did not speak of the *permission* to put away one's wife, but of the *command* to give her a bill of divorcement. "For the hardness of your heart he (Moses) wrote you this precept." Actually the word "precept" is *entoleen* in Greek which means not merely "precept," which would indicate advice, but an actual commandment that had to be obeyed. The commandment the Lord refers to in Mark 10:5 applied to the necessity of giving a bill of divorcement in protection of the innocent, dismissed wife. It could not refer to an obligation to dismiss one's wife.

39

GOD PERMITTED DIVORCE AS PART OF HIS CHASTISEMENT FOR MAN'S SIN

". . . command to give a writing of divorcement . . ."
Matthew 19:7

Actually then, God through Moses permitted divorce but commanded that the man who divorced his wife must give her a bill of divorcement when the cause of divorce was not infidelity on her part which sin would have led to death by stoning (Deut. 22:22).

From the beginning of creation to the fall of man, it was not necessary to do so because there was no divorce since there was no sin. Divorce is the direct result of man's sinfulness, and it is permitted by God as part of His chastisement. It involves the infliction of punishment.

God's Concern for the Innocent Party, Be It Man or Woman

But at the same time, God shows concern for the innocent party who suffers as a result of the specific sin of the guilty party in the marriage relationship. It was this that God through Moses wanted to regulate. The innocent victim of divorce must be protected by being given a bill of divorcement. Therefore, the bill of divorcement is something that the guilty spouse gives to the innocent one releasing her of any further attachment and responsibility toward him.

This would apply to either man or woman for before the Lord there is no difference. This is made absolutely clear in Mark 10:12 where the Lord speaks of a woman dismissing her innocent husband and marrying another. As Paul says in Galatians 3:28: "There is neither male nor

171

female: for ye are all one in Christ Jesus." Not, of course, that there should be no distinction in the sexes, but that in God's sight there is no discrimination in His treatment of a man versus a woman. The only reason why it was usually stated that the man must give his wife divorce papers was because of the low position of women in that particular society. Therefore, the word "man," or the personal pronoun in the masculine, ought to be considered in its generic sense as referring to man or woman.

The Theological Dictionary of the New Testament has a very enlightening paragraph on the subject by A. Oepke:

"The Jews staunchly maintained their singular law of divorce. At bottom, this gave the initiative only to the husband. The distinctive feature was that he could give a bill of divorcement conferring freedom to marry again ... The fact that Salome herself dissolved her marriage according to Greek custom is described as repugnant to Jewish law in Jos. Ant., 15, 259. To be sure, there were times when the Jewish wife could and should ask for divorce, e.g., when her husband forced her into a morally doubtful vow. But this, too, could be made into a strategem by men seeking divorce" (Vol. I, p. 783).
stratagem by men seeking divorce" (Vol. I, p. 783).

40

JESUS' ATTITUDE TOWARD WOMEN

Our Lord did not hesitate to break rigid Jewish custom with matter-of-fact boldness. He did not hesitate to speak with a woman (John 4:27), to teach a woman (Luke 10:39), or to show respect to a woman by calling her the daughter of Abraham (Luke 13:16). He speaks on behalf of women (Mark 12:40) and helps the needy among them more than rabbinic benefactors had ever done (Mark 1:30ff; 5:21-43; 7:24-30; Luke 7:12-17; 8:2; 13:11-17; John 11:1-44). On behalf of a sick woman, He breaks the Sabbath (Luke 13:10ff), and He does not shun contact with unclean women (Mark 1:31; 5:27ff; Luke 7:38ff). Jesus is surrounded by a band of women (Luke 8:2f) who are with Him in His suffering (Mark 15:40f) and glorification (Mark 16:1ff; John 20:1, 11ff). We never hear from the lips of Jesus a derogatory word concerning women as such. This stands in contrast to the characteristic traditional position and estimation of woman in societies such as the Persian, Greek and Jewish in which man gives thanks that he is not an unbeliever or uncivilized, that he is not a woman, and that he is not a slave.

Women in the Early Church

In the early church community as men are called brothers, so women are called sisters (Rom. 16:1; I Cor. 9:5, etc.).

Paul in Galatians 3:28 writes: "There is neither Jew nor Greek, there is neither bond nor free, there is neither male nor female; for ye are all one in Christ Jesus."

Peter in I Peter 3:7 says: "Likewise, ye husbands, dwell with them according to knowledge, giving honor unto the wife, as unto the weaker vessel, and *as being heirs together* of the grace of life, that your prayers be not hindered."

41

DE FACTO SEPARATION—THE BREAKING OF THE ONE-FLESH RELATIONSHIP

"Wherefore they are no more twain, but one flesh. What therefore God hath joined together, let no man put asunder."
Matthew 19:6

The Greek text of I Corinthians 6:12 uses the verb *exestin*, fully discussed in our examination of Matthew 19:3 where it occurs also and should be translated "Is it *permitted* for a man to put away his wife for every reason?" (See Chapters 29 and 37.) And in I Corinthians 6:12 it should not read "All things are *lawful* to me," but "All things are *permitted* to me" in the sense that, as some claim, I have the moral freedom to do whatever I want. I may engage in idolatry, in fornication or adultery, in masturbation, in homosexuality. I may steal, covet, drink, make fun of others, or just take from others whatever I wish. No law, earthly or heavenly, can force me not to engage in any or all of these things. But when Jesus Christ indwells me, I cannot do such things because this would make Him who indwells me a perpetrator of these things, and such are contrary to His character and teaching.

And in I Corinthians 6:13, Paul singles out the body and fornication, writing: "but the body not to fornication." This refers to his determination expressed in verse 12: "but I shall not be brought under the power of any" or better still, "under the authority of any."

Then go to I Corinthians 6:15: "Know ye not that your bodies are the members of Christ? Shall I then take the members of Christ and make them the members of an harlot *(pornees)?* God forbid."

And then in verse 16: "What? Know ye not that he which is joined to an harlot is one body? for two saith he, shall be *one flesh."* And to whom does the verb "saith he" refer? To Jesus Christ. He is telling us that we become "one flesh" with the person with whom we have sexual relations. When we marry, we become "one flesh" with our spouse. Therefore, extra-marital relations are prohibited, for the moment such occur, separation from one's spouse ensues and the adulterer becomes "one flesh" with a harlot. It is not necessary to do this repeatedly to be considered as having become "one flesh" with another woman. Once is enough. That person has become *pornos,* a fornicator, an adulterer. The marriage has de facto been fractured, *choorismos* has already occurred. (See the verb *choorizoo* in chapter 31 as one of the words meaning "divorce.")

God, however, can forgive once there is repentance and forsaking of one's sin. The relationship, however, of the "one flesh" of marriage is broken and the joy God intended for marriage can never be the same. That is stamped upon us as the inherent consequence of voluntary sin in our walk of faith. God can put back together what man breaks asunder, but the repair in the gluing process will always be evident.

42

WHEN IS THE MARRIAGE RELATIONSHIP REALLY BROKEN?

It is interesting to note that the verb *"joined to"* in I Corinthians 6:16 is the same verb as in Matthew 19:5: "For this reason man shall forsake the father and the mother and *shall be glued* to his very own wife." The marriage relationship is broken, not when a judge grants a divorce, but upon the first act of infidelity to one's spouse. That is a basic concept in the teaching of Christ which we must understand. The granting of a bill of divorcement is for the sake of the spouse toward whom one partner has proven unfaithful because he has ceased to be one flesh with his spouse and become one flesh with another person.

Think of the Consequences of Breaking Up What God Joined Together

In I Corinthians 6:12 Paul says, "All things are not expedient," and especially this act of infidelity a man may choose to commit because God has permitted him moral choices. That word "expedient" is *ou sumpherei,* "does not pay" or more literally, "does not pull together." It will separate a man from his wife. It will destroy the marriage and make a liar out of the person after having promised to live with his spouse "till death do us part." Indeed, it doesn't pay. It is a proven fact confirmed by the Word of God.

And this leads us to the examination of Matthew 19:6 which is a conclusion: "Therefore, (or 'wherefore' as the A.V. has it) they are no more two, but one flesh. What, therefore, God hath joined together, let not man put asunder." We hear these words of Christ at every wedding ceremony, but do we really understand their meaning?

It would be more understandable if we stated the proposition thus: "Because the two (in marriage) are no more two, but one flesh; therefore, that which God joined together, let not man separate."

That is God's law for all humans, one man marrying one woman, even as God made Eve out of Adam's rib.

In marriage the two become one flesh. That is a de facto occurrence, irrespective of whether or not these two people have faith in their Creator. He is the Manufacturer, and it is best to follow the Manufacturer's instructions for the smooth operation of the family bond. Otherwise the pre-determined results are misery for oneself and sickness and suffering for all involved. That's just what we have today: herpes, AIDS, syphilis, gonorrhea, torn and broken homes, unhappiness, frustration, neglected and needy children. Why? Because man has disobeyed God's law: one man to one woman equals one flesh with no allowance for extra-marital sexual relations, not even flirting—adultery of the eye or the hand—for this is where sin and temptation enter in.

Divorce Is Not Just a Change of Mind, But a Destruction of God's Creation of One Flesh

When we marry, Christ says, it should not be something entirely of our own doing. I decide, indeed, to be "glued to my own wife" and vice-versa, having forsaken my father and mother. This applies at that moment also to the wife leaving her own parents to attach herself to her own husband. In exercising this choice, God joins the two together. I "cleave" or "glue myself" to my wife, and my wife glues herself to me, her husband. That is our choice.

The two then become "one flesh." What brings about this fusion? God's foreordained law. Marriage involves the fusion of a sexual relationship, but is not only that. It is a spiritual relationship before it consummates into a physical one as Paul explains in Ephesians 5:22-33. If human marriage were only the sexual relationship, then animals would be considered married. It is not the mere joining of two bodies that constitutes marriage, but the fusion of two human personalities, made in God's image, who have a will, the power of choosing right from wrong. It is the spiritual union of two spirits which characterize and differentiate man from the animal creation.

178

Marriage is frequently referred to as a relationship similar to that of Christ and His Church which is a spiritual relationship. But nevertheless, the Lord never allowed divorce for any reason other than fornication. A spiritual disagreement, even as Paul also explains in I Corinthians 7:12-17, does not give a Christian the right to divorce his spouse; but fornication, or the breaking up of the oneness of the flesh, does.

43

IN MARRIAGE THE COUPLE IS ONE FLESH, YET TWO PERSONALITIES

"Wherefore they are no more twain, but one flesh. What therefore God hath joined together, let not man put asunder."
Matthew 19:6

The verb used in Matthew 19:6 referring to God's part in marriage is *sunezeuxen,* from *suzeugnuoo,* "to join together," as putting two oxen under the same yoke. It is derived from the conjunction *sun,* meaning "together," and *zeugnuoo,* "to yoke." A man by his own choice gets attached or glued to his wife and vice versa, and these two become one flesh by virtue of God's decree. But that is symbolic for the joining or fitting together of their bodies into a spiritual and sexual relationship. However, these two continue to remain separate entities whom God brings together under one yoke. Actually the word *zeugos* not only means "yoke" but also "two, a couple," as in Luke 2:24 which refers to a couple or pair of turtledoves or young pigeons for sacrifice. It is God who yokes together a couple, a man and a woman. From this verb *zeugnuoo,* "to yoke," we derive certain very important lessons for marriage:

Marriage is a pulling together of the cart of life no matter how heavy it is. One of the two may become very weak. The strong partner does not break the yoke to pull independently. A spouse must never decide to become free of the other. They must run, walk, work, play, sleep, and do all things together. They are under a common yoke which God puts over them. The verb *sunezeuxen* is in the aorist active which means that once a person decides to attach himself to a spouse of the opposite sex, God places a common yoke over both.

Is It Grounds for Divorce When Sexual Relations Must Cease?

But what about two who have become one flesh and cannot

181

continue to have sexual relations due to physical reasons? Cases have been known when allergies have developed between two spouses because of physical contact. Accidents and illnesses have left many impotent. The couple can no longer complete the marriage copulation. Does one of the two then have the liberty to break the union of marriage? We have no definitive instruction in God's Word. But since marriage is not solely and principally a sexual relationship, although that is basic, it would seem that the choice of separation is a demonstration of cruelty on the part of the separating partner. Marriage is for life till death parts the spouses, not till sickness makes it impossible for them to have sexual relations.

The Yoke Should Be Equal

It is never the Lord's will, though, to put a yoke on two who do not want to pull the same direction and exercise patience and understanding with each other. So many times I have seen in the fields of Palestine a donkey and an ox yoked together ploughing a field. They are unequal in their pull. But I have never seen two so yoked that they pull in opposite directions. Be careful not to attach yourself to someone who determinedly wants to pull in the opposite direction from you. There has to be submission to God by both husband and wife for God to yoke them together to move toward one direction and accomplish one unified purpose in their lives. Otherwise, life will be a constant, wearying struggle. You may make the attachment, but unless you are yoked together with that person in a spiritual bond, that attachment will not be able to accomplish that which marriage was meant to accomplish from the beginning.

Is Marriage Consummated in the Sexual Union?

Is marriage consummated if one of the two spouses refuses to become one flesh with his or her spouse? We have no definitive instruction on this matter, therefore we can only arrive at consequential conclusions. Two people whose marriage has not been consummated in their becoming "one flesh," among other realizations of marriage, are still two separate human beings. It is not necessary to separate two who have never actually become one flesh.

182

44

DOES ANYONE HAVE THE RIGHT TO "PUT ASUNDER"?

". . . let not man put asunder. They say unto him why did Moses then command to give a writing of divorcement, and to put her away?" Matthew 19:6, 7

What does the expression "let not man put asunder" mean? The Greek word is *choorizetoo (choorizoo),* "to set apart," from *chooros,* "space"; therefore, meaning to put in two different places or spaces.[1]

It means no man, no matter who he is, has the right to separate two people of the opposite sex who have become attached to each other and whom God has yoked together. He can do so, but if he does, he goes contrary to what God has done. Man can oppose God's work in spite of the fact that he has no right to do so, but it does not mean that he necessarily succeeds. Man can undo what God has done in a specific marriage, but man, no matter how hard he tries, cannot undo the divine institution of marriage. Man may succeed in going against a divinely instituted law, but he cannot escape suffering the consequences of his choice. Man can attempt to oppose God's physical law of gravity, but if he should throw himself from the top of a building, he will not go up; he will fall and possibly kill himself. Thus anyone attempting to separate himself from his spouse will suffer the consequences of that separation in his own life, and his partner and others, such as the children, will suffer. Thus "any man" who may attempt to separate the yoke of marriage may be a person directly involved, or any other person, such as an interfering relative or a person trying to lure one of the marriage partners. God's commandment is not to separate a married couple.

Any man can disobey any of God's laws and commandments, but no man can cancel out any of these laws or commandments as to their dependability and veracity. The choice is man's, but

183

the consequences of that choice are set not by man, but by God who made the laws. God's laws can be broken, but they cannot be cancelled.

The verb *choorizoo* is one of the words used consistently in the New Testament to indicate the dissolution of the marriage bond instituted by God. We find the same verb in Mark 10:9. It is also used in I Corinthians 7:10, 11 and 15: "And unto the married I command, yet not I, but the Lord, Let not the wife depart (*mee chooristheenai*—an indirect imperative here also) from her husband; But and if she depart (*chooristhee),* let her remain unmarried, or be reconciled to her husband; and let not the husband put away[2] his wife . . . But if the unbelieving depart, let him depart."[3]

The Pharisees answered, "Why did Moses then command to give a writing of divorcement, and to put her away?" What Jesus had stated was God's original purpose and achievement. He made two out of one when he made a woman out of man's rib, and in marriage He makes one flesh out of the two again, and He meant that union to be indissoluble. But man, in spite of God's prohibition and due to the hardness of his heart, did break God's law. But marriage is and should remain what God made it to be even as it is our duty to keep His other laws and institutions in spite of the fact that they are being broken all the time by rebellious mankind. Those who keep God's laws derive the promised benefit. Those who break them similarly reap the promised results. Both the benefits and injuries are inescapable. Man must lie in the very bed of his own making.

But what happens when man breaks the law of matrimony? The law was instituted so that evil may not get out of hand. God had to prescribe punishments for those who break His laws other than the intrinsic punishment self-evident in every disobedience of God's law. Just think for a moment of what a law is. A law defines what is evil and who are the evil-doers. It also specifies what the punishment for certain evils should be. The punishment should be commensurate to the crime, tooth for a tooth and eye for an eye. The law does not prescribe the death penalty for somebody who defrauds another of a few dollars, but only for one who takes another man's life. As Paul so aptly says in Romans 5:13: "For until the law sin was in the world; but sin is not imputed when there is no law." The law was instituted for the proper identification of sin and the proper imposition of the relative punishment in the case of its disobedience.

God Never Approved Divorce but Commanded the Consideration of the Victim or Victims of Divorce

These Pharisees referred to Moses as the transmitter of God's law in Deuteronomy 24 concerning man setting asunder those whom God had yoked together. But this law *did not* constitute an approval by God of divorce in any shape or form. It was the setting forth of a regulation of a circumstance which God neither desires nor approves—the separation *(choorismos)* of a married couple. God emphatically stated in Malachi 2:16 that He hates divorce. God hates anything that separates man from Himself and man from his fellow humans. The devil in Greek is called *diabolos,* from the verb *diaballoo* made up of the preposition *dia,* "through," implying separation, and *balloo,* "to throw." The devil is one who specializes in separating man from God, husband from his wife, nation from nation, man from his fellowman. Separation is Satan's goal but God's is union, bringing man back to Himself through Jesus Christ and man to man. You can believe the devil that separating yourself from God's commands will be "good," but is it? Man's breaking the bond of marriage when it was God's union in the first place can never bring real benefit. It is of the devil.

God never changed His mind as to His first desire for the accomplishment of the institution of marriage. Moses never contradicted God whose messenger he was. But God, through Moses, instituted the regulation governing the portion of divorce. The spouse who decides to divorce his partner is given permission to do it, but God does not necessarily approve man's choice as a free agent. But once he has made that choice, God then states the punishment that awaits the guilty transgressor of His inherent law of marriage and what protection must be granted to the innocent spouse dismissed for no adequate reason.

"Why did Moses then command to give a writing of divorcement, and to put her away?" This was quoted by the Pharisees in such a way as to set Moses in contradiction to God and Christ. Moses never said anything of the kind. Rather, we find the following three regulations governing divorce in Deuteronomy 24:1-2:

185

1. When a man decides to dismiss his wife for whatever he prefers to call "finding an uncleanness in her," he is to give her a bill of divorcement. He is to make the divorce legal so that the woman may have the right of remarriage if she so chooses. The granting of a divorce in no way affects God's attitude toward this sin, but it does affect the attitude of society toward those who are involved in a marriage contract.

2. The husband could not divorce his wife and still keep her in his house.

3. "When she is departed out of his house, she may go and be another man's wife."

This clearly was not permission by God or Moses for one to divorce his wife. But it was a law protecting the innocent wife, unjustly and unjustifiably dismissed, necessitating the issuance of a divorce certificate enabling her to remarry.

Is this man who unjustly dismisses his wife going to be punished? We believe that he cannot escape God's immediate condemnation and the ultimate punishment prescribed for all his evil perpetrated on earth.

II Corinthians 5:10 unquestionably gives us the answer although not specifically designating the extent of the punishment. "For we must *all* appear before the judgment seat of Christ." This includes those who divorced their spouses for any reason other than the one acceptable to Jesus Christ as valid. "That everyone may receive the things done in his body, according to that he hath done, *whether it be good or bad.*" And what sin is greater than fornication as far as the sins "done in the body?" The reason why the Lord has not specified the punishment may be due to the fact that the sin results in such varying degrees of consequences hurting so deeply other people such as the children or parents in addition to the spouse divorced.

So in Christ's answer to the Pharisees there is no acceptance of the inferred accusation that Moses approved divorce on behalf of God. Moses commanded the giving of "a book of divorcement,"[4] a document permitting one to stand away from someone with whom he had made a covenant to stay.

God through Moses did not order the dismissing of one's wife but rather required the granting of a certificate of divorce by the one who dismissed his wife. The divorce is contrary to God's will, but the provision of the bill of divorcement by the one who has decided to send away his wife is a requirement of God. There is a tremendous difference between this and God commanding divorce. He commands what man must do to mitigate somewhat the evil perpetrated upon his wife.

[1]The imperative is in the third person singular which makes it an indirect imperative.

[2]Another verb is used also in the indirect imperative, *mee aphienai*, from *aphieemi*, "to send away from oneself."

[3]*Choorizetai, choorizesthoo*—again in the indirect imperative indicating that he can do so although it is not required. (See Chapter 31 for the three Greek words used for "divorce" in the New Testament. Also see related discussions elsewhere in this book and the one on I Corinthians 7.)

[4]*Biblion*, meaning "little book or writing," and *apostasion* from *apo*, "from," and *stasion* from the verb *histeemi*, "stand." This word *apostasion* occurs only in Matt. 5:31 and 19:7 and Mark 10:4, all three instances referring to separation from one's spouse.

45

DISTINCTION BETWEEN DISMISSING ONE'S SPOUSE AND THE GRANTING OF A CERTIFICATE OF DIVORCE

The verb used in Matthew 19:7 in the phrase "to give a writing of divorcement and *to put her away"* is *apolusai (apoluoo),* "to set loose from oneself." The phrase, "to put her away," does not refer then to the certificate that a man grants his wife, but rather to setting her free or loosing her from her bond to him. She is only loosed with innocence if the bill of divorcement is granted her. Otherwise whatever she decides to do, stay single or remarry, she will be considered as unchaste, an adulteress.

And what was Jesus' answer to the question of these Pharisees? "He saith unto them, Moses because of the hardness of your hearts, suffered you to put away your wives, but from the beginning it was not so."

Christ Clears Moses of Any Contradiction With Himself

The Lord Jesus first clears Moses of any contradiction in his law against God's intent in relation to divorce.

Moses did not *order* anyone to dismiss his wife. The verb which the Pharisees used in their question in verse 7 was *"eneteilato" (entellomai),* "did command." But Jesus answered by saying that Moses did not *command,* but he *permitted, epetrepsen (epitrepoo).* There is a tremendous difference between what God through Moses commanded and what He permitted. What He commands we are morally obligated to do. But His permission may be due to a situation created by us or because of original sin in the process of time. God does not order an accident, but He may permit something in the here and now to accomplish something greater in the context of eternity and infinity. When He allows us to do something, it is because He

189

will not abrogate our right of choice since we are made in His image. God is responsible for what He directs, but for the results of our own free choice, He is not responsible. Once man has chosen to do that which may be permissible but not directed, God allows the predetermined consequence of his choice. And in the case of divorce, God determines what happens to both the guilty and the innocent party involved. Moses, Jesus said, *permitted* you at a certain instant in time to dismiss your wives. The verb *epetrepsen* is in the aorist tense which means He did it at a specific time, and that time, of course, was consequent to man's sin.

First One Separates Himself and Then Puts Away His Wife

Interestingly enough, in Matthew 19:7 the Lord does not use the verb *choorizoo* used in verse 6 in the expression "let no man put asunder," but the verb *apoluoo,* "to set loose or apart," and this word represents the second step in the process of divorce. The verb *choorizo* is "to separate," or establish that first cleavage or estrangement between husband and wife. Once this has occurred and the two bodies have ceased to be one, then the estranged spouse is dismissed. This latter part in the process is what God permitted through Moses. If *you,* Christ says, have separated *(choorizoo)* yourself from your spouse, that's your decision in the divorce for which you must bear responsibility, but give her the proper divorce papers to enable her to remarry and not be considered an adulteress. If this is not done, then the sin is compounded against her by causing her to be considered by society as an adulteress. Therefore, the word *apoluoo* which is used in this verse indicates God's permission to grant divorce papers to protect the wife's right to dignity and the privilege of remarriage.

46

WHY "FROM THE BEGINNING" GOD DID NOT PERMIT THE DISMISSAL OF ONE'S SPOUSE

". . . that he which made them at the beginning made them male and female." Matthew 19:4
". . . from the beginning it was not so." Matthew 19:8

In Matthew 19:4 the Lord Jesus said, *"from the beginning* God made that which he made, male and female."* He made one for one to stay together for life. It was never His plan for them to be separated, to be broken up, but nevertheless, they did separate. So in verse 8 He adds again, *"from the beginning* it was not thus."* From the beginning it was not necessary for God to order the giving of a writing of divorcement and the setting free of a wife who was innocent so she could remarry and adultery not be committed against her. The Lord did not have to institute "setting loose" procedures for the innocent spouse until man sinned in separating himself from his wife. A law and a judge were not needed against a particular sin until the sin was perpetrated, and then the result of that sin had to be regulated.

God Had to Counter Man's Sin Head On

What caused the establishment by Moses of the divorce law, actually of letting the innocent wife loose? "The hardness of your hearts" caused it all, said the Lord Jesus. The expression in Greek, *pros teen skleerokardian humoon*, "toward the hard-heartedness of yours" is the literal translation of Matthew 19:8.

The use of the preposition *pros*, "toward," is interesting since it is used instead of the more common preposition *dia* which could be more naturally used in such an instance indicating cause with the accusative *skleerokardian*. The preposition *pros* is more direct indicating that God had to

191

encounter man "head on" to meet the hardness of his heart. The word *skleerokardia,* from *skleeros* meaning "hard" and *kardia* meaning "heart," occurs only in the two contexts of divorce here and in Mark 10:5, plus one other reference in Mark 16:14 when the Lord referred to the hardness of the disciples' hearts. The disciples did not believe the report of those who had seen Jesus risen from the dead, and He chided them for their hard-heartedness because they failed to believe in the available evidence. The disciples, in exercising unbelief, hardened their hearts. So man hardened his heart toward God who originally told him to obey His word stating that He had created one woman for one man and in that lay man's basic conjugal happiness. The resultant circumstances are not what God commanded, but only what he permitted so that an unpleasant, unhappy situation created by man's sin might be properly handled.

God did not harden man's heart. Man did it himself through his decision to believe in his own plan that he could be happier in dismissing his wife in order to marry another. The law of divorce was for the purpose of handling the result of man's sinful choice to separate himself from his original wife.

When a Spouse Is Permitted to Put Away His or Her Partner

The Lord added His own clarification as to the only circumstance that would permit someone to actually dismiss his or her spouse. He said in verse 9: "And I say unto you, Whosoever shall put away his wife, except it be for fornication, and shall marry another, committeth adultery: and whoso marrieth her which is put away doth commit adultery."

DIFFERENCES BETWEEN MATTHEW 19:9 AND MATTHEW 5:32

"But I say unto you, That whosoever shall put away his wife, saving for the cause of fornication, causeth her to commit adultery: and whosoever shall marry her that is divorced committeth adultery." Matthew 5:32

"And I say unto you, Whosoever shall put away his wife, except it be for fornication, and shall marry another, committeth adultery: and whoso marrieth her which is put away doth commit adultery." Matthew 19:9

There are some differences between this last saying of Jesus and that in Matthew 5:32 although in its essence it is the same with Matthew 19:9 although a little more comprehensive.

Let us first examine the differences:

In Matthew 5:32, our Lord begins with the personal pronoun *egoo*, "I," in addition to the suffix "*oo*" indicating "I" in *legoo*. In Matthew 19:9 the emphatic "I", *egoo,* is missing.

In Matthew 5:32 (UBS text), the word *pas,* translated "whosoever" is used. It actually refers to anyone, no matter who it may be. It allows no exception. It is a rule applying to everybody and anybody.

In Matthew 19:9, the relative pronoun *hos* is used, as also in the Textus Receptus text in Matthew 5:32, meaning "he who" or "whosoever" referring exegetically back to the person under discussion in Matthew 19:3: "Is it lawful or permissible for a man to put away his wife for every cause?" Verse 9 is an answer to that interrogation of Jesus by the Pharisees. Christ's answer is an emphatic "No, it is not lawful or permissible for a man to put away his wife for every cause." There is only one cause for which such an action is permissible, and that is the sexual infidelity of the wife or the husband.

In Matthew 5:32 (UBS text), the present participle of the verb *apoluoo, ho apoluoon,* is used whereas in Matthew 19:9

193

the suppositional preposition *an*, "if," is used followed by the subjunctive of the same verb *apoluo, an apolusee,* "if he shall dismiss." "But I say to you that if anyone dismisses his wife, but for fornication, and he marries another, he commits adultery." Essentially the participle *apoluoon* of Matthew 5:32 has also the meaning of hypothetical action as the Textus Receptus clearly has it through the use of the *an*, "if," with the subjunctive *apolusee.* It is not something that God desires or commands. He simply sets the consequence of such hypothetical action by man.

In Matthew 5:32, the exception clause is introduced with the word *parektos,* an adverb derived from *para,* "at," and *ektos,* "without." The meaning of *parektos* is exactly "except." This adverb is used only here and in Acts 26:29 translated "except" and II Corinthians 11:28 translated "without." After the adverb *parektos,* there is the noun *logou* here meaning "reason" or "on account of" as in Romans 14:12; Hebrews 13:17; I Peter 4:5. The clause, therefore, reads "except on account of fornication." In Matthew 19:9, the expression is *ei mee epi porneia,*[1] "if not for fornication." Both expressions refer to the exception of fornication.

The great difference between Matthew 5:32 and 19:9 is that the latter adds the phrase "and marry another." Matthew 19:9 confirms that the very reason for granting a divorce to the innocent party is that she or he may have the opportunity of remarriage without the stigma of her being considered as an adulteress. She is considered that anyway when her husband dismisses her and does not give her a divorce certificate, but doubly so when she remarries, although she has the right to if she so chooses. The granting of a bill of divorcement was not for the purpose of liberating the guilty party, but the innocent one.

Matthew 5:32 finds Christ declaring that the one dismissing his wife for any reason other than unfaithfulness—fornication— causes her to be considered as an adulteress. This does not refer to what his wife may have done before she was married, but to what she does after her marriage. The verb *apolusee* is in the aorist tense which indicates punctiliar action in the future. This involved a definite action this husband was going to take at a definite time in the future. This action was to be based not in the review of his wife's history, but in the examination of her behavior after she was married to him. If he dismisses her in the future for any reason other than her own infidelity to him, personally he commits adultery against her, or causes her to be considered as an adulteress if he does not give her a bill of divorcement. That's as far as Matthew 5:32 goes.

But Matthew 19:9 declares Christ as saying something more. He adds the element of remarriage on the part of the licentious husband who dismisses his wife. He says, "Whosoever shall put away his wife, except for fornication, *and shall marry another,* committeth adultery." (On this particular difference in Matthew 19:9, see chapter 48.) What happens to the innocent party against whom the adulterous husband has committed adultery by lusting after another woman? Is she left without any redress? Who would know why she has been dismissed by her husband? The bill of divorcement according to Deuteronomy 24:1, 2 was for the purpose of enabling her to remarry: ". . . then let him write her a bill of divorcement, and give it in her hand, and send her out of his house. And when she is departed out of his house, *she may go and be another man's wife."*

[1]TR; and *mee epi porneia* in the UBS text omitting the *ei,* "if," of the TR.

195

48

BEING HUMANE IN THE PURSUIT OF A MARRIAGE DISSOLUTION

In Matthew 5:31 Jesus said, "It hath been said, Whosoever shall put away his wife, let him give her a writing of divorcement." The Pharisees did not care for what reason they dismissed their wives, as long as they could give them a bill of divorcement which would enable their former wives to remarry. But in reality, the Deuteronomy 24:1 and 2 passage demanded a bill of divorcement be given only if a mate was dismissed for a reason other than unfaithfulness in marriage.

In other words, since a divorce document was to be granted to an innocent wife, the Pharisees abused the command by considering it an easy way to get rid of an undesired wife. They would have gotten rid of her anyway, but they justified their action by misquoting Scripture. They thought the choice was theirs to give or not to give the bill of divorcement.

That's not the way it is, Jesus said. "But I say unto you that he who, no matter who it is, dismisses his wife except on account of fornication, causes adultery against her." And if that is so, he ought to clear her name by giving her a bill of divorcement. It is to such an innocent wife that a bill of divorcement belongs and not to anyone else. If she has been unfaithful, it is not necessary to give her a divorce.

Marrying an Unjustifiably Dismissed Woman Who Has Not Been Given a Bill of Divorcement (Matt. 5:32b and 19:9b)

When an unfaithful marital partner dismissed a faithful spouse, Christ taught that the utmost consideration be exercised toward the innocent spouse. In Biblical times, dismissing an innocent spouse without granting a bill of divorcement was like declaring the innocent one guilty. In other words, the innocent

197

wife was caused to suffer adultery against her.

In Matthew 19:9b, however, Christ adds another clause: "But I say unto you that whosoever dismisses his wife except for fornication (i.e. her infidelity) *and marries another* he commits adultery." The new element inserted in this verse which is not found in Matthew 5:32 is the phrase "and marries another." It is as if our Lord reveals the reason why such a person dismissed his innocent wife in the first place. Such a cause for dismissing his wife is implicit in the description of the lustful man who looks upon a woman and caresses her found immediately prior to the divorce verses of Matthew 5:31 and 32, i.e. Matthew 5:27 to 30. Here in Matthew 19:9, however, the Lord explicitly says, "He who dismisses his wife except for fornication *and marries another* commits adultery."

There is a further difference in the two verses. In Matthew 5:32a the Lord says, "He causes adultery against her." But in Matthew 19:9, simply the verb *moichatai* is used which refers to committing adultery against himself. The verb *moichatai* is in the passive form as in Matthew 5:32, but in Matthew 5:32 it specifically singles out who is affected by the man's actions— *poiei auteen moichasthai* (infinitive passive). It's against the innocent wife who, unbeknown to her and without personal participation, is considered as a *moichalees,* "an adulterer," unless a bill of divorcement is given to her to clear her of guilt and to enable her to remarry without the stigma of adultery. But in Matthew 19:9, the verb *moichatai,* "commits adultery," stands alone.[1] The action of adultery is committed by the man and returns to himself. Therefore the Lord says in Matthew 19:9: "Whosoever dismisses his wife except for fornication and marries another, becomes (or makes himself) adulterous." He is responsible for his own action.

A Guilty Husband Marrying Any Other Woman Commits Adultery

The word for "another" in the Greek text of "and shall marry another" is *alleen,* which means another woman of the same kind. She is not *hetera* which is another word in Greek meaning "another of a different kind." No matter what qualities another woman has that differ from that of a man's wife, they do not give him the right to discard her for one with different qualities, be it physical attraction or whatever.

This word *alleen* cannot refer to a divorced woman. It refers to just another woman who, if he were not married, would be perfectly legitimate for him to marry. If she were otherwise, she would have been referred to as *apolelumeneen,* "a dismissed woman" as in the immediate following clause which says, "and whoso marrieth her which is put away." Thus one becomes an adulterer not merely by marrying a dismissed woman but by marrying another woman, any woman, arithmetically another, other than his wife.

Marrying a Dismissed Woman

Now what does the clause following immediately in Matthew 19:9b mean? "And he who marries her which is put away doth commit adultery."[2] The participial noun refers to any unjustly divorced woman. The definite article *ho* refers to the man, any man, who marries an innocent divorcee.

Now, who is this dismissed woman? Is she any dismissed woman? It cannot be. It must be an innocent, dismissed woman. If she were not such, she would have been a licentious, unfaithful woman who would have been under the condemnation of stoning to death.

"Who so marries," in Greek is *ho gameesas.*[3] The literal translation is "who when he married" or "having married at a particular time in the past."

The second verb "commits adultery" *moichatai,*[4] is in exactly the same form as in the previous clause occurring for the second time in Matthew 19:9. He who marries a woman who has been dismissed by her husband for reason other than fornication, "doth commit adultery" says the Authorized Version. Now how can a man who marries a woman who has been unjustly released by her licentious husband commit adultery? As we explained in the study of Matthew 5:32b, the verb *moichatai* is passive with middle voice meaning. This man by marrying such an innocent dismissed wife brings upon himself the stigma of adultery since his wife has been carrying this public charge from the moment her first husband dismissed her. And she will carry this stigma of adultery for life as indicated by the present indicative *moichatai* showing continuity. The man who chooses to marry an unjustly dismissed wife who has not been granted a bill of divorcement by her former husband assumes the stigma of adultery although unwarranted. That is what the sin of the first truly adulterous husband has caused. This can be called vicarious adultery. It is a stigma caused by another.

The second clause of Matthew 19:9 "and whoso marrieth her which is put away doth commit adultery," meaning that he who marries a dismissed woman suffers vicarious adultery, is not found in the UBS text. It is, however, in the Textus Receptus which we accept as valid since Matthew 5:32b, which says the same thing, is in all the texts.

[1]Third person singular of *moihaomai*. In other words it has middle meaning since in form the middle voice is the same as the passive voice.

[2]In the Greek text, this clause is almost the same as in Matthew 5:32b. In Matthew 5:32b, it says: "And whosoever ('he who'— *hos*) if *(ean)* dismissed one *(apolelumeneen)* he shall marry *(gameesee)* commits adultery against himself, *(moichatai)*."

In Matthew 19:9b, the relative pronoun *hos*, "whosoever" or "he who," is missing. It has instead the definite article *ho*, "the," which refers to the participial noun *gameesas*, "he who did marry" at a particular, definite time in the past (aorist). This is followed by the participial noun *apolelumeneen*, "a dismissed woman" (feminine perfect passive participle of *apoluoo*). There is no definite article in the accusative *teen* before the participle which would identify this dismissed woman as the very one the licentious man dismissed.

[3]First aorist active masculine singular participle of *gameoo*, "to marry" with the definite article *ho*, "the."

[4]The present indicative of the passive *moichaomai*.

49

WAS AN UNFAITHFUL SPOUSE ENTITLED TO A BILL OF DIVORCEMENT?

The bill of divorcement was not to be given to a woman or a man who was unfaithful.

In Deuteronomy 22:13-19, we are told of the following case: If a maid marries a man and is then accused of having not been a virgin, the father of the maid is to prove that she was. The man is to be fined "because he hath brought up an evil name upon a virgin of Israel: and she shall be his wife; he may not put her away all his days" (Deut. 22:19). But if the accusation be true then "the men of her city shall stone her with the stones that she die" (Deut. 22:21).

If the damsel was found not to have been a virgin when she was married, nowhere do we find that she was to be given a divorce. She was to be stoned to death (Deut. 22:21). If she were to be proven a virgin, then the punishment was prescribed against her husband and he was obliged also to keep her as his wife (Deut. 22:19). How then could some interpreters, by any stretch of the imagination, make the expression "except for fornication" to mean the possibility that the girl was not a virgin is a mystery to us. It is rather an attempt to fit Scripture into our preconceived ideas which is a very dangerous philosophy of Bible interpretation.

That God always meant the protection of the innocent party is manifest from the reading of Deuteronomy 22:22-30:

"If a man be found lying with a woman married to a husband, then they shall both of them die, both the man that lay with the woman, and the woman: so shalt thou put away evil from Israel.

"If a damsel that is a virgin be betrothed unto a husband, and a man find her in the city, and lie with her; then ye shall bring them both out unto the city, and ye shall stone them with stones that they die; the damsel, because she cried not, being in the city;

and the man, because he hath humbled his neighbor's wife: so thou shalt put away evil from among you.

"But if a man find a betrothed damsel in the field, and the man force her, and lie with her: then *the man only that lay with her shall die: but unto the damsel thou shalt do nothing; there is in the damsel no sin worthy of death:* for as when a man riseth against his neighbor, and slayeth him, even so is this matter: for he found her in the field, and the bethrothed damsel cried, and there was none to save her.

"If a man find a damsel that is a virgin, which is not betrothed, and lay hold on her, and lie with her, and they be found; then the man that lay with her shall give unto the damsel's father fifty shekels of silver, and she shall be his wife; because he hath humbled her, *he may not put her away all her days.*

"A man shall not take his father's wife, nor discover his father's skirt."

In Deuteronomy 24:1 and 2, since God decrees a bill of divorcement to be given to a dismissed wife "because he hath found some uncleanness in her" and not death to be imposed upon her, it must be concluded that such "uncleanness" found in her must be a reason far less serious than fornication fabricated by the husband as an excuse for dismissing his wife. If this were fornication, according to the law she should have been put to death and not be given a bill of divorcement for the express purpose of clearing her of guilt so she could remarry.

The Case of Joseph and Mary

Do we have any indication, however, as to what the actual practice was if a woman was dismissed having been proven unfaithful?

In the case of Joseph, he, being a just man, felt he could have put away Mary had he not found that her child was of the Holy Spirit. And he was not obligated to give her a bill of divorcement in that case for just dismissing her "would make her a public example." Not wanting to do that, he was going to put her away privily—i.e., not making her case public. No mention is made of providing a bill of divorcement had she been guilty of infidelity, for this was reserved only for cases when the spouse was innocent and was not dismissed for such a reason.

The private dismissal referred to by Joseph was a way

devised to save a guilty person from public embarrassment or perhaps even stoning. But nowhere do we read that the bill of divorcement was to be given to a guilty spouse.

Of course, it is to be remembered that at the time of Joseph and Mary, a betrothal or engagement constituted a ceremony binding one to the other, not as far as immediate conjugal union was concerned, but as far as one remaining purely and exclusively for the other. Unfaithfulness in engagement was therefore equivalent to unfaithfulness in actual marriage (see Genesis 24:53-67).

It seems that the law of putting to death the unfaithful spouse was not strictly adhered to. Since Joseph intended to put away Mary secretly had he found her truly unfaithful, it seems that this was one way of dealing with such persons without giving such a one a bill of divorcement. No concern for the remarriage of such a guilty person was to be demonstrated. The divorce bill was not meant to ever become the substitute of putting the guilty party to death by stoning.

The Woman Caught in Adultery Who Was Brought to Jesus

The fact that even at the time of Jesus' ministry a woman allegedly caught in the act of adultery was brought to Him by the Pharisees, claiming that in the law Moses had commanded that such should be stoned, is evidence that the practice of stoning a sexual transgressor may still have been in effect (John 8:3-11). The command by Jesus to cease sinning was proof that she was indeed a sinner. But also the "sin no more" injunction of Jesus brought restoration to her inasfar as Jesus was concerned, and consequently before her accusers and society in general. Again we have the law of forgiveness established whenever there is cessation from one's sins. He or she is no more condemned by Jesus.

Today, however, a divorce is obtainable for reasons other than infidelity. Having a divorce document is not automatic scriptural authority to remarry. In the context of the Holy Scriptures, one only can remarry if he or she is the innocent party having been dismissed by the guilty spouse or if the innocent partner separated because of the unfaithfulness of the spouse.

50

SHOULD A FAITHFUL PARTNER SUBMIT TO AN UNFAITHFUL SPOUSE?

What should a faithful husband or wife living with an immoral spouse do? Just stop having marital relationships because otherwise he makes his or her body one with a harlot or fornicator? The Apostle Paul's rules must then come into consideration. Here is what he says in I Corinthians 6:15: "Know ye not that your bodies are the members of Christ? Shall I then take the members of Christ, and make them the members of an harlot? God forbid." This word "harlot" must not be taken to refer merely to a professional prostitute. The Greek word is *pornee,* meaning "one committing fornication."

But how is this attitude affected by what Paul says in I Corinthians 7:4 to 6? "The wife hath not power of her own body, but the husband: and likewise also the husband hath not power of his own body, but the wife. Defraud ye not (do not deprive) one the other, except it be with consent for a time, that ye may give yourselves to fasting and prayer; and come together again, that Satan tempt you not for your incontinency." This clearly relates to two believers. But it is possible for one believer to sin sexually. What then is the faithful partner to do?

A Private Decision of a Spouse Living With a Sexually Unfaithful Partner

In verse 6 Paul adds something of utmost significance. He says: "But I speak this by permission, and not of commandment."

In other words, Paul admits that there are things in the Christian life that must be left to the individual Christian conscience to decide. Christ left no definitive commandments to regulate certain detailed aspects of our lives. And where Christ was silent, Paul could not give definitive answers but only

205

guidelines which would help the individual Christian decide. Would to God that more of us would imitate Paul in this attitude and allow our fellow Christians to decide some things for themselves.

It seems that the determination of the attitude of an innocent marriage partner toward a licentious spouse is one of those matters for individual decision.

Should an innocent wife continue to live with her husband whom she knows is having extra-marital relations? Should she submit herself to him knowing that she is submitting her body, which is a member of Christ, and making it a member of her adulterous husband (I Cor. 6:15)? Should she deprive her husband of his marital privilege, and vice versa, a husband his unfaithful wife?

The Apostle Paul and I Corinthians 7

Paul's comment in I Corinthians 7:5 and 6, referring to mutual abstention from marital relations presupposes the purpose of a mutual desire on the part of both husband and wife to engage in prayer and fasting. This in turn presupposes that both the husband and wife live a holy life and are walking with the Lord. Therefore, if one spouse has given himself or herself to fornication, this principle of abstention from one another by mutual agreement obviously does not apply.

According to Scripture, the choices that a faithful spouse has in facing life with a sexually unfaithful partner are the following two:

1. A faithful partner has the right, if he or she wishes to exercise it, to dissolve the marriage. This is clearly taught by the Lord Jesus in Matthew 5:32 and 19:9.

2. The innocent spouse may choose to continue to live with the unfaithful partner, but in this case gives himself or herself to forced adultery. The innocent spouse in this instance, out of love for her husband and following the Lord's example, makes herself redemptively sinful even until death. Jesus became sin for us and died to redeem us, although He had no sin. So a faithful partner may decide to follow after Christ.

In this relationship of one spouse being *pistos,* "faithful," and another *apistos,* "unfaithful," the terms refer to being a believer and an unbeliever. We examine this in a separate volume of a full exegetical exposition of I Corinthians 7.

An unbeliever may be either sexually faithful or unfaithful to his spouse. And on the other hand, one who professes faith in Jesus Christ may be faithful or unfaithful to his or her spouse. This is handled by Paul in I Corinthians 7:12 to 15 fully covered in our volume entitled *May I Divorce and Remarry?* on I Corinthians 7.

Our discussion here pertains to the attitude of a morally faithful spouse toward a morally unfaithful partner inasfar as marital sexual relations are concerned.

The Choice Is Between Two Evil Situations

If the faithful partner gives herself or himself knowingly to an unfaithful partner then as a member of Christ's body, he or she also becomes a member of a harlot (I Cor. 6:15). Is refusal to the licentious spouse therefore permissible?

If there is refusal if such a conjugal relationship is still desired by the licentious partner, it may precipitate a divorce. That is a possible consequence of such an attitude that the faithful partner must face versus other evils which may arise such as:

1. The scandal in the community in which the couple lives. A Christian sometimes may decide to suffer privately to save one's public testimony as long as that public testimony is not compromised.

2. If they have children, what is going to happen to them? They are precious lives that a faithful Christian mother or father must consider. Is it worthwhile for a Christian mother or father to sacrifice and personally compromise in giving herself or himself to an unclean partner for the sake of the children? Who is to tell such a mother or father what to do? Who would want to shoulder that responsibility? It's a decision which has to be made personally with the Lord's direct leading as one weighs in the deepest recesses of his heart what is God's will in the case.

None of us can live totally untainted by sin. This is not a situation for which one bears the entire responsibility. Circumstances are forced upon a person sometimes in which he or she must make a choice that cannot hold a "yes" or "no" answer applicable as a general rule. And what one decides to do must never be pronounced as something all others must follow.

207

It is good to remember Paul's admonition in Galatians 5:1: "Stand fast therefore in the liberty wherewith Christ hath made us free, and be not entangled again with the yoke of bondage." And in Galatians 2:4: "And because of false brethren unawares brought in, who came in privily to spy out our liberty which we have in Christ Jesus, that they might bring us into bondage." In all this, however, we must also remember the admonition "For, brethren, ye have been called unto liberty; only use not liberty for an occasion to the flesh, but by love serve one another."

Privately Consider Which Is the Lesser of Two Evils

Many times, in life, the Christian has the opportunity of choosing the better of two good things. But even more difficult is the necessity of choosing the lesser of two evils. If we are forced into a choice in such a situation, we should be willing to sacrifice something of self instead of putting self first. Being redemptive is better than being vengeful. That which is for the general good of others should have preeminence over that which is rather for the limited good of others or self. The end never justifies the means, but sometimes painful means must be chosen to achieve the lesser of two evils or the better of two goods. The faithful spouse, and he or she alone, is the one who must determine what would be most pleasing and honoring to God in facing a life with an unfaithful partner. May God spare us from ever having to make such a choice.

Is Divorce of a Sexually Unfaithful Partner Required?

This is a serious dilemma which the believing spouse must face. From our examination of the Scriptures, we would come to the conclusion that divorce in such a case is not necessarily required. The Christian spouse may continue to live with the unfaithful spouse and be personally guided by God as to their marital relationship.

Forgiveness of an Unfaithful Spouse

Should the sexual marital relationship be restored between an unfaithful spouse and a faithful one once the unfaithful one repents and ceases from his sin? In such a case, the spirit of forgiveness should prevail and the law of restoration should be practiced as promulgated by Christ in Matthew 18:21 to 23. Nevertheless, let no one be deluded in thinking that the stigma and consequence of infidelity can be completely eliminated. Sin demands a heavy price. The abscess may be removed, but the scar remains. The advice of Paul in I Timothy 5:22 is to be strictly adhered to: "Keep thyself pure." Obedience will never bring regret.

51

WHY DOES THE LORD PERMIT A FAITHFUL PARTNER TO PUT AWAY A MORALLY UNFAITHFUL SPOUSE INSTEAD OF DEMANDING FORGIVENESS?

It is wise to note that Matthew 19 follows the Lord's teaching about forgiveness in the 18th chapter, verses 21 to 35. But the disciples, having heard how austere the Lord's teaching was in Matthew 5:27 to 32 about divorcing one's mate for reasons other than fornication, realized that there is a limitation even to forgiveness. A spouse may forgive an unfaithful marital partner, but it is not a requirement. Divorce in such a case is permissible. And having done so, one will not be charged by Christ as unforgiving. There must be a reason why the Lord permits this. In fact, the words "forgive" and "dismiss" are one word in Greek—*aphieemi.* (See Chapter 31 in this book.) It means to let such a person stand *(hieemi)* away *(apo)* from you thus protecting your purity, but to continue to be concerned about the forgiveness *(aphesis)* of his or her sins, i.e., the removal or standing away of these sins from the unfaithful partner. Of course this would simultaneously entail the forsaking of sin.

The Lord is concerned about His child as a member of His body. If the Lord insisted that a member of His body whom He loves be forced to live with an unchaste, licentious marital partner, He would thus cause the indirect defilement of His body through His very institution of marriage. This is the very reason that the Lord does permit a faithful partner in marriage to put away from himself or herself *(aphieemi,* the same word as "forgive") a licentious partner, especially when there seems to be no interest in the forgiveness *(aphesis,* "removal of sin from oneself") involving the forsaking of his or her sins.

The Lord Does Not Eliminate the Possibility of Redemptive Action by His Faithful Child

The Lord does not mandate any of His faithful members to put away their morally unfaithful partners. If He did, He would then make divorce obligatory. He would then eliminate the possibility of compassionate personal suffering with redemptive purposes by a faithful member of His body. The Lord Himself certainly suffers with us as He is the Head of His body and we constitute its members. We are not always pure and perfect. We defile His body willingly and unwillingly. It grieves and hurts Him, but He does not choose to cut us off from His body. He redemptively tolerates us.

In our marital relationship, as a faithful believer living with an unfaithful unbeliever or believer spouse, we must seek to be equally as redemptive as our Master. But if we find that the continuation of such a relationship with a licentious spouse dangerously defiles the body of Christ, then the Lord allows us the freedom to act in removing the cause of the defilement even if that means putting away a licentious spouse. We are permitted to follow our conscience in separating from our spouse who, through our mutual association, endangers the whole body of Christ. Our decision to put away or not to put away an unfaithful spouse, to have marital relations with such a one or not, must depend on the effect that that relationship may have on the total body of Christ. It must not rest merely on personal convenience or inconvenience alone.

The Consequences of Deliberate Disobedience to God's Commands

Thus one who dismisses his partner for any reason other than infidelity and remarries has deliberately disobeyed God and must suffer the consequences. The Lord in His day of judgment will avenge the injustice done against the innocent party since restitution is impossible. The one perpetrating the injustice must live the rest of his life in consequence of his sin from which it is impossible to extricate himself. It will be recorded in the books of life (Rev. 20:12; II Cor. 5:10).

To totally escape the consequence of this sin is contrary to God's justice toward the person sinned against. God cannot be manipulated because He is a God of forgiveness. For forgiveness,

212

there had to be an acceptable payment for sin in the blood of God's Son, but that does not give us license to sin. "Of how much sorer punishment, suppose ye, shall he be thought worthy, who hath trodden under foot the Son of God, and hath counted the blood of the covenant, wherewith he was sanctified, an unholy thing, and hath done despite unto the Spirit of grace?" (Heb. 10:29).

The forsaking of sin is an integral part of forgiveness, but the consequences of sin usually remain upon the sinner and the one he may have harmed. This is the reason the Lord commands us to go and find the one who has something against us (Matt. 5:23-26). Restoration of the evil done is commanded. But if it is impossible by virtue of a situation such as divorcing one's innocent and faithful marital partner, there must be some punishment on the offender when final justice is executed. Otherwise God's justice is in reality a mockery.

Forgiveness is not license to please ourselves and do another unjustifiable harm for life. The only forgiveness that can be had in such a case is that one's name would not be eliminated from the Lamb's Book of Life. This sin cannot be bypassed and ultimately will result in diminished rewards for the doer. It will meet God's justice and punishment because it is a sin from which there is no redress.

The one who claims that God will forgive even if he deliberately sins must think also of His justice toward the person that he injured morally or otherwise and who must now bear that burden till death. In spite of Christ's utter desire to forgive as expressed in Matthew 18, He was not about to encourage one of His children to enter into a state of sinfulness from which there was no way or ability to bring about the necessary escape.

52

DIVORCE AND REMARRIAGE
IN MARK 10:2-12

"And the Pharisees came to him, and asked him, Is it lawful for a man to put away his wife? tempting him." Mark 10:2

"The Pharisees also came unto him, tempting him, and saying unto him, Is it lawful for a man to put away his wife for every cause?" Matthew 19:3

For our study to be complete, it is necessary to examine every passage of the New Testament in particular where divorce and remarriage are discussed.

The third passage in order of occurrence in the books of the New Testament is in Mark 10:2-12. Essentially, this passage is the same as that of Matthew 19:3-12. It is a repetition of the same occasion. It occurred when Jesus left the region of Galilee for the last time before His crucifixion and came to Perea, the area in Judea beyond the river Jordan some nineteen miles away from Jerusalem.

Jesus Was Cross-Examined for the Purpose of Being Tempted in Regard to Divorce and Remarriage

There are, however, some important differences in these two very important narratives about divorce and remarriage which must be dealt with.

In Matthew 19:3 we read: "And the Pharisees came unto him, tempting him, and saying." Matthew shows the purpose of their questioning Jesus. It was to tempt Him, or to trip Him so that no matter what He said they would find fault with Him. Sincere inquiry for the purpose of learning was not their desire. It is therefore amazing that the Lord even pursued the conversation.

In Mark 10:2 we read: "And when the Pharisees came (to Him) and were questioning him." Our Authorized Version has simply "asked" as the translation of the Greek verb *epeerootoon*, but such a translation is unwarranted.[1] It means "to interrogate, to question," and not merely to ask. A special usage is for a request for a decision in a disputed issue. And certainly divorce and remarriage were disputed issues among the Jews in the days of Christ as they are in our day. The Pharisees were saying to Jesus that they wanted a decision on that issue. Thus in the two words, *peirazontes*, "tempting" of Matthew 19:3, and *epeerooton*, "were questioning" of Mark 10:2, we have a definite expression of the attitude of these Pharisees. *Eperootaoo* and the noun *eperooteema*[2] refer to a judicial questioning to find out the truth in a certain matter. Thus we can say that the *epeerootoon*, "questioned," of Mark 10:2 refers to the method the Pharisees used in finding out the truth about divorce and remarriage, and the *peirazontes*, "tempting," of Matthew 19:3 refers to their motive in questioning. Thus the two do not conflict in their reporting, but complement each other.

Both tenses of these verbs indicate that the tempting and the questioning did not occur only once but were repeated contentions of the Pharisees.

"Man" Means Husband

In Matthew 19:3 the question is, "If it is permitted for man[3] to dismiss his wife."

In Mark 10:2 the word for husband is more definitive, *andri*,[4] for a "husband" to dismiss a woman. *Anthroopos*, not in its generic sense, can be translated as "a male," but *aneer* (husband or male) cannot be translated as "man" generically, referring to mankind.

What Did the Pharisees Mean by Dismissing One's Wife?

In Matthew 9:3 the question the Pharisees asked of Jesus was: "Is it permitted for a man (a husband) to dismiss his own wife *for every cause?*" That expression "for every cause" is missing from Mark 10:2: "And when the Pharisees came, they questioned him if it is permitted for a husband to dismiss a wife, tempting him."

Is there a contradiction between the two evangelists? No, there isn't. Matthew gives us the direct question asked, undoubtedly one of many if we are going to take into account that the verb *epeerootoon*, "were questioning, or cross-examining," involved more than one question even as in a court case where the whole interrogation procedure is called *eperooteema,* "questioning." Furthermore, the verb *epeerootoon* is in the imperfect tense which indicates a series of questions, one of which is the exact question given in Matthew's record. "Is it permitted for man (a husband) to dismiss his wife for every cause?"

There may well have been a lot of other questions asked by a number of Jesus' conversationalists. That this was so is indicated by Mark's record: "And when the Pharisees came to him they questioned him if it is permitted for a husband to dismiss a wife (a woman), tempting him." This does not constitute a direct questioning as in Matthew where the question is introduced by the participle "saying," *(legontes).* Mark records that one of the many questions was "if it is permitted for a husband to dismiss a wife."

"A Dismissed Wife" Means One Dismissed for Reasons Other Than Infidelity

Essentially, when the Pharisees were questioning Jesus about a husband dismissing a wife, they understood and inferred just what Matthew says explicitly, "for every cause." They wanted a loophole which would allow divorce for reasons other than fornication. They clearly knew that the Old Testament was specific about the right of the husband not only to dismiss a wife for being unfaithful to him, but to cause her to be stoned to death.

The study of this whole matter of questions to Jesus and His answers will be very confusing unless one understands that the term "dismissed wife," *apolelumeneen,* or the verb "dismiss," *apoluoo* refers to the one who did not deserve to be dismissed because of immorality. That matter was settled in the minds of all who knew the law. An unjustifiably dismissed wife was to be given a bill of divorcement. If she were guilty, she could be dismissed but usually no bill of divorcement was granted to her by her dismisser. She was actually to be put to death (Lev. 20:10, Deut. 22:22), but whether she was or not is another matter. But that was the law. The Pharisees needed no further clarification on the matter. However, it seems that they totally ignored the fact that the law also clearly stated that the male adulterer was also to be put to death. In their double standard, they grasped only that part of the law which referred to the woman while overlooking that which referred to men as is

217

clearly seen in the story of the woman caught in adultery (John 8:1-11).

When the Pharisees were questioning Jesus about " dismissing a wife," they *always* implied that it was for a reason other than the legitimate cause of infidelity on her part. Divorce of their wives was practiced by the Israelites during their captivity in Egypt as slaves at the time when Moses began leading them out of captivity. Moses had nothing to do with instituting divorce. He simply attempted to regulate it by law and to avenge the innocent party. The whole concern and subject was dismissing wives *for reasons other than fornication.*

Due to the fact that in those days a woman was but a chattel, a piece of property for whom one could pay or work (Gen. 34:12; Ex. 22:16, 17; Deut. 22:29; Josh. 15:16; I Sam. 18:25), the husband as her proprietor thought he could dispose of her just like selling an animal or some other piece of property which he owned.

Jesus corrects this injustice with His teaching. A woman is a creature of God, His special creation. She is not a thing. This is why Paul over and over again stresses, and particularly in Galatians 3:28, "There is neither Jew or Greek, there is neither bond nor free, *there is neither male nor female:* for ye are all one in Christ Jesus."

Notice what Paul says that a Christian husband's attitude should be toward his wife in I Peter 3:7: "Likewise, ye husbands, dwell with them (your wives) according to knowledge, giving honor unto the wife, as unto the weaker vessel, and *as being heirs together of the grace of life;* that your prayers be not hindered." Apparently, the double standard maintained even by believers of that day was hard to overcome.

[1]The word for "ask" in Greek is *erootaoo.* The verb used here is a commonly used compound verb made up of the intensive preposition *epi,* meaning "on top, over," and the verb *erootaoo,* "to ask." It is a word favored by Mark. It is used for judicial examination as in Mark 14:60f and also for investigation or counter-questioning (Mark 15:44, Acts 23:34).

[2]Only in I Peter 3:21 unfortunately translated "answer" instead of "questioning."

[3]*Anthroopoo,* dative of *anthroopos.*

[4]The dative of *aneer.*

218

53

DID MOSES COMMAND OR PERMIT A BILL OF DIVORCEMENT TO BE GIVEN TO A DISMISSED WIFE?

"And they said, Moses suffered to write a bill of divorcement, and to put her away." Mark 10:4

In Matthew 19:7 the Pharisees are reported to have asked Jesus: "Why did Moses then *command (eneteilato, entellomai)* to give a writing of divorcement, and to put her away?"

But in Mark 10:4 we find the Pharisees answering Jesus' question, "What did Moses command *(eneteilato)* you?" (v. 3), in this manner: "Moses *permitted* a writing of divorcement to be written and dismiss (her)."

In Matthew we have the Pharisees asking, "Why did Moses *command* it?" Jesus answered, "Moses *permitted* it."

In Mark we find Jesus asking, "Why did Moses *command* you?" The Pharisees answered, "Moses *permitted* a writing of divorcement to be written to dismiss her."

Notice how shrewd these Pharisees were. When asking Jesus, they put forward the idea that Moses *commanded* that those who dismiss their wives should give them a bill of divorcement. They knew full well that Moses only *permitted* it, the whole thing—divorce—a most detestable thing in the sight of God. He permitted it, but he did not command it. But when it came to the granting of the bill of divorcement to exonerate the innocent wife, then Moses *demanded* that a bill of divorcement be given.

When in Mark the Lord queries them, He puts their own words in their mouth by asking: "What did Moses command you?" They were caught in their subtlety. They really did not mean what they said that "Moses commanded for a bill of divorcement to be given" because that, as Jews loyal to Moses, would put them under obligation.

Here is how they must have reasoned:

"If truly Moses commanded us to give a bill of divorcement, that is proof that the wife is innocent. If she is innocent, then the husband who dismisses her is guilty because she is not put to death being declared as an adulteress. But if no bill of divorcement is granted her, nor is she put to death by stoning, she is in limbo. We would rather have it that way. Just send her away without making any acknowledgement one way or another. In this manner, no false guilt is brought upon her."

She could not be stoned to death unless her guilt was proven, and that they could not do. To accuse an innocent wife that she was an adulteress would not help them, for their aim was marrying another one. Maybe the reason that we have no record of any adulterer or adulteress ever having been put to death was because it would have been easy, especially for a man, to falsify proof of the adultery of his wife. But why proceed to the proof of adultery which could involve the killing of an innocent person since they could obtain their basic purpose of remarrying by simply dismissing one's marital partner?

The easiest and most convenient way of achieving their ultimate goal, which was marrying another, was to put away their wives "for any cause" and leave it at that. The most beneficial thing for them was to believe and have it affirmed that Moses permitted the granting of a divorce document, instead of commanding that they do so. That is why, as we find in Mark, when they were asked by Jesus, "Did Moses command you to give a writing of divorcement?" they immediately reversed themselves and said, "No, we didn't mean 'commanded,' we meant 'permitted.' " That is Pharisaic shrewdness. They would rather have the choice as to whether or not to grant a divorce document to declare or not declare their wives innocent of guilt.

That was a prime example of situational ethics—something being bad or good depending on circumstances. There is nothing evil or good in itself, reasoned the Pharisees then. That's exactly how today's situational moralistic humanists reason. Everything is relative, they say; nothing is absolute–a philosophy that is bound to lead one astray. Jesus says that if a wife is dismissed "for any cause" other than her infidelity, she is to be officially declared innocent by receiving a divorce document; and by so doing, the husband declares himself guilty of adultery. But who would be willing to do that? The Pharisees weren't.

Jesus Stated That Moses Commanded a Dismissed, Innocent Spouse Be Given a Bill of Divorcement

Observe also how Jesus confirms that Moses did not merely permit the giving of a document of divorce declaring the innocence of the wife by what He refers to as Moses' provision. Rather, He calls it "a commandment." Here is what Mark 10:5 says: "For the hardness of your heart he (Moses) wrote you this *precept.*" That word "precept" in Greek is *entoleen (entolee)* which is the substantive of the verb *entellomai,* used in Matthew 19:7 and Mark 10:3. It is not a mere precept to be understood as an admonition. It is a legal order, a commandment, *entolee,* just as the Decalogue is known as the Ten Commandments (See Matt. 15:3, 6, Rom. 7:8, 9, II Pet. 3:2, I Jn. 3:22, 23, 24, etc.).

The Lord says: "It is a commandment absolutely binding upon you, if you dismiss your wife for reason other than fornication, that you declare her innocent by granting her a bill of divorcement which will enable her, if she so desires, to remarry." In other words, as there was the law of stoning by death for those guilty of adultery (Lev. 20:10), so there was *the law* of granting a document of divorce declaring the innocence of a wife.

54

IF YOU CANNOT LEGITIMATELY DISMISS A WIFE, WHY MARRY IN THE FIRST PLACE?

"And in the house his disciples asked him again of the same matter. And he said unto them, Whosoever shall put away his wife, and marry another, committeth adultery against her."
Mark 10:10, 11

Mark 10:10 tells us that Jesus was now alone with the disciples in the house. Therefore, they were uninhibited in asking some questions which brought out the weaknesses of human nature, even theirs. When you really understand the disciples' question, you would easily conclude that they were just as human as we are today. Here is what they asked the Lord Jesus: If it is so that the only charge or legitimate reason that a man can get rid of his wife is fornication, then it is better or it does not pay to get married.

Isn't that what the philosophy of marriage has developed to be in our day?—I don't want to get married at all if the only way I can legitimately divorce my spouse and marry another is for the cause of fornication, i.e. if she sexually deviates. Therefore, let's not bind ourselves legally, let's just live together and forget marriage!

Now let's examine Matthew 19:10 word for word to see if this is actually the true meaning of the Greek text.

"His disciples say unto him, If it is this way", *ei* "if," *houtoos,* "thus, in this way, so." Observe that the disciples were not ready to accept the word of Jesus as final. They hesitated. It seemed beyond their comprehension. They were wondering if He had really meant what He had said, that fornication on the part of one's spouse was the only legitimate reason for breaking the marriage. Their hesitancy proves that the word of Jesus on the matter of divorce made it difficult and not easy. Man always tends to accept as normal that which can more easily satisfy his flesh. It is the restrictiveness of man's moral freedom that makes people reject the Gospel. How can I get married and be stuck with the same woman all my life if I find we don't get along? In fact some of the books on divorce which I have been perusing in my study of the subject run with this philosophy in mind:

God is a God of forgiveness.

His purpose for the life of His people and all people is for them to be happy. Therefore, if you are unhappy with your spouse, go right ahead, divorce her or him and marry someone you will be happy with. God will forgive you. Your happiness is God's main concern.

And then the idea of the Church's obligation to accept such a philosophy is promulgated.

The fallacy of such a philosophy of moral behavior is whether God's forgiveness overrules His sense of justice and expectation of holiness. It must be remembered that the total plan of man's salvation was for the purpose of bringing to man not what he thinks he needs, but what God as his Maker knows he needs in order to bring satisfaction to his total being.

The heart of the Gospel proclaims: "For God so (or thus) loved the world that he gave his only begotten son, that whosoever believeth in him should not perish, but have everlasting life" (John 3:16). It does not say that God gave man the ability to have more of what he had already seized on his own— disobedience to God's commandment, sin, but what God knew he needed, restoration of himself to God. How was that achieved? Not through outright forgiveness but first through the satisfaction of God's righteousness and justice in and through Jesus Christ dying on Calvary's cross to pay the price of redemption for sin.

The consequence of sin can never be bypassed. The cost must be paid by someone. Since there was no way man could make full restitution, God decided to provide in His Son, the Lord Jesus, the penalty for man's sin. And though that has been accomplished; man is not automatically pardoned because of this action on God's part. He has to repent of his sin and accept God's offer of forgiveness through Christ's satisfaction of God's justice.

What does the rest of John 3:16 say? "That whosoever believeth on him, should not perish, but have everlasting life."

This is equivalent to acquiring God's nature, becoming *makarios,* "blessed" (the word in the Beatitudes). God did not want just to provide for the penalty of man's sin, but to provide for a supernatural way whereby man could become just and sin no more as a matter of acquiring God's holy nature.

It can never be conceived that all that God intended to do in and through Christ was to provide automatic forgiveness *in our sin* but to provide forgiveness and liberty *from our sin.* "Shall we continue in sin, that grace may abound? God forbid. How shall we, that are dead to sin, live any longer therein?" are the potent questions asked by Paul in Romans 6:1 and 2.

55

IS MARRIAGE WITHOUT DIVORCE EXCEPT FOR FORNICATION TOO HARSH?

"His disciples say unto him, If the case of the man be so with his wife, it is not good to marry." Matthew 19:10

The disciples were shocked by the seriousness and severity of Jesus Christ in regard to this matter of marital obligation. So much so that they said: "If the case of the man be so with his wife, it is not good to marry."

The Greek word translated "the case" is *aitia* which means "cause, reason," from the verb *aiteoo*, "to ask, request, require." It is the same word found in Matthew 19:3 in which the Pharisees questioned: "Is it lawful for a man to put away his wife for every *cause (aitia)?*" Observe that the word *aitia* in Matthew 19:10 has before it the definite article *hee aitia*, "the cause" (femine gender).

"If," to put it in modern vernacular, "the only cause or charge that a man can bring against his wife to legitimately dismiss her is her sexual unfaithfulness, what's the use of marrying and getting stuck?"

In the phrase, "the case of the man," *hee aitia tou anthroopou*, the last two words are the subjective genitive which refers to the fact that the only charge a man can bring against his wife is fornication. Man, the husband here, is the subject and not the object. It is not the charge that can be brought *against* the husband but *by* the husband. The phrase, *meta tees gunaikos*, "with his wife," speaks of the relation that this man has with his wife. If only this charge of fornication is what man can bring in relation to his wife, it may be better not to marry.

That last expression in Greek is *ou sumpherei gameesai*, "it is not good to marry." The *ou* means "does not." *Sumpherei*,[1] when used absolutely as in Matthew 19:10, means "to be of benefit, to be profitable, advantageous, or bring together for the benefit of another." Here it is used impersonally. It is not advantageous to marry. The word for "to marry" here is *gameesai*,[2] It refers to getting married at one particular time. It is not advantageous to take this once-in-a-lifetime action and be bound to that one woman from whom the only release to be had would be her fornication. Man's freedom thus becomes restricted by the woman's action. Only if she is unfaithful can the husband be free to dismiss her and remarry.

How can one know whether the wife he marries is going to help or hinder in the proper execution of one's higher calling? She may be a hindrance, they reasoned, and so it may be better to remain single. We would be willing to give up marriage if it would jeopardize our ministry.

Although the disciples may have thought it to be advantageous to be free from marital obligation, they were not selfishly motivated as is the natural man. Their concern may have been that, after all, when one marries, he can have no control over what his spouse does. He or she may adversely affect one's testimony for Christ. Thus marriage may diminish the possibility of the disciple of Christ accomplishing his or her utmost for Christ's highest call.

Natural Man's Selfish Motive

The natural man thinks similarly but from a different motive. Man wants to be free to do as he pleases instead of being bound by marital restrictive obligations. He wants to be free to gratify his selfish wishes, and if marriage permanently ties him to one person for life, he would rather by-pass marriage altogether. Isn't this the hedonistic philosophy so prevalent today?

Jesus' Answer to the Disciples

In spite of the disciples' objection, which admittedly is difficult to understand, the Lord Jesus did not alter His rule. His law stood then and it stands today, no matter how they felt or how we feel about it. Marriage for life may have risks, but it is God's way and His way is always in man's best interest.

It is conceivable that the disciples wanted this strong Christian moral code to be relaxed so that more might follow Jesus. Let's throw open our doors to all so that our teaching will be more acceptable, may have been their reasoning. But the Lord Himself in Matthew 7:13 spoke of the narrow gate and the straight way. To make the door wide and the way easy so that people will think they are in the Kingdom of God even though they have not turned from their sins is an ever-present temptation for many of us.

[1]The third person present indicative of *sumpheroo,* from the conjunction *sun,* "together," and *pheroo,* "to bring." Actually, it literally means "to bring together."

[2]The first aorist infinitive active of *gameoo,* "to marry."

56

MAN'S PREROGATIVE TO HAVE NO ROOM FOR GOD'S RESTRICTIONS, BUT!

"But he said unto them, All men cannot receive this saying, save they to whom it is given." Matthew 19:11

When the disciples expressed the opinion that it is not advantageous to restrict oneself to one wife for life, Jesus said to them: "All men cannot receive this saying, save they to whom it is given." This admittedly is not an easy answer to understand.

The first thing we must determine is the meaning of the word "saying." The Greek is *logon touton*, "word this one."

Was the Lord referring to the disciples' comment that it was not advantageous to marry if the only way whereby one could get rid of his wife was if she committed fornication? Impossible. The Lord could not possibly agree to anything of the kind for in this manner He would have contradicted His saying in Matthew 19:4 that:

1. God had originally created male and female for the obvious purpose of marriage.

2. Man should forsake his father and mother and be attached to his own wife. He did not say that man or woman were meant to stay in celibacy, a state He deemed more advantageous than that of marriage.

3. That the two shall be one flesh.

4. That once God yokes together a man and a woman, nobody should put them apart.

5. That Moses, by commanding a bill of divorcement to be granted to the innocent party, made a law to take care of a situation not originally designed by God, but to regulate the result of man's sin. There would be no need of law if it were not for transgression from the law God originally wrote in man's heart.

6. That one could not dismiss his wife and marry another, except if his wife gave herself to fornication.

7. That he who marries a woman released by her husband because of fornication commits adultery since he marries an adulteress.

These pronouncements of Jesus in Matthew 19:4-9 are what is meant by "this saying" *(logon touton)* of verse 11.

What Jesus stated is that not all men have room for this kind of a saying or these sayings, because in the word *logon* we must see the entire teaching of Jesus relevant to the fidelity of and permanence of the marriage bond. "Not all" in Greek is *ou pantes,* which refers to humanity as a whole. This included unbelievers such as the Pharisees who initiated the discussion in Matthew 19:3 and believers such as the disciples in Matthew 19:10 who expressed their opinion that the strictness of Christ was excessive in the matter of the marital bond.

Man Has No Room for Christ's Teaching

But the word *pantes* also refers to the individuals within the totality. Not any person in his natural, sinful state, nor all of human beings, sinful as they are, have room for such sayings. Man is a fallen creature, whether an unbeliever or even a believer. And even a believer's redemption is spiritual and only partially physical since he is still in this body of sin. Romans 8:23 states that the believer's redemption of the body is yet to come. Man in his present condition of being an unbeliever, or a believer only partly delivered from the sinful state of the world, has no room for these laws of God's Kingdom promulgated by Jesus.

The verb in Greek for "have no room" is *ou choorousi*[1], in this instance, figuratively used and means "are capable of receiving mentally." What the Lord is here confirming is that the carnal mind cannot receive the things of the Spirit of God (I Cor. 2:14, 15; 3:1-3). Man in his natural mind considers God's marital law foolishness, thinking it is not to his advantage to receive it and practice it.

One may object, however, that even believers, even disciples, are lumped into that category.

In Matthew 15:10 and 11, we find Christ saying to the multitudes: "Hear and understand: Not that which goeth into the mouth defileth a man; but that which cometh out of the mouth, this defileth a man."

We would think that Jesus' disciples would understand what He meant. But they didn't. We read in Matthew 15:12: "Then came his disciples, and said unto him, Knowest thou that the Pharisees were offended, after they heard this saying?"

The next verse essentially says what the second part of Matthew 19:11 declares: "but to them that it is given." In other words, only those understand to whom it is given by God's Spirit to understand. Now note what Matthew 15:13 says: "But he (Jesus) answered and said, Every plant, which my heavenly Father hath not planted, shall be rooted up."

And then pass on to Matthew 16:21 where we find Jesus at Caesarea Philippi telling His disciples of His impending suffering in Jerusalem where He was determined to go. Did Peter understand Jesus' words? No. Peter tried to dissuade Him from going. He could not accept the grim future Christ depicted for Himself. And who can forget the stern words of Jesus that were spoken to Peter in verse 23: "Get thee behind me, Satan: thou art an offence unto me: for thou savourest not the things that be of God, but those that be of men."

And then in Matthew 17:17-20, we find Jesus having descended from the Mount of Transfiguration facing a demoniac boy whom the disciples could not heal. In verse 17 we find Jesus saying to the disciples: "O faithless and perverse generation, how long shall I be with you? how long shall I suffer you? Bring him hither to me."

Is it therefore any wonder that the words of Jesus concerning divorce find difficult acceptance not just by the Pharisees but by His own disciples also?

Hasn't the subject of divorce brought havoc in the ranks of Christendom? "Not all have room for these sayings concerning it but those to whom it has been given." Man, whether an unbeliever or a believer, cannot accept as valid and useful the restrictions for marital life which Jesus gave, strict though they may be.

God Gives the Ability to Comprehend the Profitability of His Order of Things

But what does the phrase "but to those that it (the saying

233

about divorce) is given" mean? The Greek word translated "given" is *dedotai*,[2] to give as a free gift. By whom has it been given? By God Himself. The perfect passive voice indicates that this ability to understand Christ's saying concerning divorce was given by God. The ability to comprehend it belongs to such people to whom it has been given to understand. In other words, the capacity to handle the all-important matter of marriage is not an ability of the natural man, but it is a gift of God even as faith is. This reminds us of Ephesians 2:8: "For by grace are ye saved through faith; and that not of yourselves: it is the gift of God."

The Lord is teaching that God gives to people, unbelievers and believers, certain capacities inasfar as sexual appetites are concerned. It is a gift just like other gifts of God and entails a responsibility before God as any other thing He has given us. Paul speaks of the ability to stay single as he was as a *charisma* in I Corinthians 7:7: "For I would that all men were even as I myself. But every man hath his proper gift of God *(charisma)*, one after this manner, and another after that."

God Gives Us Grace to Behave Sexually

The Lord gives His grace enabling us to behave sexually. That is what Christ said to His disciples. To Paul He gave the grace to remain single in order to accomplish the work of an itinerant evangelist and apostle. God's grace is always sufficient to enable any of His children to be what He wants them to be. It would have been wrong for Paul to insist that because he was single, all should be single. There are laws of sexual behavior for each class of people—for the unmarried: chastity; for the married: to be one flesh within the bonds of matrimony, and within this bond to remain faithful to one's partner. The only time that remarriage is permitted is definitely prescribed in the Bible, i.e., when a spouse dies or when he or she has proven unfaithful. The natural man will say that he can't live like that. However, God will give the grace to do His will according to each one's individual need. Our needs are as varied as our appearances. Even as we don't all look alike, let us not presume to impose our way of life, even our sexual conduct, on others.

No religious leader should demand that all those serving God must be celibate. On the other hand, those who decide that such is God's will for them in order to accomplish tasks for Him they could in no other way accomplish should not look down upon those who are married and vice versa. To each one, God gives His particular grace.

I know of one missionary who felt called to go to the cannibals of Irian Jaya. As the pontoon plane settled on the water near the cannibals in the middle of the jungle, he and his expectant wife fearfully disembarked. Much to their surprise, they were treated with great respect by these wicked savages, and many came to know the Lord through their ministry there. Years later, this man learned that it was his wife's advanced state of pregnancy that afforded them protection since the natives considered pregnancy as a revered state of being. Surely, it was God's will for this man to be married, otherwise he would have only been food for the cannibals.

A very wonderful verse to remember is Romans 12:3: "I say, through the grace given unto me, to every man that is among you, not to think of himself more highly than he ought to think; but to think soberly, according as God hath dealt to every man the measure of faith." So does He give, through faith, the ability to properly behave sexually. The person who remains continent must not think it is his own achievement. It is by God's grace. If one feels he does not have the grace to be sexually poised according to God's purpose, he must ask of God who "giveth to all men liberally," and then claim such promises as I Corinthians 10:13: "There hath no temptation taken you but such as is common to man: but God is faithful, who will not suffer you to be tempted above that you are able; but will with the temptation also make a way of escape, that ye may be able to bear it." No one can ever say, "I don't have what it takes to be sexually the man or woman God wants me to be." He gives the measure of the particular grace needed.

Let Us Prescribe Limitations to Our Own Freedom

In the Greek, the phrase "not to think of himself more highly than he ought to think; but to think soberly," we have the use of some intriguing words that defy translation. The word for "think" is *phroneoo* which refers to the exercise of prudence in our inter-human relationships. A prudent person is *phronimos,* one who knows how to behave toward his wife and vice versa

235

and toward others. Paul says that we should not think more highly than we ought to, *huperphronein, (huper,* "above and over," and *phronein,* "to think or behave prudently"). We must not stand above others and look down upon them as their critic. We are to stand alongside of them. We are prudent when we think soberly or soundly. *Soophroneoo,* here translated "think soberly," actually means to have the ability to prescribe limits to one's own freedom, thought, and behavior.

By learning that, a happy marital relationship or a happy single life can almost be guaranteed. God gives the grace needed, the measure of faith to prescribe the necessary limitations to one's own freedom. That is a gift of God even in our sexual relationships and behavior, our Lord tells His disciples in Matthew 19:11. God will give grace to be chaste if unmarried, deserted or widowed.

"Not all can receive this saying." Naturally you cannot, but supernaturally—by God's grace—you can. Therefore, seek His grace to be what He has directed or permitted you to be.

[1]*Ou choorousi* in the present indicative of *chooreo.*

[2]Third person singular perfect indicative passive of *didoomi.*

57

THE LIFE OF ABSTINENCE—
FOR WHOM?

"For there are some eunuchs, which were so born from their mother's womb: and there are some eunuchs, which were made eunuchs of men: and there be eunuchs, which have made themselves eunuchs for the Kingdom of heaven's sake. He that is able to receive it let him receive it." Matthew 19:12

If God wanted all people to be single, He wouldn't have instituted marriage. He would have implemented some other method for the propagation of the race. The fact that from the beginning He made male and female, one for one, is because He wanted marriage to be the basis of the preservation and multiplication of the race.

But the fact remains that not all men and women can marry. They are unequally distributed on this earth. No single person, therefore, must feel that being single is being out of God's will for him or her. Nor should a married person despise an unmarried one as if not blessed of God. Marriage is not for all and celibacy is not for all. It is as God gives grace in His directive or permissive will. His children are most fulfilled not in what they desire to be in their natural selves, but in their God-ordained status.

To further clarify His teaching, the Lord Jesus proceeded to give an illustration in Matthew 19:12 which constitutes something unique and which He never said anywhere else. Here it is:

"For there are some eunuchs, which were so born from their mother's womb: and there are some eunuchs, which were made eunuchs of men: and there be eunuchs, which have made themselves eunuchs for the kingdom of heaven's sake. He that is able to receive it, let him receive it."

What Is a Eunuch?

What is a eunuch? The Greek word is *eunouchos,*[1] "one

237

who goes to or has a bed alone." It came to mean a keeper of the bed or bedchamber, a chamberlain. A eunuch, therefore, is a man either naturally impotent or castrated. In olden times, eunuchs had the charge of the bedchamber and the care of the women in the palaces of the Eastern princes. We have in Acts 8:27 reference to a eunuch of Queen Candace of Ethiopia. A eunuch, in a figurative sense or in a real sense, is one who on religious account mortifies his natural inclinations and refrains even from marriage.

A eunuch is one who either demonstrates no sexual desire or who voluntarily does not engage in sex.

There Are Eunuchs

The first thing the Lord Jesus asserts in the Scripture is that there are such people. "There are, therefore, eunuchs." Not all humans have the same degree of sexual appetite.

Then the Lord goes on to say that there are such eunuchs because:
1. They were born like that
2. Others brought it upon them
3. They decided to bring about this state of being on themselves.

Is this an acceptable state? Not for all, but for some, as the Lord stated in verse 11. And concluding this whole section on marriage and divorce, He says, "He that is able to receive it, let him receive it."

Born Eunuchs

That there are people born into the world without sexual proclivity and appetite, there is no doubt. As to who is responsible for this state we cannot tell. There may be second causes, such as physical illnesses, but these second causes are possible only because the first cause, God Himself, permits such a state. He may not so direct it to be, but He permits it. Therefore, we could safely say that being a eunuch is a special state, call it an exception to the rule, of a human being born into the world sexually impotent.

Such a state is also possible through physical castration caused by others. In the Old Testament, the castration of both men and animals is forbidden, for it contradicts the divine will of creation. Thus, there were no eunuchs in Israel itself. The royal courts were an exception. In Deuteronomy 23:1 it specifies that no eunuch is to be received into the congregation of Jehovah. There is a different emphasis in the prophets. In Isaiah 56:3-5, we find eunuchs were to be allowed to enter the congregation, be that a local place of worship or the congregation of the righteous in general.

That the passage in Matthew 19:12 cannot refer to the servants of the Lord, to priests or ministers, is apparent because Paul's advice for both deacons and bishops (1 Tim. 3:2, 12, Titus 1:6) is that they be married, husbands of one wife. That is God's general rule. And yet Paul himself who penned these pastoral epistles was unmarried. There can be exceptions to the rule only as God gives His grace.

In the Old Testament, marriage was an unconditional duty. There is only one known instance of a celibate rabbi, Ben Azzai. He was sharply blamed by other rabbis. Therefore, what Christ says in Matthew 19:12 does not specifically pertain to those who particularly minister His Word, but to all men and particularly to believers. There are some who "were born eunuchs from their mother's womb." If you are such, be satisfied to be what God permitted you to be. Should you seek marriage? Only for the sake of companionship and not for being one flesh with your spouse. Be honest about your state. The rule set down by Paul in I Corinthians 7:5 would apply in this case which would necessitate sexual abstinence on common agreement between the spouses.

Then there are those who were made eunuchs, eunuchized *(eunouchistheesan)* by men. The verb *eunouchizoo* is used only here in Matthew 19:12, and it is used twice. It is in the aorist tense which signifies an operation performed on them by others at a particular time. There is absence of opinion by the Lord as to this procedure. Here, again, the Lord speaks of a practice by men even as He spoke of men divorcing their wives for the hardness of their heart. But from the beginning it was not thus. One has to measure the evil that one's sexuality can cause in open society versus his castration. Such castration might have been for the protection against raping for the particular service a castrated individual could render as in a palace, for instance. The only point the Lord is making is that only "those to whom it is given," who may receive special grace, may be in such a state.

Eunuchs by Voluntary Sexual Abstinence

And then finally our Lord says: "And there are eunuchs who *eunuchized* themselves," or "made themselves eunuchs." This must refer to a figurative meaning, not necessarily those who castrated themselves but those who voluntarily submerged and sublimated their sexual instinct, even as Paul did, "for the kingdom of the heavens." Origen, the ancient church father, took this literally and had himself castrated, an act which he apparently later regretted.[2]

A Way of Life That Is Only for Some

Such a life is not for all, but only for some. And this the Lord stresses with the words: "He that is able to have room, let him have room." That is the literal translation from the Greek text. It does not constitute a direct command with an imperative in the second person plural which would have been directly spoken to His disciples, but it is in the indirect third person singular, *chooreitoo,* "let him have room, he who is able" *(ho dunamenos choorein),* that is, he who has the power or is able to have room for such a way of life. And who is able? The one who is born like that or is rendered so by others or who by His own volition, for a higher cause, chooses such a life of celibacy or sexual abstinence within marriage.

[1]This compound word is derived from *eunee,* "a bed," which is a derivative of *heis, henos,* "one, of one, alone," and *echoo,* "to have, keep."

[2]Kittel, *Theological Dictionary of the New Testament,* Vol. II, pp. 765-768, Eerdmans, 1964.

58

JESUS' PRIVATE TEACHING TO HIS DISCIPLES CONCERNING DIVORCE AND REMARRIAGE

The words which Jesus spoke as recorded in Matthew 19:11 and 12 and Mark 10:11 and 12 were spoken privately to His disciples in a house, apparently not in the hearing of the Pharisees who had engaged Him with questions in the presence of His disciples.

Look at Matthew 19:10: "His disciples say unto him," and Mark 10:10: "And in the house his disciples asked him again on the same matter." What therefore we have recorded in Matthew 19:11 and 12; Mark 10:11 and 12 was said by Jesus privately to His disciples and must be taken in that context.

Apparently Jesus' remarks to the disciples were stimulated by their question found only in Matthew 19:10: "If the case of the man be so with his wife (that he has to live with her for life with the only basis of divorce being fornication), it is not good to marry."

Jesus patiently explained to them that:

1. God gives His grace for people to be that which God permits them to be by birth, by circumstances, or by individual choice. A person cannot be what God wants him to be in his natural self and choice. He has to allow God to make him to be what He wants him to be. That answer is expressed in Matthew 19:11 and 12 and has already been fully explained.

2. Anyone who dismisses his own wife and marries another, commits adultery against her.

He left out, in this instance, what Matthew 19:9 records, "Except for fornication." He had just said it to the Pharisees who were questioning Him. Why, therefore, did He have to repeat what He had just said? He said it once, or perhaps repeatedly, to the Pharisees in the presence of His disciples. And He also said it to the disciples in the hearing of the crowds

241

(Matt. 5:1 and 2) as part of the Sermon on the Mount in Matthew 5:32. He did not have to say it in exactly the same manner to His disciples since they heard it explicitly on at least two occasions as Jesus taught publicly.

In this instance, when speaking to His disciples alone, He said, "Whosoever shall put away his wife, and marry another, committeth adultery against her." In the very word *apolusee,* "shall dismiss" in the aorist with punctiliar future indicates an act at a definite time in the future. He was implicitly referring to the dismissal of one's wife "for any cause," or a reason lesser than fornication on the part of a wife. Such a one would therefore dismiss an innocent wife for the sake of marrying another. The word for "another" is *alleen* as in Matthew 19:9. He then commits "adultery on her." That is exactly what the Greek text says, *ep' auteen,* "on her." Who is *her?* His wife whom he dismisses. This is obvious. The new wife he marries may already be an adulteress or may not be. The verb here in Mark 10:11 is *moichatai,* exactly the same as in Matthew 19:9. The only difference is that in Matthew 19:9 there is nothing after *moichatai.* The verb stands by itself. It is the passive form with middle meaning by the fact that the object of his adultery is imposed upon himself. "He becomes adulterous" should be the translation of Matthew 19:9.

But in Mark 10:11 there is the object of the verb *moichatai* explicitly stated as *ep' auteen,* "on her." This can only mean on the innocent wife he is divorcing. The preposition *epi,* "on," should be better translated "against" as the preposition has that particular meaning of against since the pronoun *auteen* is in the accusative as also in Matthew 26:55 *(epi leesteen,* "upon or against a robber"). If the new woman he marries is meant, how can he commit adultery against her? It is not the marrying of another that has been Jesus' concern in this entire discussion, but the innocent wife dismissed by her husband. In other words, Jesus could have left out the phrase "and shall marry another" and He would have meant the same thing. It would have then run like this: "Whosoever shall put away or dismiss his own wife... commits adultery against her." By dismissing her without the cause of fornication and not giving her a bill of divorcement, he allows her to be thought of as an adulteress. And this Jesus would not permit against an innocent wife.

Matthew, by omitting the *ep' auteen,* "against her," uses the verb *moichatai* in a middle voice sense; i.e. that the adultery is upon or against himself.

Thus putting these two passages together, the thought becomes complete. A husband who dismisses his wife for a reason other than fornication commits adultery first against himself and then against the wife he dismisses. Of course, the one dismissing can also be the wife.

59

WHEN A WIFE DISMISSES HER HUSBAND AND MARRIES ANOTHER

"And if a woman shall put away her husband, and be married to another, she committeth adultery." Mark 10:12

This is the first time thus far in any discussion concerning divorce that we find a woman taking the first step in that direction. Matthew consistently presents Christ castigating the man who lusts after another woman and, in order to marry her, divorces his own wife.

The Lord thus far forbade a man to dismiss his wife but for reason of fornication. The very use of the word *apoluoo,* "to dismiss or put away," implies dismissal for reasons less than the unfaithfulness of the wife.

But now Mark presents Christ as having something to say about the wife who takes the initiative. Christ said in Mark 10:12: "And if a woman shall put away her husband, and be married to another, she committeth adultery."

Mark, unlike Matthew who writes primarily to the Jews, writes to Gentiles. The attitude of the Jew was that only the man could exercise the prerogative of divorce. Woman occupied such a low place that she was just like a chattel to be acquired and exchanged at will.

But such was not the case among the Gentiles. A woman had rights too. So Mark presents Christ emphasizing that His teaching concerning divorce is not restricted to the husband, to the male only, but applies equally and unreservedly to the wife, to the female as well. It is to be remembered also that in Matthew 19 the Lord spoke directly to the Pharisees who were questioning Him while in Mark 10:10 we see that the Lord was speaking only to His disciples. These disciples needed instructions by Christ on dealing with divorce and remarriage, not only in

245

relation to the Jews, but also in relation to the Gentiles to whom they were also to preach the Gospel.

Although commentator R.C.H. Lenski admits that it was not customary for Jewish women to divorce their husbands, yet cases of this kind did occur. He refers to Josephus, the Jewish historian (Antiquities 15, 7, 10), who reports that Salome, sister of Herod the Great, even sent her husband, Costobarus, a bill of divorcement. However, Josephus remarks that the sending of this bill was not according to Jewish laws.

He further mentions Herodias who left her husband, Philip. And then he comments: "To say that these were prominent abnormalities does not dispose of them. Because the people involved were prominent, history reported their cases. It is rather difficult to believe that wives were completely bound to their husbands, and that, while husbands constantly got rid of their wives, the hardness of heart never extended to Jewish women to do the same with their husbands. It has been established that they, too, could obtain a divorce. The case is simply this, Jewish law recognized a certain easy procedure for the husband but provided nothing that was equal for the wife. She would either have to desert her husband or apply to the difficult local courts for release. This formal difference is immaterial to Jesus. In His estimation the sin consisted in the disruption of the marriage, no matter by what means this was effected.

"In all His utterances Jesus treats only the immorality that is involved in the disruption of marriage, whether this immorality emanates from the husband or from the wife; and not the legal actions of any court of law. Even when he refers to Deuteronomy 24:1 and what was considered legal among the Jews (among whom, however, the husband required no court action but only the wife if she wanted to be freed) Jesus treats only the moral side, namely, the hardness of the heart and the consequent defection from God's creative intention. Confusion results when this is overlooked, and when we speak of divorce, meaning a court action, and then apply the utterances of Jesus to that. The sin of destroying a marriage is in the heart and in the action of the husband or the wife (possibly of both); this is what destroys the marriage. Running to the court for a legal edict is only a subsequent result and not the main point. A disrupted marriage is a disrupted marriage and thus a vicious sin against the will, Word, and command of God, whether some court action follows, as it does in our day, or is not needed at all, as was the case in Jesus' day.

"In all His utterances on this subject Jesus blames only the one who disrupts the marriage and not the one whose marriage is disrupted. The mistranslations of Matthew 5:32 should not confuse us on this point, nor the exegesis that operates with these mistranslations. I Corinthians 7:15 is exactly the same as Matthew 5:32; 19:9, and the passages in Mark. The innocent party in a disrupted marriage is not bound as Paul states, nor does Jesus declare that party bound."[1]

And so Jesus says, "And if a woman," or "a wife." The word in the Greek text is *gunee,* the generic name for "woman" which, however, is used for a wife. There is no definite article before *gunee.* Therefore it would be wrong to say "the woman or the wife" making her to be the wife either dismissed by the husband of the previous verse or the other woman whom the divorcing husband has chosen to marry. Verses 11 and 12 are unrelated inasfar as the personalities involved are concerned. The word *gunee,* "a woman or a wife," refers to any woman who is married.

"Having dismissed her own husband." The verb in Greek is *apolusasa,* "she having dismissed."[2] This refers to an action by the wife in the past. What was the reason for her dismissing her husband? It certainly could not be for the legitimate reason of his unfaithfulness. The word *apoluoo* here, as in the previous verse, agrees fully with the explicit reason stated in Matthew 5:32 and 19:9, "except for fornication." It implies that the dismissal was not for reason of his fornication, which if it were, she would have had the right to legitimately dismiss him and have him stoned to death. But in this verse, she is the guilty party and he is the innocent.

"Her own husband," is *ton andra autees,* "the husband of her own." The idea is that she was duly and legitimately married to him. Marriage in Scripture is never left to be understood as mere cohabitation. It is a contract binding two into an indissoluble union.

"And be married to another, she commits adultery against herself." The verb "be married," in Greek is *gameethee.*[3] It means that at a definitive time she gives herself for marriage to another other than her husband. Evidently that is the very purpose of her divorcing her first husband who is innocent of any charge of fornication. The man always marries *(gameoo,* active) and a woman is married *(gameomai—gamatai,* third person passive).

The word for "another" is *alloo* in the dative which refers to any man. It makes no difference who this is, as long as he is a man other than her husband. It is not the person she marries that is the important consideration here, but the innocent husband whom she dismisses.

The verb *moichatai* is translated "she committeth adultery." Actually the verb is exactly the same as in the second clause of Matthew 5:32 and in both clauses of Matthew 19:9. It is in the passive voice form which is the same form also as the middle voice. The passive voice refers to action brought upon by a person other than oneself, and the middle voice refers to action which a person brings upon oneself. This woman who divorced her husband for no valid reason and married another makes herself adulterous. But she also has adultery committed with her through her new marriage.

Thus we can say that the verb *moichatai* is both middle and passive in meaning. She brings upon herself a situation of adultery for life, indicated by the present indicative tense of the verb. She continuously commits adultery against herself and against her new husband.

[1]*Commentary on Mark,* pp. 421-423. The Wartburg Press, Columbus 15, Ohio.

[2]First aorist participle feminine active of *apoluoo.*

[3]First aorist subjunctive passive of *gameoo,* "to marry."

60

DIVORCE AND REMARRIAGE IN LUKE 16:18a

"Whosoever putteth away his wife, and marrieth another, committeth adultery." Luke 16:18a

The only passage in the Gospel of Luke where divorce and remarriage are mentioned is Luke 16:18. This verse forms part of a small parenthesis of five verses between two of the most significant parables of our Lord, that of the steward of unrighteousness (money) in Luke 16:1-13, and that of the rich man and Lazarus in Luke 16:19-31.

The Background

What are these five verses that are given parenthetically? Realizing the concern of these verses will help us to know the motive of our Savior's words on divorce and remarriage.

The Lord was speaking to His disciples in Luke 16:1. In Luke 15:1 and 2 we find all kinds of sinners and publicans who were hated tax collectors coming to hear Him. Undoubtedly, among them were some who were real harlots and some women who were dismissed by their Jewish husbands for no valid reason and who were stigmatized as harlots without really being of that group.

That bothered the Pharisees and the scribes. We read in Luke 15:2, "And the Pharisees and scribes murmured (grumbled), saying, This man (Jesus) receiveth (welcomes with open arms) sinners, and eateth with them." Jesus' remarks in Luke 15 and 16 were in reality an answer to this attitude of the Pharisees and scribes who were critical of His hearty welcome of sinners and outcasts to Himself. They thought of this as unbecoming for one who claimed to be God's prophet. Recall what such a Pharisee said when he saw a woman, known for her past immorality, approach Jesus and rub His feet with ointment. "This man

(Jesus), if he were a prophet, would have known who and what manner of woman this is that toucheth him; for she is a sinner" (Luke 7:39). It is interesting that this saying and the context of the Lord found eating in a Pharisee's house occur particularly in Luke's Gospel.

Now observe what this parenthesis of five verses in Luke 16:14 to 18 contains:

The Pharisees Were Covetous

Verse 14 tells us that the Pharisees who were listening to Jesus' teaching about how to handle money as good stewards in Luke 16:1 to 13 derided him, for they were covetous. They preferred money above people, a typical characterization of a covetous person.

Now notice what Jesus said to them after their demonstration of their true character. In Luke 16:15 we read: "Ye are they which justify yourselves before men; but God knoweth your hearts: for that which is highly esteemed among men is abomination in the sight of God."

His actual charge to them was: You do whatever you like and then try to justify it as being according to God's will. You divorce your wife and then you say: "That's what God wants me to do! I'm doing God's will!"

Isn't the same being done by religious people today? To do evil is one thing, but then to attempt to align it as God's will compounds the abomination before the Lord. The charge followed: God knows your hearts. He knows not only what you do, but why you really do it.

The Pharisees Were Misusing the Scriptures

And then in Luke 16:16 and 17, Jesus makes reference to the Old Testament of which the Pharisees and scribes were great proponents. They called upon their Scriptures to justify their actions without impunity. These Scriptures stood for 430 years from Malachi till John the Baptist appeared on the scene. Then for some three years plus, Jesus preached the kingdom of God. But to be found in the kingdom was not an automatic thing. Because Jesus was a Jew, it did not mean that every Jew was by his hereditary right included in Jesus' kingdom. No. It takes an individual decision to believe and accept. Don't fail to enter it by neglecting to exercise faith. That's how the kingdom of God has always been entered, by individual faith and not by heredity.

Luke 16:17 goes on to affirm that the Scriptures can never be used as justification for evil, the constant attempt of the Pharisees. Follow Jesus' discussion with them in Matthew 19:1 to 12 and Mark 10:1 to 12. They were tempting Jesus to affirm that Moses altered God's original plan of one man for one woman as his wife for life. Moses permitted, they said, for a husband to put away his wife for any reason. The rascals! They had even the disciples almost believing it. Can you imagine the disciples saying: "If the case of the man be so with his wife, it is not good to marry."

The Lord went on to tell them that no matter how hard they tried to cut up the Scriptures to fit their behavior, not the least part of the Word of God was going to be abrogated. "It is easier for heaven and earth to pass, than one tittle of the law to fail." And especially this is so, insofar as the scriptural provision is concerned about the matter of marriage, divorce, and remarriage. The theme, then, is the permanence of God's Word. It must stand no matter what man's behavior is in regard to marriage.

And then follows Luke 6:18: "Whosoever putteth away his wife, and marrieth another, committeth adultery." That is the first statement.

It is similar to Matthew 5:32, Matthew 19:9, and Mark 10:11, but not entirely identical.

Let me first of all point out the differences with an exact literal translation from the Greek.

In Matthew 5:32 the Mere Unwarranted Dismissal of an Innocent Wife Causes Her to Be Considered an Adulteress

Matthew 5:32: "But I say unto you that he who (referring to the man who plays around with a woman other than his wife by constantly looking at her and caressing her with his right hand; see Matt. 5:28, 30), if he puts away or dismisses his wife for a reason other than fornication, causes adultery against her."

The verb periphrastically translated here referring to the committal of adultery is in the passive voice, *moichatai.* He makes her to suffer adultery, to be counted as an adulteress because he has dismissed her for a reason other than fornication on her part without giving her a bill of divorcement.

No mention is found in this verse about his remarriage being wrong. The wrongness is in the plain fact of his unwarrantly divorcing his wife.

Matthew 19:9: "But I say unto you, that he who, if he dismisses or puts away his wife if not for fornication *and* should marry another *(alleen),* he commits adultery." The verb is *moichatai,* essentially as in Matthew 5:32a. However, in Matthew 5:32a we have the exception that the principle verb is *poiei,* "he makes," with the direct object being *auteen,* "her," and the indirect object being the present infinitive *moichasthai* (TR), the present infinitive of the passive form *moichaonai* or the first aorist passive infinitive *moicheutheenai* (UBS—also of the passive verb *meicheuomai).* In each case the verb is passive, either the present infinitive of the passive verb *moichaomai* or the first aorist passive infinite of the verb *moicheuomai.* In the final analysis, both forms cannot be other than passive. But it must be remembered at all times that a verb in the passive form can have either a passive meaning (the action from another to oneself) or a middle meaning (the action from oneself to oneself).

Thus in Matthew 5:32, the very dismissal of a woman by a wicked husband causes her *poiei auteen,* to suffer adultery as a result of his action against her in dismissing her.

In Matthew 19:9 We Have the Reason Why a Husband Dismisses His Wife: to Marry Another

In Matthew 19:9 there is the additional action on the part of the sinful husband of marrying another. But since Matthew 5:32a lays the cause of adultery on behalf of the wicked husband simply and merely on the charge of his dismissing his wife and not on his remarrying another, the first must be considered as the basic cause of adultery on his part. The second is the further explanation of why he did it and involves the spreading of the evil to another woman who may have been spared participating in this sin if he were not to lust after her and marry her.

The verb in Matthew 19:9a is *moichatai,* the present indicative of the passive verb *moichaomai.* This can be taken with the passive meaning in that his action caused his innocent wife to be stigmatized as an adulteress by his mere action of dismissing her without giving her a bill of divorcement. This, as we have explained previously, was tantamount to an absolution certificate insofar as her personal guilt was concerned. And it can also be taken with the middle meaning in that he himself, the wicked husband, brings upon himself the proper and justified accusation of adultery.

Mark 10:11 Refers to Both the Dismissal of One's Wife and Marrying Another

In Mark 10:11 we have: "And he (Jesus) says to them: he who, if he should dismiss his wife and should marry another *(alleen),* causes her to suffer adultery," or "adultery is brought against her."

The Greek expression is *moichatai ep 'auteen,* literally, "adulters or adulterates upon or against her." Again the verb *moichatai* is the present indicative of the passive *moichaomai.* Since the object is explicitly given, "against her," this has a passive meaning. "He" refers to the wicked husband who does the double wrong to dismiss his wife and marry another one. We must then conclude that the meaning of the passive voice form is passive, meaning that the action of the wicked husband is suffered by the dismissed, innocent wife. But it also has, merely by deduction, a middle meaning since he at the same time inevitably commits adultery against himself. The principal sufferer, however, is the dismissed wife.

Thus the literal translation of Luke 16:18a is: "Every one *(pas,* the same word used in Matthew 5:28 and not *hos* (TR) of Matthew 5:32a, 19:9a, and Mark 10:11 meaning 'anyone,' not referring to a particular person) who, dismissing his wife and marrying another *(heteran),* commits adultery."

Differences of Luke 16:18 From Matthew 5:32 and 19:9

There are some differences in this Lucan rendering from the Matthean and Marcan sayings. In Matthew (TR) and Mark we have the verb *apoluoo,* in the aorist subjunctive *hos an apolusee,* "he who if he should dismiss." In Luke we have the verb in the present active participle *ho apoluoon,* "the dismissing one," as in the UBS text of Matthew 5:32a. Constancy and repeated habitual action is involved by this tense. Remember that our Lord was speaking to the Pharisees for whom dismissing a wife was no different then getting rid of an object. Marriage for them lost its permanent status. The Lord really is concerned about marriage itself as a divine institution. These Pharisees apparently were constantly and repeatedly shedding their wives. Hence we have the stricter word of Jesus without the exception clause found in Matthew 5:32 and 19:9.

We find for the first time in any of these divorce and remarriage pronouncements of Jesus that the verse used in Luke 16:18 is in the active voice. It is *moicheuei* instead of *moichatai* as heretofore. Why? The active voice means something more than the passive. *Moichatai* is somewhat less direct—he causes adultery to be suffered by himself or against his innocent wife. This has been the charge thus far. Now, however, suddenly it is *moicheuei.*

I believe this was spoken at a different time. Most probably it was spoken in the order and sequence that it is recorded in Luke's Gospel in association with the other charges contained in this parenthesis of Luke 16:14 to 18. The Lord is charging the Pharisees with deliberately and directly disobeying and breaking the Sixth Commandment, *ou moicheuseis,* "Do not commit adultery," in the active voice. This commandment does not say *ou porneuseis,* "Do not commit fornication," which would have been a far more general sexual prohibition. It would have applied more directly also to single people who had not married since *porneia,* "fornication," is primarily the sexual activity of single people while adultery implies a married person. What was the purpose of the Sixth Commandment? The forbidding of illicit sex? Yes, but not primarily. It was the commandment on the preservation of the sanctity of the human family as instituted by God Himself directly. The engaging in illicit sex by a married person was the direct destruction of marriage and family. When a man dismisses his wife, he destroys his family and family life in general. It is a slap at God Himself and not merely the hurt and harm brought upon three individuals: the innocent wife, the perpetrator, and the person who may marry the dismissed innocent wife, not to mention the children who may be involved. The person who believes in the principle of being able to dismiss his innocent wife at any time, *moicheuei,* actively perpetrates the crime of destroying what God has established, marriage and the family.

There are yet two more differences in this Lucan pronouncement than the parallel ones in Matthew 19:9 and Mark 10:11. It does not say "and if he should marry another," using the word *alleen,* "another (merely numerically)," but it says *heteran,* "another of a different kind or qualitatively different." Why do we find this change? Because of some little difference that these Pharisees could see in other women thus wanting to marry them, and consequently rejecting their own wives. Look what she has that my wife doesn't have, they reasoned. Taste and pleasure were the guiding principles instead of love and dedication to a person with whom they were joined for life. Just as it is today, so it was then, and this continued on to the third and fourth wife, etc.

The other difference in the Lucan pronouncement is the verb *gamoon,* "marries another." It is not as the Authorized Version has it, "and marrieth" or "marries another" in the third person subjunctive as in Matthew 19:9 and Mark 10:11 or *gameesee,* but *ho gamoon,* "the one marrying another." The definite article *ho* applies to both present participles, *apoluoon,* "the one dismissing," and *gamoon* "the one marrying." It was not done just once but constantly and repeatedly. Hence the use of the verb *moicheuei* in the present indicative, i.e., he is with his actions constantly, actively destroying the institution of marriage.

It is much stronger than Matthew 5:32a where no remarriage is mentioned. There, the hurt is only upon the dismissed, innocent wife, upon himself, and the one who would marry such a dismissed wife. But here the harm is upon the institution of marriage itself and an active fight and affront against God.

61

MARRIAGE TO A
GUILTY DIVORCEE

"And whosoever marries her that is put away from her husband commits adultery." Luke 16:18b

The second part of Luke 16:18 is also somewhat different than Matthew 5:32b and 19:9b.

Matthew 5:32b says as we have interpreted it: "And he who if he should marry a dismissed woman, takes upon himself the stigma of adultery." Since the dismissal of a wife without the cause of fornication stigmatizes her as an adulteress, naturally he who marries her takes upon himself her stigma.

The only difference between Matthew 5:32b and Matthew 19:9b is that instead of the subjunctive,[1] "if he should marry a dismissed one," we have[2] "and he who having married a dismissed woman."

In Luke 16:18b we have,[3] "anyone (without exception) who marries (*ho gamoon,* as a matter of principle) a woman dismissed by a husband commits adultery."

The verb in Luke 16:18b is in the present participle, *ho gamoon,* "the marrying one, the one who marries" either for the second or multiple time, who marries over and over even as the *apoluoon,* the one dismissing his wives one after the other to marry another and yet another. That is the meaning of these two present participles, the one dismissing and the one marrying.

He marries one at a time, but one after the other is the implication of this present participle versus the first aorist participle *ho gameesas* in Matthew 19:9b referring to one single remarriage. Thus in Luke 16:18 we have the constantly recurring dismissal of wives and the remarrying of others. Among these others there can be those wives who dismissed themselves from their husbands. In fact, for the first time this dismissal *"from a husband" apo andros,* is specifically mentioned in Luke 16:18b: "and everyone marrying a woman dismissed from a husband (*apo andros*) commits adultery."

The reason why the specific expression *apo andros* occurs here is because the guilt for such separation must not be attributed to the husband in this case but to the wife who has separated herself from her husband.

Edward Robinson in his *Greek and English Lexicon of the New Testament* says in a discussion of the use of the preposition *apo* which is used in Luke 16:18b: "If it were *hupo* 'by,' the blame would have fallen directly upon the husband as heretofore in the discussion of *apolelumeneen,* 'the dismissed wife.' But it is possible that a woman is loosed from her husband not because of his fault but hers. In Matthew 5:32b and 19:9b it just says *apolelumeneen,* 'released or loosed or dismissed.' "

Only Luke 16:18b says "from a husband" which attributes the blame on the separating wife. Remember that Luke even as Mark writes primarily for Gentiles, unlike Matthew whose primary target is the Jews. Among the Gentiles, the action by a woman to separate from her husband was more common than among the Jews. Therefore Mark 10:12 speaks of a woman dismissing her husband and Luke 16:18b speaks of one marrying a woman who dismisses herself from a husband.

Robinson says that *apo* is put after neuter and passive verbs to mark the author and source of the action; but not where the author is to be concerned of as *personally and immediately active.* Now let us look at this Lucan expression, *apolelumeneen apo andros,* "dismissed or loosed or released from a husband." The participle *apolelumeneen* is the feminine perfect passive of *apoluoo,* "to set loose from oneself" (*apo,* "from" and *luoo,* "to loose"). The question to determine is who sets loose whom? Is it the husband who sends his wife away and therefore "she is loosed by him?" If this were the case, the preposition used here should have been *hupo* or *para* meaning "by." But the preposition is *apo* indicating an action not by the husband but by the wife. It is she who dismisses *her* husband. And since the verb *apoluoo* in all the tenses in the contexts of divorce in the two Synoptists, as we have already seen, refers to dismissing one's partner for reasons other than moral infidelity, it must also mean the same here in Luke 16:18b. This woman has released herself from her husband for reason other than her husband's unfaithfulness. Therefore she is the guilty party, hence she is truly an adulteress. Her adultery upon her remarriage is doubly affirmed.

Here is the sentence again: "And anyone (or whosoever) marrying a woman who dismisses herself from (her) husband (for no valid reason) commits adultery."

The participial noun, *apolelumeneen,* "dismissed (woman)," although in the passive form must take the middle voice meaning thus indicating that this woman releases herself from her husband instead of being released by her husband. If it is taken to have a passive meaning, then it would refer to an innocent wife unjustifiably dismissed by her husband. But how then would a man who marries her truly commit adultery since that is what he is said to do as the verb *moicheuei,* being in the active present indicative, indicates exactly? Why should any man marrying an innocent woman who was dismissed by her guilty husband be penalized by being considered as actually and continuously committing adultery?

Remember that the verb "commits adultery" in Luke 16:18b is the active present indicative, *moicheuei,* which refers to the one who marries this woman as truly committing adultery. He was not an adulterer until this moment. This verb *moicheuei* is in the present indicative and refers to true adultery and not that imputed to him by association as in the case of man described in Matthew 5:32 where the verb *moichatai* is in the passive voice. If the woman were the innocent party, the preposition *hypo* or *para,* "by," with the husband doing the dismissing would have been used before *andros,* "husband," instead of *apo,* "from," indicating the action taken by a guilty wife. If she were the innocent party, she could remarry without causing her new husband (providing he was a bachelor or a non-guilty divorcée or a widower) to be an actual adulterer. The only guilt of adultery he could assume would be that of the stigma of his wife if she were unjustifiably dismissed by her husband. But here the wife who remarried has unjustifiably dismissed her husband and separated herself from him. She, therefore, is the guilty party in the divorce, and he who marries her indeed commits adultery.

It is to be remembered, as we already mentioned, that Luke is writing primarily to Gentiles, and therefore the mention of a wife divorcing her husband for reason other than fornication is more relevant in the Gentile context than in the Jewish context of Matthew's Gospel.

The meaning, therefore, of the second clause of Luke 16:18

259

is: Anyone who marries a woman who unwarrantedly divorces her first husband in order that she may marry him commits adultery. This clearly refers to a man who may not have any guilt of adultery to this moment taking upon himself such guilt of adultery for life by marrying a divorcée who unjustifiably divorced her own husband in order to marry him.

The verb for the second time in Luke 16:18 for "commits adultery" is again *moicheuei* in the active present indicative, which means to directly commit adultery as in the previous clause. The word *moicheuei*, "commits adultery," therefore, here indicates an active, destructive effort of the divine institution of marriage. This refers to the man who goes after another woman who in turn divorces her husband because she simply doesn't want him anymore so that she may marry the new man now courting her. The woman referred to here is not one who divorces her husband because of his unfaithfulness.

The sin of such a man who marries a guilty, divorced woman could have been expressed by the more general verb *porneuei*, "commits fornication," but it says *moicheuei*, "commits adultery." Why? In order that such a man may also equally bear the guilt of the breaking up of a family which is clearly implied in the verb *moicheuei*.

Please recall our discussion about the commandment God gave being, "Thou shalt not commit adultery" (Ex. 20:14), and not "Thou shalt not commit fornication." The Lord was concerned not merely with the evil of defiling one's body through fornication, but clearly with the preservation of the family which is the basis of the survival of a structured society. This man who marries a woman who divorces herself from her husband to marry him breaks up the family which she had with her former husband. In addition to defiling his own body, precious children, if they exist, will be left without one of their rightful parents.

The obvious conclusion in the progression of sin is evident: the look, the touch, the divorce, and then the breakup of the home and family—a grievous sin in the eyes of God which causes one to live in a state of adultery all his life.

[1]*ean gameesee*

[2]*ho*, "he who"—the definite masculine article "the," *gameesas*,

first aorist participle, "having married" or "when he marries" (a dismissed one) in the past or at some definitive time.

[34]"And anyone who," *pas,* the same word as in Matthew 5:28 (also in the UBS text of Matthew 5:32a) and also in Luke 16:18a.

62

REMARRIAGE IN ROMANS 7:1-3

"Know ye not, brethren, (for I speak to them that know the law,) how that the law hath dominion over a man as long as he liveth? For the woman which hath an husband is bound by the law to her husband so long as he liveth; but if the husband be dead, she is loosed from the law of her husband. So then if, while her husband liveth, she be married to another man, she shall be called an adulteress; but if her husband be dead, she is free from that law; so that she is no adulteress, though she be married to another man." Romans 7:1-3

Romans was written by Paul in Corinth toward the end of his three-month stay there at the conclusion of his third missionary journey (Acts 20:1-6; 24:17).

His main subject in Romans 7 is the law and its binding force and the freedom of the believer in Jesus Christ from the law of Moses. The reference to the binding relationship of marriage between partners is offered as an illustration. Paul begins by saying, "Know ye not, brethren, (for I speak to them that know the law,) how that the law hath dominion over a man as long as he liveth?" (Rom. 7:1). Obviously, the law does not pursue dead people in an attempt to punish them.

Then Paul illustrates this from the marriage relationship. Certain facts are implicit in relation to the institution of the marriage bond.

1. Marriage involved two human beings, a man and a woman (verse 2).

2. Marriage is not the result of the mutual consent of a man and a woman to just live together. It is a binding contract by divine law, instituted by God and continuing in its recognition by men. Read verse 2 carefully: "For the woman which hath an husband is bound by the law to her husband. . . ."

The expression "the woman which hath a husband" in Greek is *hee hupandros gunee.* Here is the only place that the word *hupandros,*[1] "the one having an husband," is used. It means "one who is under a husband, a covered woman, one under the shelter of a man." This word is used the same way several times in the Septuagint (Num. 5:20, 29; Pr. 6:24; 29) and also by Polybius, Plutarch, Diodorus Siculus, and Athenaeus.

3. It is the married woman that is held bound *(dedetai)* by law *(nomoo*—dative of means).

Why does it speak of the woman being bound? Because this law is the Mosaic or Jewish law which peculiarly bound a woman to her husband. Deuteronomy 24:1-4 speaks of the husband who sends his wife away and the obligation he has to give her a bill of divorcement, but it does not give explicitly the same privilege to a wife. This binding was also common among the Romans, although not to as great a degree. (See Mark 10:12 where a woman dismisses her husband, and Luke 16:18 where a woman separates herself from her husband without his being the guilty party. Both Mark and Luke in their writings are addressing themselves to Gentiles, not Jews.)

Furthermore, a woman is a type of the Church. As the Church is related to Christ, so is a woman bound to her husband. And as the law binds a woman to her husband, so God's grace— which always stands as the higher counterpart of the law— stands as the binding ingredient of the Church to Christ. (See Eph. 5:22-32.)

4. A woman is legally bound to her husband as long as he lives. Verse 2b: "But if the husband be dead, she is loosed from the law of her husband." Verse 1b: "the law hath dominion over a man as long as he liveth." Therefore when a husband dies the wife is free to remarry.

5. The conclusion is given in verse 3: "So then if, while her husband liveth, she be married to another man, she shall be called an adulteress."

Here we have the case of a woman who, while her husband is alive, arbitrarily marries another. The Greek word for "another" is *heteroo* which means another of a different kind, perhaps one she likes better than her own husband. Actually the Greek text says, "if she becomes another man's." In that case "she shall be called an adulteress." She will actually be a bigamist. If, however, her first husband dies, then she is free from that law.

Remember the teaching of Jesus who forbade divorce for any reason other than the unfaithfulness of the marital partner

(Matt. 5:32). In Romans, we have a woman who divorces her husband while he is still alive in order to marry another man, a different kind of man, whom she may like better for some reason. This assumes that her husband has not been unfaithful, for if he had been, then according to both the Mosaic law and Christ's teaching, she would be fully justified in divorcing him and would not be called an adulteress.

"But if her husband be dead, she is free from that law; so that she is no adulteress, though she be married to another man." The law does not have to declare her free to remarry. That freedom comes automatically and inherently after her husband's death.

Therefore, within the limits of this illustration of the marriage relationship, a wife is bound by law to her husband as long as he lives. When he dies, she is free to remarry if she wishes. However, while he is alive, she is not free to do so (unless the one exception taught by Christ applies, that her husband proves unfaithful). This would also apply in case the wife should die, at which time the husband would be free.

Thus as the married woman is freed from the law to marry another after her husband has died, so Christ, the Church's bridegroom, has freed us all in Him from the law that bound us in our sinful state so that we now belong to another, entirely different *(heteroo)*. And who is this one so qualitatively different *(heteros*—Rom. 7:3, 4, 23)? It is the risen Christ. He is our "different husband," spiritually speaking.

[1]Actually *hupandros* is a compound word made up of the preposition *hupo,* "under," and *andros (aneer),* genitive, "of a husband."

Greek-English Index

Greek	English	Scripture	Page
agapaoo	to love	Eph. 5:25, 28, Col. 3:19	35
agapee	love		62
agoreuoo	to speak		143
aiteoo	to ask		227
aitia	reason	Matt. 19:10	147, 227
akatharsia	uncleanness	Gal. 5:19	95
allos (alloo)			
allee (alleen)	another	Mark 10:11, 12	198, 199, 242, 248, 252, 253, 255
an	if	Matt. 5:32	112, 194
an apolusee	if he *dismisses,*	Matt. 5:32	113, 194
androphonia	*killing,* of man		98
aneer	*male* partner		9, 25, 161, 162, 216, 218, 265
anthroopos	man	Matt. 19:5	161, 162, 216, 218, 227
ap archees	from *beginning*	Matt. 19:4	156
aphesis	forgiveness		211
aphieemi	to *put away,*		46, 106, 145, 211
apo	from		73, 141, 145, 178, 211, 258, 259
apistos	unfaithful		206
apo andros	from a *husband,*	Luke 16:18	257, 258
apolelumenee			
apolelumenos	the *dismissed* one,	Matt. 5:32	68, 69, 135, 199, 200, 217, 258, 259
apoluoo	to dismiss	Matt. 5:32	11, 46, 84, 112, 135, 141, 145, 189, 190, 193, 194, 200, 217, 242, 245, 247, 248, 253, 255, 257, 258
apostasion	*divorce* document	Matt. 5:31	62, 73, 187

arsen	male	Matt. 19:4	152, 166
arsenokoitees	abuser of oneself with mankind or *homo-sexual,*	I Cor. 6:9, I Tim. 1:10	99, 166
ascheemon pragma	*shameful* or uncomely thing		142
aselgeia	lasciviousness	Mark 7:22	95
a-sheema	without *shape,*		142
autee (n)	her	Matt. 5:28, Mark 10:11	84, 114, 115, 132, 242, 252
autou	his own	Matt. 5:32	142
balloo	to *throw,*		185
biblion	little book of writing,		187
biblion apostasiou	a small *book* of divorce-ment or estrangement	Matt. 19:7	73
blepoo	to *look,*	Matt. 5:28	60, 116
charisma	gift	I Cor. 7:7	234
chooreoo	to fit in space		236
chooreetoo	receive		240
choorismos	separation		176, 185
choorizomai	to *separate oneself,*		46, 187
choorizoo	to *separate,*		145, 176, 183, 184, 190
chooros	space		183
dia	through		185, 191
diaballoo	to falsely *accuse,* to place something in be-tween		185
diabolos	devil		185, 186
didoomi	to *give,*		264
didoomi (dedotai)	given		234, 236
ean	if	Mark 10:12	32, 200
ean gameesee	if he *marry,*	Matt. 5:32, Mark 10:11	260
echoo	to have, *keep,*		240
egoo	*I* (emphatic)		193
ei	if		195, 223
ei mee epi porneia	if not for *fornication,*	Matt. 19:9	194
eimi	to be		140
eis porneian me	unto *fornication,* he attracted		
ephelkusato	me		89
ekporneuoo	to live very licentiously,		88, 93
ektos	without		194
emoisheusen auteen	committed *adultery,* against her	Matt. 5:28	119
emoicheusen met autees	committed *adultery,* with her		119
en porneia	in *fornication,* he		
emoicheuthee	committed *adultery*		89, 97

268

269

ho gameesas	who when he married or having *married,* at a particular time in the past		199, 257
ho gammoon	the one *marrying* another		255, 257
hoi duo	the *two*	Matt. 19:6	163
hoi . . . prassontes	the ones *doing,*		109
hos	he *who*	Matt. 5:31	61, 79, 80, 112, 120, 135, 193, 200, 253
hos an	whosoever		80, 112, 121,
hos ean			125, 253
hos an apolusee	he who if he *dismisses*		
teen gunaika autou	the wife of his		111, 112, 113
hoti	that, *which*		115
houtos	*this* one		253
hupandros	the woman having a husband, *married* woman		25, 265, 264
huper	above and *over*		236
huperphroneoo	to *think* more highly		236
hypo	by		258, 259, 265
hupotaktikee	a word which is under another action or state, *subjected*		113
hupotassomai	to *subject* one	Eph. 5:22	37
kai	and		120, 135
kainee	qualitatively *new,* of a better quality	John 13:34	80
kardia	heart		192
kata	an *intensive* preposition		160
kata	down		141
kata	according or against		143
kataleipoo	*leave* behind		159
kataluoo	to *destroy*	Matt. 5:17	57, 141
kata pasan aitian	for any *reason*	Matt. 19:3	143
kateegoreoo	to speak against or to *accuse*		143
kaollaomai glue oneself	to be *attached* to, Matt. 19:5, Mark 10:7		161
legoo	to *say* or speak intelli- gently	Matt. 19:9	193, 217
leipoo	leave		160
logon touton	*word* this one		231, 232
logos	word, *reason* or an account of		194, 232
luoo	to *loose*		141, 258
makarios	blessed		255
malakos	effeminate	I Cor. 6:9	99, 166
mee aphienai	not to *put away*		187

273

English – Greek Index

275

276

278

279

Index of Subjects

Scripture Index

287

Bibliography

Specialized Books

Gray, James Comper, *The Biblical Encyclopedia and Museum,* Cleveland, OH, F.M. Barton, 1900.

Staton, Julia, *What the Bible Says About Woman,* Joplin, MO, College Press Publishing Company, 1980.

Tuck, Robert, *A Handbook of Biblical Difficulties,* London, Elliot Stock, 1886.

Wight, Fred H., *Manners and Customs of Bible Lands,* Chicago, IL, Moody Press, 1953.

Articles on Marriage, Divorce and Remarriage

Abbott, Lyman, "Marriage and Divorce", *The Christian World Pulpit,* vol. 49, pp. 204-07, 1896.

Horton, R.F., "Christ's View of Divorce," *The Christian World Pulpit,* vol. 99, pp. 282-84, London, 1981.

Simpson, James Gilliland, "The Message of Malachi," *The Christian World Pulpit,* vol. 82, London, James Clarke and Company, 1912.

Dictionaries and Reference Works on the Greek Language

Analytical Greek Lexicon, The, New York, Harper and Brothers.

Arndt, William F., and Gingrich, F. Wilbur, *A Translation of Walter Bauer's Griechisch-Deutsches Worterbuch zu den Schriften des Neuen Testaments und der Ubrigen Urchrislichen Literatur,* Chicago, IL, The University of Chicago Press, 1957.

Brown, Colin, *Dictionary of New Testament Theology,* 3 volumes (*Theologisches Begriffslexikon Zum Neuen Testament),* Grand Rapids, MI, Zondervan Publishing House, 1975.

Bullinger, Ethelbert W., *A Critical Lexicon and Concordance to the English and Greek New Testament,* London, The Lamp Press, Ltd., 1957.

Cremer, H., *Biblico--Theological Lexicon of the New Testament,* Edinburgh, T & T Clark, 1954.

Douglas, J.D., *The New Bible Dictionary,* Grand Rapids, MI, William B. Eerdmans Publishing Company, 1970.

Friberg, Barbara and Timothy, *Analytical Greek New Testament,* Grand Rapids, MI, Baker Bookhouse, 1981.

Grant, F.W., *The Numerical Bible,* New York, Loizeaux Brothers, 1899.

Gray, James Comper, *The Biblical Encyclopedia and Museum,* Cleveland, OH, F.M. Barton, 1900.

Hastings, James, *A Dictionary of the Bible,* 5 volumes, Edinburgh, T & T Clark, 1901.

Hastings, James, *A Dictionary of Christ and the Gospels,* 2 volumes, Edinburgh, T & T Clark, 1906.

Hastings, James, *Dictionary of the Apostolic Church,* 2 volumes, Edinburgh, T & T Clark, 1951.

The Interpreter's Dictionary of the Bible, 4 volumes, New York, Abingdon Press.

Kittel, Gerhard, translated by Geoffrey W. Bromiley, *Theological Dictionary of the New Testament,* 10 volumes, Grand Rapids, MI, William B. Eerdmans Publishing Company, 1968.

Lampe, G.W.H., *A Patristic Greek Lexicon,* 5 vol., Oxford, Clarendon Press, 1968.

Liddell, Henry George, and Scott, Robert, *A Greek-English Lexicon,* Oxford, Clarendon Press, 1958.

McClintock, John, and Strong, James *Cyclopedia of Biblical, Theological and Ecclesiastical Literature*, 12 volumes, Grand Rapids, MI, Baker Bookhouse, 1968.

Meillet, A., *Apercu D'une Histoire de la Langue Grecque* (in French), Paris, Librairie Hachette, 1935.

Moulton, J.H., and Milligan, G., *A Vocabulary of the Greek Testament,* Grand Rapids, MI, William B. Eerdmans Publishing Company, 1957.

Nestle, Eberhard, *Novum Testamentum Graece cum Apparatu Critico Curabit,* Stuttgart, Wurttemburgische Bibelanstalt, 1952.

Parkhurst, John, *A Greek and English Lexicon to the New Testament,* London, 1769, published by AMG Publishers, 1980.

Richardson, Alan, *A Theological Word Book of the Bible,* New York, The Macmillan Company, 1959.

Robertson, Nicoll W.; Stoddart, Janet; Moffat, James (eds), *The Expositor's Dictionary of Texts,* William B. Eermans Publishing Company, Grand Rapids, MI, 1953.

Robinson, Edward, *A Greek and English Lexicon of the New Testament,* Edinburgh, T & T Clark, 1829.

The Septuagint Version of the Old Testament and Apocrypha, with an English translation and various readings and critical notes, London, Samuel Bagster and Sons, Ltd.

Smith, William, *Dictionary of Greek and Roman Antiquities,* London, Taylor, Walton, and Maberly, 1848.

Strong, James, *Exhaustive Concordance of the Bible,* New York, Abingdon Cokesbury, 1943.

Thayer, Joseph Henry, *A Greek English Lexicon of the New Testament* (Grimm's Wilke's Clovis Nobi Testamenti), Edinburgh, T & T Clark, 1956.

Trench, Richard C., *Synonyms of the New Testament,* Grand Rapids, MI, William B. Eerdmans Publishing Company, 1953.

Vine, W.E., *An Expository Dictionary of New Testament Words,* Westwood, NJ, Fleming H. Revell Company, 1966.

Weigle, Luther A., *The New Testament Octapla,* New York, Thomas Nelson and Sons, 1946.

Commentaries on Matthew

Abbott, Lyman, *An Illustrated Commentary on the Gospel According to Matthew*, New York, A.S. Barnes, 1875.

Anderson, Edward E., *The Gospel According to St. Matthew*, Edinburgh, T & T Clark, 1909.

Bagot, Daniel, *An Exposition of the First Seventeen Chapters of the Gospel According to St. Matthew*, London, R. Groombridge & Sons.

Barclay, William, *Gospel of Matthew*, Vols. 1 and 2, Edinburgh, Scotland, The St. Andrew Press, 1958.

Carr, A., *The Gospel According to St. Matthew*, Cambridge, University Press, 1906.

De Valdes, Juan, *Commentary Upon the Gospel of St. Matthew*, London, Trubner and Company, 1882.

Ford, James, *The Gospel of St. Matthew*, London, Joseph Masters, 1859.

Gaebelein, A.C., *The Gospel of Matthew*, New York, Our Hope Publishers, 1910.

Glover, Richard, *A Teacher's Commentary on the Gospel of Matthew*, Grand Rapids, MI, Zondervan Publishing House, 1956.

Gundry, Robert H., *Matthew, A Commentary on His Literary and Theological Art*, Grand Rapids, MI, William B. Eerdmans Publishing Company, 1982.

Hendricksen, William, *New Testament Commentary on Matthew*, Edinburgh, The Banner of Truth Trust, 1973.

Henry, Matthew, *An Exposition of the Old and New Testament*, London, 1875.

Ironside, H.A., *Expository Notes on the Gospel of Matthew*, Neptune, NJ, Loizeaux Brothers.

Kelly, William, *Lectures on the Gospel of Matthew*, London, G. Morrish, 1868.

Lenski, R.C.H., *The Interpretation of Matthew*, Minneapolis, MN, Augsburg Publishing House, 1961.

Maclaren, Alexander, *The Gospel of St. Matthew*, London, Hodder and Stoughton.

Micklen, Philip A., *St. Matthew*, London, Methuen & Company, Ltd., 1917.

Morison, James, *Commentary on the Gospel According to Matthew*, London, Hamilton, Adams & Company, 1870.

Nicholson, Edward B., *A New Commentary on the Gospel According to Matthew*, London, C. Kegan Paul and Company, 1881.

Porteus, Beilby, *Lectures on the Gospel of St. Matthew*, London, T. Cadell and W. Davies, 1810.

Rice, Edwin W., *People's Commentary on the Gospel According to Matthew*, Philadelphia, PA, The American Sunday School Union, 1893.

Robinson, Theodore H., *The Gospel of Matthew*, London, Hodder and Stoughton, 1928.

Thomas, David, *The Gospel of St. Matthew*, Grand Rapids, MI, Baker Bookhouse, 1956.

Commentaries on Mark

Alexander, J.A., *Commentary on the Gospel of Mark,* Grand Rapids, MI, Zondervan Publishing House, 1858.

Allen, W.C., "The Gospel According to St. Mark," *The Oxford Church Biblical Commentary,* London, Rivingtons, 1915.

Barclay, William, *The Gospel of Mark,* Edinburgh, The St. Andrew Press, 1958.

Bennett, W.H., *The Life of Christ According to St. Mark,* London, Hodder and Stoughton, 1907.

Branscomb, B. Harvie, *The Gospel of Mark,* London, Hodder and Stoughton, 1948.

Burn, John Henry, *A Homiletic Commentary on the Gospel According to St. Mark,* New York, Funk and Wagnalls Company.

Chadwick, G.A., *The Gospel According to St. Mark,* London, Hodder and Stoughton, 1887.

Eaton, Robert, *The Gospel According to St. Mark,* London, Burns, Oates and Washbourne, Ltd., 1920.

Erdman, Charles R., *The Gospel of Mark,* Philadelphia, PA, The Westminster Press, 1917.

Exell, Joseph S., "St. Mark," *The Biblical Illustrator,* London, James Nisbet and Company.

Exell, Joseph S., "St. Mark," *The Pulpit Commentary,* New York, Funk and Wagnalls Company.

Glover, Richard, *A Teacher's Commentary on the Gospel of St. Mark,* London, Sunday School Union, 1912.

Gould, Ezra P., *Critical and Exegetical Commentary on the Gospel According to St. Mark,* Edinburgh, T & T Clark, 1896.

Hiebert, D. Edmond, *Mark, A Portrait of a Servant,* Chicago, Moody Press, 1974.

Hobbs, Herschel H., *An Exposition of the Gospel of Mark,* Grand Rapids, MI, Baker Bookhouse, 1970.

Hort, A.F., *The Gospel According to St. Mark,* Cambridge, University Press, 1914.

Horton, Robert F., *The Cartoons of St. Mark,* London, James Clarke and Company, 1894.

Hunter, A.N., *The Gospel According to St. Mark,* London, SCM Press, Ltd., 1962.

Ironside, H.A., *Mark,* Neptune, NJ, Loizeaux Brothers, Inc., 1948.

Lenski, R.C.H., *The Interpretation of St. Mark's Gospel,* Minneapolis, MN, Augsburg Publishing House, 1964.

Maclaren, Alexander, *The Gospel of St. Mark,* London, Hodder and Stoughton, 1893.

Maclear, G.F., *St. Mark,* Cambridge, University Press, 1891.

Marshall, F., *The School and College St. Mark,* London, George Gill and Sons, Ltd.

Morison, James, *A Practical Commentary on the Gospel According to St. Mark,* London, Hodder and Stoughton, 1884.

Oldham, H.W., *Studies in the Gospel According to St. Mark,* London, Student Christian Movement, 1904.

294

Rawlinson, A.E.J., *St. Mark,* London, Methuen and Company Ltd., 1927.

Ryle, J.C., *Expository Thoughts on the Gospels, Mark,* London, James Clarke and Company, 1955.

Sadler, M.F., *The Gospel According to St. Mark,* London, George Bell and Sons, 1899.

St. John, Harold, *An Analysis of the Gospel of Mark,* London, Pickering and Englis Ltd., 1956.

Sumner, John Bird, *A Practical Exposition of the Gospel According to St. Mark,* London, J. Hatchard and Son, 1847.

Swete, Henry Barclay, *The Gospel According to St. Mark,* Grand Rapids, MI, William B. Eerdmans Publishing Company, 1936.

Books on Marriage, Divorce and Remarriage

Adams, Jay E., *Marriage, Divorce & Remarriage in the Bible,* Phillipsburg, NJ, Presbyterian and Reformed Publishing Company, 1980.

Bontrager, G. Edwin, *Divorce and the Faithful Church,* Kitchener, Ont., CAN., Herald Press, 1978.

Bustanoby, Andre, *But I Didn't Want a Divorce, Putting Your Life Back Together,* Grand Rapids, MI, Zondervan Publishing House, 1979.

Duty, Guy, *Divorce and Remarriage,* Minneapolis, MN, Bethany Fellowship, Inc., 1967.

Ellisen, Stanley A., *Divorce and Remarriage in the Church,* Grand Rapids, MI, Zondervan Publishing House, 1980.

Emerson, James G. Jr., *Divorce, the Church, and Remarriage,* Philadelphia, PA, The Westminster Press, 1961.

Epp, Theodore H., *Marriage and Divorce,* Lincoln, NE, Back to the Bible Broadcast, 1968.

Hosier, Helen Kooiman, *The Other Side of Divorce, A Christian's Plea for Understanding and Compassion,* Nashville, Abingdon, 1975.

Kilgore, James E., *Try Marriage Before Divorce,* Waco, TX, Word Books, Publisher, 1978.

Kysar, Myrna and Robert, *The Asundered, Biblical Teachings on Divorce and Remarriage,* Atlanta, John Knox Press, 1978.

Lee, Mark, *Creative Christian Marriage,* Glendale, CA, Regal Books, 1977.

Leman, Kevin, *Sex Begins in the Kitchen, Renewing Emotional and Physical Intimacy in Marriage,* Ventura, CA, Regal Books, 1981.

Lovett, C.S., *Divorce Problem,* Baldwin Park, CA, Personal Christianity, 1964.

Meier, Paul D., *You Can Avoid Divorce,* Grand Rapids, MI, Baker Bookhouse, 1978.

Murray, John, *Divorce,* Philadelphia, PA, The Orthodox Presbyterian Church, 1953.

Nordie, Donald L., *Divorce and the Bible,* New York, Loizeaux Brothers, 1958.

Plekker, J. Robert, *Divorce and the Christian: What the Bible Teaches,* Wheaton, IL, Tyndale House Publishers, Inc., 1980.

Rice, John R., *Divorce, The Wreck of Marriage,* Murfreesboro, TN, Sword of the Lord Publishers, 1946.

Richards, Larry, *Remarriage, A Healing Gift from God,* Waco, TX, Word Books Publisher, 1981.

Snowman, Preston W., *New Light on Divorce and Remarriage,* Salisbury Center, NY, Select Publications, 1978.

Stott, John R.W., *Divorce,* InterVarsity Press, Downers Grove, IL, 1973.

Thomas, J.D., *Divorce and Remarriage,* Abilene, TX, Biblical Research Press, 1977.

Toussaint, Stanley D., Portland, OR, Multnomah Press, 1980.

Williams, John, *For Every Cause? The Question of Divorce,* Neptune, NJ, Loizeaux Brothers, 1981.

Williams, H. Page, *Do Yourself a Favor: Love Your Wife,* Plainfield, NJ, Logos International, 1973.

Reference Works in Greek Only

Archaioi Helleenes Sungrapheis (Ancient Greek Writers), 150 volumes, Athens, Zacharopoulos, 1954.

Bibliotheekee Helleenoon Pateroon Kai Ekkleesiastikoon Suggrapheoon (Library of Greek Fathers and Ecclesiastical Writers), 15 volumes, Athens, Apostoliki Diakonia, 1955.

Demetrakou, D., *Great Dictionary of the Greek Language (Mega Lexikon Tees Helleenikes Glossees,* in Greek), 9 volumes, Athens, Demetrakos, 1949.

Eleftheroudakis, *Enclyclopedic Lexicon* (in Greek), 12 volumes, Athens, Eleftheroudakis, 1927.

Great Greek Encyclopedia (in Greek), Pursou, 24 volumes, Athens, P.G. Makris.

Helios, *Newer Enclyclopedic Lexicon* (in Greek), *Neoteron Egkuklopaidikon Lexikon,* 18 volumes, Athens.

Ioannou tou Chrisostomou ta Hapanta (Complete Works of John Chrysostom), Kalaraki, Michael and Nikolas Galanos, 1899.

Martinos, Ath., *Encyclopedia of Religion and Ethics* (written in Greek), 12 volumes, Athens, A. Martinos, 1962.

Papaoikonomou, George L., *Lexikon Anoomaloon Rheematoon (Lexicon of Irregular Verbs),* Athens, Kagiaphas.

Roosse, John, Th. (in Greek) *Grammar of the Ancient Greek Language and Especially in Attic Dialect,* Athens.

Triantaphullou, I. Delee (In Greek), *Grammatical Skills, The Content and the Methodical Teaching of the Ancient Greek Grammar,* Athens, 1972.

Grammars of the Greek Language

Blass, F. and Debrunner, A., Translated from the German by Robert W. Funk, *A Greek Grammar of the New Testament and Early Christian Literature,* Chicago, IL, The University of Chicago Press, 1961.

Burton, Ernest De Witt, *Syntax of the Moods and Tenses in New Testament Greek,* Edinburgh, T & T Clark, 1966.

Buttmann, Alexander, *A Grammar of the New Testament Greek,* Andover, Warren F. Draper, 1891.

Cartledge, Samuel A., *A Basic Grammar of the Greek New Testament,* Grand Rapids, MI, Zondervan Publishing House, 1959.

Chamberlain, William Douglas, *An Exegetical Grammar of the Greek New Testament,* Grand Rapids, MI, Baker Bookhouse, 1941.

Curtius, George, *A Grammar of the Greek Language,* London, John Murray, 1882.

Green, Thomas Sheldon, *A Treatise on the Grammar of the New Testament Dialect,* London, Samuel Bagster and Sons, 1842.

Harper, William Rainey, *An Introductory New Testament Greek Method,* New York, Charles Scribner's Sons, 1911.

Jay, Eric G., *New Testament Greek, An Introductory Grammar,* London, S.P.C.K., 1958.

Jelf, William Edward, *A Grammar of the Greek Language,* 2 volumes, Oxford, John Henry and James Parker, 1859.

Marshall, Alfred, *New Testament Greek Primer,* Grand Rapids, MI, Zondervan Publishing House, 1982.

Metzger, Bruce M., *Lexical Aids for Students of New Testament Greek,* Princeton, NJ.

Moulton, James Hope, *A Grammar of New Testament Greek,* 2 volumes, Edinburgh, T & T Clark, 1957.

Moulton, James Hope, *An Introduction to the Study of New Testament Greek,* The Macmillan Company, 1955.

Robertson, A.T., *A Grammar of the Greek New Testament in the Light of Historical Research,* New York, George H. Doran Company, 1923.

————————, Practical and Social Aspects of Christianity, 1916.

————————, Pictures in the New Testament, Nashville, TN, Broadman Press, 1933.

Seager, John, *Hoogeveen's Greek Participles,* London, A.J. Balpy, 1829.

Smyth, Herbert Weir, *Greek Grammar,* Cambridge, Harvard University Press, 1959.

Sonnenschein, E.A., *A Greek Grammar, Accidents,* London, Swan Sonnenschein and Company, Ltd., 1909.

Summers, Ray, *Essentials of New Testament Greek,* Nashville, TN, Broadman Press, 1950.

Thomson, George, *The Greek Language,* Cambridge, W. Heffer and Sons, Ltd., 1960.

Vine, W.E., *New Testament Greek Grammar,* Grand Rapids, MI, Zondervan Publishing House, 1965.

Wenham, J.W., *The Elements of New Testament Greek,* Cambridge, Cambridge University Press, 1981.

Winer, G.B., *A Treatise on the Grammar of the New Testament Greek,* Edinburgh, T & T Clark, 1882.

Commentaries on the Bible

Abbott, Edwin A., Clue, *A Guide Through Greek to Hebrew Scripture,* London, Adam and Charles Black, 1900.

Alford, Henry, *The Greek Testament,* 4 volumes, London, Rivingtons, 1880.

Barnes, Albert, *Notes on the New Testament,* Explanatory and Practical, Grand Rapids, MI, Baker Bookhouse, 1949.

Bengel, John Albert, *Gnomon of the New Testament,* Edinburgh, T & T Clark, 1863.

Bloomfield, S.T., *The Greek Testament Notes,* Critical Philological and Explanatory, 2 volumes, London, Longman, Brown, Green and Longmans, 1845.

Churton, Edward and Jones, William Basil, *The New Testament of Our Lord and Saviour Jesus Christ,* 2 volumes, London, John Murray.

Commentary Wholly Biblical, London, Samuel Bagster and Sons.

Criswell, W.A., *The Criswell Study Bible,* Nashville, TN, Thomas Nelson Publishers, 1979.

Dalton, W., *An Explanatory and Practical Commentary of the New Testament,* Dublin, William Curry, Jun. and Company, 1840.

Driver, Samuel Rolles; Plummer, Alfred; Briggs, Augustus Charles, *The International Critical Commentary of the Holy Scriptures of the old and New Testaments,* Edinburgh, T & T Clark, 1907.

Ellicott, Charles John (Ed), *A Bible Commentary for English Readers,* London, Cassell and Company, Ltd.

Jacobus, Melancthon, *Notes on the Gospels, Critical and Explanatory,* New York, Robert Carter and Brothers, 1866.

Jamieson, Robert; Fausset A.R.; and Brown, David, *A Commentary Critical, Experimental, and Practical on the Old and New Testaments,* Glasgow, William Collins Sons and Company, 1870.

Lange, John Peter, *A Commentary on the Holy Scriptures, Critical, Doctrinal, and Homiletical,* New York, Charles Scribner's Sons, 1884.

Lapide, Cornelius A., *The Great Commentary,* translated by Thomas W. Mossman, Edinburgh, John Grant, 1908.

Luckock, Herbert Mortimer, *Footprints of the Son of Man,* pp. 41-48, London, Rivingtons, 1889.

Meyer, Heinrich August Wilhalm, *Critical and Exegetical Handbook of the Gospels of Mark and Luke,* Edinburgh, T & T Clark, 1880.

Morgan, G. Campbell, *The Gospel According to Matthew, Mark, and Luke,* New York, Fleming H. Revell Company, 1929.

The New Testament with English Notes, etc., (Greek), London, A.J. Balpy, 1831.

Nicoll, W. Robertson, *The Expositor's Greek Testament,* Grand Rapids, MI, William B. Eerdmans Publishing Company, 1956.

Nicoll W. Robertson (Ed.), *The Expositor's Bible,* Grand Rapids, MI, William B. Eerdmans Publishing Company, 1956.

Olshausen, Hermann, *Biblical Commentary on the Gospels,* Edinburgh, T & T Clark, 1855.

Owen, John J., *A Commentary, Critical, Expository, and Practical on the Gospels of Matthew and Mark,* 1861.

Patrick, Lowth, Arnald, Whitby, and Lowman, *A Critical Commentary and Paraphrase on the Old and New Testament, and the Apocrypha,* London, William Tegg and Company, 1853.

Peloubet, F.M., *The Teacher's Commentary on the Gospel According to St. Matthew,* London, Oxford University Press, 1901.

Rebuilders' Guide, Institute in Basic Youth Conflicts, 1982.

Schaff, Philip, *A Popular Commentary on the New Testament,* Edinburgh, T & T Clark, 1879.

Tuck, Robert, *The Preacher's Homiletic Commentary on the New Testament,* New York, Funk and Wagnalls.

Webster, William and Wilkinson, William Francis, *The Greek Testament with Notes Grammatical and Exegetical,* London, John W. Parker, 1855.

Weiss, Bernhard, *A Commentary on the New Testament,* translated by G. Schodde and E. Wilson, with an introduction by James S. Riggs, New York, Funk and Wagnalls Company, 1906.

Whitby, Daniel, *A Paraphrase and Commentary on the New Testament,* London, Awnsham and John Churchill, 1710.

Wordsworth, Chr., *The New Testament,* 3rd Edition, London, Rivingtons, 1864.

Young, Robert, *Literal Translation of the Holy Bible,* Grand Rapids, MI, Baker Bookhouse, 1956.

GUIDE TO TRANSLITERATION – FROM GREEK TO ENGLISH

Capital Letter	Small Letter	Greek Name	Trans-literation	Phonetic Sound		Example
A	α	alpha	a	a	as in	father
B	β	beeta	b	b	as in	bed
Γ	γ	gamma	g	g	as in	go
Δ	δ	delta	d	d	as in	do
E	ε	epsilon	e	e	as in	met
Z	ζ	zeeta	z	dz	as in	adze
H	η	eeta	ee	e	as in	prey
Θ	θ	theeta	th	th	as in	thin
I	ι	ioota	i	i	as in	pin or machine
K	κ	kappa	k	k	as in	kill
Λ	λ	lambda	l	l	as in	land
M	μ	mu	m	m	as in	men
N	ν	nu	n	n	as in	now
Ξ	ξ	xi	x	x	as in	wax
O	o	omicron	o	o	as in	obey
Π	π	pi	p	p	as in	pet
P	ρ	rhoo	rh*,r	rh	as in	Rhine
				r	as in	fur
Σ	σ, ς˙	sigma	s	s	as in	sit
T	τ	tau	t	t	as in	tell
Y	υ	upsilon	hu*,u	hu	almost like who
				u	as in	German ü – über French u – tu
Φ	φ	phi	ph	ph	as in	graphic
X	χ	chi	ch	ch	as in	German buch, ich
Ψ	ψ	psi	ps	ps	as in	hips
Ω	ω	oomega	oo	o	as in	tone (not oo as in moon or foot, but just a long o)

* At beginning of words
˙ At end of words

300

COMBINATIONS OF CONSONANTS

γγ	gamma	+ gamma	= ng	as in sing
γκ	gamma	+ kappa	= nk	as in sink
γξ	gamma	+ xi	= nx	as in lynx
γχ	gamma	+ chi	= nch	as in synchronize
θθ	theeta	+ theeta	= tth	as in Matthew
ρρ	rhoo	+ rhoo	= rrh	as in pyrrhic

DIPHTHONGS (DOUBLE VOWELS)

ΑΙ	αι	alpha + ioota	= ai as in aisle
ΑΙ	ᾳ	alpha with ioota subscript*	= a' as in ah
ΑΥ	αυ	alpha + upsilon	= au, ou as in our
ΕΙ	ει	epsilon + ioota	= ei as in eight
ΕΥ	ευ	epsilon + upsilon	= eu almost as in feud
ΗΙ	ῃ	eeta with ioota subscript*	= ee, e' as in prey
ΗΥ	ηυ	eeta+ upsilon	= eeu, eu almost as in feud
ΟΙ	οι	omicron + ioota	= oi as in boil
ΟΥ	ου	omicron + upsilon	= ou as in group
ΥΙ	υι	upsilon + ioota	= ui as in quiet
ΥΙ	ὑι	rough upsilon + ioota	= hui, whi as in while
ΩΙ	ῳ	oomega with ioota subscript*	= oo', o as in tone
ΩΥ	ωυ	oomega + upsilon	= oou, ou as in thou

BREATHINGS (Occur only with initial vowels)

(') Smooth –, not transliterated or pronounced. When words begin with vowels, it may occur at the beginning of words with every vowel or double vowel (diphthong). ἔργον – ergon, work; εὐχή – euchee, vow.

(') Rough = h. When words begin with vowels, it may occur at the beginning of words with every vowel or double vowel (diphthong). Pronounced like h. ἁμαρτία – hamartia, sin; υἱός – huios, son.

ῥ) rho = r) When they begin a word, they always have the
ὑ) upsilon =u) rough breathing. There they are transliterated rh, hu, respectively. ῥέω – rheoo, flow; ὑπο-μονή – hupomonee, patience.

*Ioota subscript is silent.

' In our transliteration we cannot distinguish between vowels with and without ioota subscript.

VII

GUIDE TO TRANSLITERATION – FROM ENGLISH TO GREEK

Trans-literation	Greek Name	Greek Symbol Capital Letter	Small Letter	Phonetic Sound	Example
a	alpha	Α	α	a as in	father
b	beeta	Β	β	b as in	bet
g	gamma	Γ	γ	g as in	go
d	delta	Δ	δ	d as in	do
e	epsilon	Ε	ε	e as in	met
z	zeeta	Ζ	ζ	dz as in	adze
ee	eeta	Η	η	e as in	prey
th	theeta	Θ	θ	th as in	thin
i	ioota	Ι	ι	i as in	pin or machine
k	kappa	Κ	κ	k as in	kill
l	lambda	Λ	λ	l as in	land
m	mu	Μ	μ	m as in	men
n	nu	Ν	ν	n as in	now
x	xi	Ξ	ξ	x as in	wax
o	omicron	Ο	ο	o as in	obey
p	pi	Π	π	p as in	pet
rh,*r	rhoo	Ρ	ρ	r (rh as in Rhine, beginning of words (r as in fur, other positions	
s	sigma	Σ	σ, ς	s as in	sit
t	tau	Τ	τ	t as in	tell
hu,*u	upsilon	Υ	υ	u (German ü as in über, beginning of words (French u as in tu, other positions	
ph	phi	Φ	φ	ph as in	graphic
ch	chi	Χ	χ	ch as in	German buch, ich
ps	psi	Ψ	ψ	ps as in	hips
oo	oomega	Ω	ω	o as in	tone (not oo as in moon or foot, but just a long o)

* At beginning of words
˙ At end of words

302

COMBINATIONS OF CONSONANTS

ng	gamma + gamma	= γγ	ng	as in	sing
nk	gamma + kappa	= γκ	nk	as in	sink
nx	gamma + xi	= γξ	nx	as in	lynx
nch	gamma + chi	= γχ	nch	as in	synchronize
rrh	rhoo + rhoo	= ρρ	rrh	as in	pyrrhic
tth	theeta + theeta	= θθ	tth	as in	Matthew

DIPHTHONGS (DOUBLE VOWELS)

ai   alpha   + ioota   = Αι, αι ai as in aisle
a·   alpha   + ioota subscript* = Αι, ᾳ a as in ah
au   alpha   + upsilon = Αυ, αυ ou as in our
ei   epsilon + ioota   = Ει, ει ei as in eight
eu   epsilon + upsilon = Ευ, ευ eu as in few (approximate)
ee·   eeta with ioota subscript* = ΗΙ,ῃ e as in prey
eeu   eeta   + upsilon = Ηυ, ηυ eu almost as in feud
oi   omicron+ ioota   = ΟΙ, οι oi as in boil
ou   omicron + upsilon = Ου, ου ou as in group
ui   upsilon + ioota   = Υι, υι ui as in quiet
hui   rough upsilon + ioota = Υι, υι hui whi as in while
oo·   oomega with ioota subscript* = Ωι, ῳ o as in tone
oou   oomega + upsilon = ΩΥ, ωυ ou as in thou

BREATHINGS (Occur only with initial vowels)

— Smooth ('), not transliterated or pronounced. When words
  begin with vowels, it may occur at the beginning of words
  with every vowel or double vowel (diphthong). ergon,
  ἔργον - work; euchee, εὐχή - vow.

h Rough ('), may occur at beginning of words with every vowel
  or double vowel (diphthong). Transliterated h. hamartia,
  ἁμαρτία — sin; υἱός, huios — son.

r = rho - 'ρ) When they begin a word, they always have the
u =upsilon- ὑ) rough breathing. There they are transliterat-
                ed rh,hu, respectively. rheoo, 'ρέω - flow:
                hupomonee, ὑπομονή - patience.

*Ioota subscript is silent.
In our transliteration we cannot distinguish between vowels
with and without ioota subscript.

Other Books by Dr. Spiros Zodhiates

Studies on Luke

Studies in John's Gospel

Studies on James

Three-Volume Set in handsome slip cover

Miscellaneous Titles

305